Separation of the People, Separation of the Land

*The Parallel Literary Structures of Ezra 9–10
and Nehemiah 1–3*

NICHOLAS J. CAMPBELL

WIPF & STOCK · Eugene, Oregon

SEPARATION OF THE PEOPLE, SEPARATION OF THE LAND
The Parallel Literary Structures of Ezra 9–10 and Nehemiah 1–3

Copyright © 2024 Nicholas J. Campbell. All rights reserved. Except for brief quotations in critical publications or reviews, no part of this book may be reproduced in any manner without prior written permission from the publisher. Write: Permissions, Wipf and Stock Publishers, 199 W. 8th Ave., Suite 3, Eugene, OR 97401.

Wipf & Stock
An Imprint of Wipf and Stock Publishers
199 W. 8th Ave., Suite 3
Eugene, OR 97401

www.wipfandstock.com

PAPERBACK ISBN: 979-8-3852-2301-5
HARDCOVER ISBN: 979-8-3852-2302-2
EBOOK ISBN: 979-8-3852-2303-9

VERSION NUMBER 11/20/24

Contents

Preface | vii

Chapter 1	Introduction	1
Chapter 2	Return Accounts: Ezra 1–2, 7–8, and Nehemiah 1–3	16
Chapter 3	The Literary Structure of the Return Migrations	56
Chapter 4	Dissolving Marriage: Ezra 9–10, Nehemiah 9–10, and 13:23–29	89
Chapter 5	The Literary Structure of Ezra 9–10, Nehemiah 9–10, and Nehemiah 13:23–29	109
Chapter 6	The Literary Structure of Ezra 9–10 and Nehemiah 1–3	134
Chapter 7	Purifying the Land: Ezra 9–10 and Nehemiah 1–3	140

Bibliography | 171

Subject Index | 187

Scripture Index | 191

Preface

There are numerous people who have helped me throughout my time at SBTS and even in the planning and logistics of beginning a PhD program. However, I specifically want to show appreciation for the professors that have critiqued my papers during my time here. I have been encouraged to pursue topics that interest me even when they are as strange as animal bones in archaeological sites or normalization rates of biconsonantal roots into triconsonantal roots in the Targums. Even beyond encouragement, I have received invaluable critiques that have helped develop my writing and thought in ways I did not realize were possible. I am also grateful for the guidance on dissertation topics Dr. Garrett has provided and the insights he has given to me for clear and concise writing and thinking.

Nicholas J. Campbell

Louisville, Kentucky
September 2022

Chapter 1

Introduction

THE RESEARCH QUESTION THAT prompts this study is why the migration narrative of Neh 1:1–3:32 does not follow the literary structure of the other two migration narratives (Ezra 1–2; 7–8) and why Ezra 9–10 does not follow the same pattern as Neh 9–10 and 13:23–28 (the other narratives mentioning foreign wives).

The return migrations of Sheshbazzar and Ezra are close to what Robert Alter would define as a "type-scene."[1] They contain significant exodus motifs and include similar literary features in the same order. For example, each begins with a decree, the leader receives items for the temple, and the narratives conclude with a list of returnees. This makes the Nehemiah return stand out starkly as the narrative lacks many of these elements.

The three narratives about putting away foreign wives are all very different. Regardless of whether they are recasting a single historical event or three different historical events, their literary features are unique. Nehemiah 9–10 only briefly references separating from foreign wives while addressing a variety of stipulations in the decree, primarily regarding temple donations. Nehemiah 13:23–28 addresses intermarriage but is explicitly concerned with the language that the children speak. Ezra, however, focuses only upon the marriage issue, unlike Neh 9–10, and only briefly mentions children but not any language or cultural problems, unlike Neh 13:23–28.

Several scholars have tried to bring these thematically related chapters together. For the return migrations, many scholars claim that Ezra-Nehemiah have a repeating literary structure. For example, a recent argument

---

1. Alter, *Art of Biblical Narrative*, 60–61.

by George Van Pelt Campbell, which was earlier put forth by H. G. M. Williamson and Lester Grabbe, is that Ezra 1–10 parallels Neh 1–10.[2] However, this chapter by chapter paralleling ignores major narrative points listed above. For example, one parallel that is suspicious is Ezra 2 and Neh 3. These are placed under the vague heading "List," most likely because they are clearly different types of lists (Neh 3 is a list of builders unlike Ezra 2 and Ezra 8, which are both lists of returnees). A similar structural argument has been presented by Raeyong Kim as a repeated cycle in Ezra 1–6, 7–10, and Neh 1–13 consisting of five elements: decree/permission, list/people, enemy, work, result.[3] However, this falls into the same issue as Campbell's organization. In order to make these parallels, the narrative categories must be extremely broad like "decree/permission," which are two very different types of speech (even in literary terms, Neh 2:1–8 is a dialogue in recorded speech, but Ezra 1 and 7 contain recorded decrees that the narrative suggests are independent documents inserted into the text).

One common method of examining the intermarriage crisis is to focus upon Ezra 9–10 and draw other passages in later as comparisons.[4] Another frequent method is to claim that Neh 9–10 originally came between Ezra 8 and 9 or after Ezra 10, but reading the text this way tends to distract from analyzing the passages in their current setting.[5] Some have even argued that Ezra 9–10 is a reworking of Neh 13:23–28.[6] Even if the historical events behind the narratives are the same, the portrayal of the events are dramatically different. The portrayal of the events in Ezra 9–10 as it stands in the

---

2. Campbell, "Structure, Themes, and Theology in Ezra-Nehemiah," 394–411; Williamson, *Ezra, Nehemiah*, xlix; Grabbe, *Ezra-Nehemiah*, 64–66.

3. Kim, "Historiographic Characteristics of Ezra-Nehemiah," 112.

4. Janzen, *Witch-Hunts, Purity and Social Boundaries*; Moffat, *Ezra's Social Drama*; Saysell, *"According to the Law"*; Johnson, *Holy Seed Has Been Defiled*; Southwood, *Ethnicity and the Mixed Marriage Crisis in Ezra 9–10*.

5. See Allen and Laniak, *Ezra, Nehemiah, Esther*, 71; Schoville, *Ezra-Nehemiah*, 118; Rudolph, *Esra und Nehemía Samt 3. Esra*, 154–55; Clines, *Ezra, Nehemiah, Esther*, 12; Williamson, *Ezra, Nehemiah*, 310. Juha Pakkala believes that Neh 8 is part of the Ezra Memoir but Neh 9–10 is a later stratum of text. Pakkala, *Ezra the Scribe*, 180–211. However, Goswell rejects this insertion on literary grounds. Goswell, *Study Commentary on Ezra-Nehemiah*, 168–69.

6. Myers, *Ezra-Nehemiah*; Hensel, "Ethnic Fiction and Identity-Formation," 133–48; McConville, *Ezra, Nehemiah, and Esther*; Williamson, *Ezra, Nehemiah*; Fensham, *Books of Ezra and Nehemiah*; Breneman, *Ezra, Nehemiah, Esther*; Shepherd and Wright, *Ezra and Nehemiah*. See arguments against reading these as a single historical event in Becking, *Ezra-Nehemiah*, 134.

Introduction

current Masoretic Text is unique and should be examined separately from the questions of historicity or an original ordering of the chapters.

A parallel that has not been examined is Ezra 9–10 and Neh 1:1–3:32. The narrative movements of these passages align surprisingly closely: a small group of leaders present a problem to the prominent character[7] in direct speech; the prominent character performs actions of mourning; a penitential prayer is recorded; an individual proposes a solution to the prominent character in direct speech; the prominent character changes location; the prominent character is in Jerusalem for three days; a plan of action is proposed in direct speech and there is an investigation of the problem (this is reversed in Nehemiah); and finally, a list of people involved in resolving the problem presented at the beginning is provided.

Thematic similarity is often what directs scholars to find similarity in literary structure. However, the most structurally similar narratives among those listed above are not, on the surface, identical in content.

THESIS

In this work, I will argue that the narrative structures of Ezra 9–10 and Neh 1:1–3:32 are intentionally shaped to draw the passages together.[8] This connects the two books but, more importantly, highlights the overlapping theological connection of building the community through exclusive ownership of the land. Many scholars have highlighted the sociological aspects

---

7. The term "prominent character" is being used rather than main or primary character. This terminology is intended to clarify that the narratives are not about the characters, but the prominent characters are the primary individuals acting within the narrative. For example, Ezra 9–10 is about putting away foreign wives, so Ezra is the prominent character acting and speaking but he is not the main or primary character in the sense that the narrative is about Ezra himself.

8. Hebrew literary and rhetorical devices are used in my analysis of the text. However, they will not be discussed in the history of the research because few of them analyze these passages in Ezra-Nehemiah in depth. In addition, I utilize literary concepts shared by a variety of scholars but do not follow one literary methodology religiously. This work attempts to follow the narrative of the text rather than apply a literary method to the text. For literary studies that provide the background to my literary analysis see Alter, *Art of Biblical Narrative*; Bar-Efrat, *Narrative Art in the Bible*; Gunn and Fewell, *Narrative in the Hebrew Bible*; Jobling, *Sense of Biblical Narrative: Structural Analyses in the Hebrew Bible I*; Jobling, *Sense of Biblical Narrative: Structural Analyses in the Hebrew Bible II*; Walsh, *Style and Structure in Biblical Hebrew Narrative*; Zeelander, *Closure in Biblical Narrative*.

Separation of the People, Separation of the Land

of the exclusion of foreign wives in Ezra 9–10.[9] Likewise, many scholars have noted the sociological and land associations in Neh 1–3.[10] However, neither of these views read Ezra 9–10 and Neh 1–3 together.

Other scholars have attempted to read the separation from foreign wives and city wall building together. The "citizen-temple community" concept claims that the Jerusalem temple owned land and so membership in the temple-community provided political rights and land.[11] Tamara Eskenazi's interpretation of Ezra-Nehemiah is a three stage process of building the temple, then the community, and finally broadening the temple (or holy precinct) to the entire city of Jerusalem.[12] However, none of these interpretations address the details of the narrative sequences in Ezra 9–10 and Neh 1–3. Instead, they read either the entire text of Ezra-Nehemiah or even postexilic literature generally within their interpretive model.

In this work, the two texts will be analyzed together both from a literary structure viewpoint and thematic interpretation. In each of the literary movements of Ezra 9–10 and Neh 1–3, a connection between the land and the Judean community will be shown. Within the texts, the leader of each narrative shows how foreigners must be excluded from the land of Judah. Nehemiah builds the community and removes foreigners by including Judeans in building the wall of Jerusalem but telling the adversaries that they have no ownership or claim there (Neh 2:20). Likewise, Ezra builds

---

9. Wright, "Writing the Restoration," 27; Wright, "New Model for the Composition of Ezra-Nehemiah," 335; Bertheau, *Bücher Esra, Nechemia und Ester*; Throntveit, *Ezra-Nehemiah*, 50–51; Clines, *Ezra, Nehemiah, Esther*, 116–17; Myers, *Ezra-Nehemiah*, 77; Rudolph, *Esra und Nehemía Samt 3. Esra*, 89; Williamson, *Ezra, Nehemiah*, 160–61; Ackroyd, *I & II Chronicles, Ezra, Nehemiah*, 261–63; Smith-Christopher, "Mixed Marriage Crisis in Ezra 9–10 and Nehemiah 13," 249; Janzen, "Sacrifice as Cultic Expression of the Law," 196; Redditt, *Ezra-Nehemiah*, 34; Esler, "Ezra-Nehemiah as a Narrative of (Re-Invented) Israelite Identity," 413–26; Moffat, *Ezra's Social Drama*; Janzen, "Scholars, Witches, Ideologues, and What the Text Said," 61; Oswald, "Foreign Marriages and Citizenship in Persian Period Judah," 1–17; Johnson, "Ethnicity in Persian Yehud," 177–86; Rothenbusch, "Question of Mixed Marriages between the Poles of Diaspora and Homeland," 65; Goswell, *Study Commentary on Ezra-Nehemiah*, 166.

10. Grabbe, "Law of Moses in the Ezra Tradition," 110; Esler, "Ezra-Nehemiah as a Narrative of (Re-Invented) Israelite Identity," 422; Wright, "New Model for the Composition of Ezra-Nehemiah," 334; Fried, "Who Wrote Ezra-Nehemiah—and Why Did They?," 75–97; Sapolu, "Reconciling Identities," 113–56. A related view is that it was political and created a national identity. See Knauf, "Bethel," 291–349. Another related view is that it was economic. Lipschits, *Fall and Rise of Jerusalem*, 168–73.

11. Weinberg, *Citizen-Temple Community*.

12. Eskenazi, *In an Age of Prose*.

Introduction

the community and removes foreigners by excluding foreign women and emphasizing that they must not even seek peace or welfare with outsiders lest they jeopardize their inheritance in the land (Ezra 9:12).

EZRA-NEHEMIAH STUDIES

Much of the research on Ezra-Nehemiah can be divided along literary and redactional lines.[13] Though these inform each other, this study is intended to focus primarily upon literary structure rather than editorial phases. The final shaping of the text will be part of the analysis, but this will be discussed in terms of its final form and not the process that produced the current text. Extended literary and redactional analyses of Ezra 9–10 and Neh 1:1–3:32 are typically concerned with either one of the texts but not both. So, I will treat the studies of Ezra 9–10 and Neh 1:1–3:32 separately and then discuss the studies that advocate for parallel passages between Ezra-Nehemiah. I will then address studies that advocate for a unitary or separate reading of Ezra-Nehemiah as a whole. A final area of research that will be discussed is the sociological angle. These studies are not always text-centered, but they derive their social models from the events within the text of Ezra-Nehemiah.

Literary Studies of Ezra 9–10

Many literary studies of Ezra 9–10 have been conducted, but most of them either focus upon redaction schemes or thematic similarities. One example of this is Juha Pakkala's study of the variance between terms and phrases in Ezra 9 and 10 suggesting two separate sources that have been edited together.[14] This is especially poignant in the statements about Israel taking

---

13. Archaeological studies have focused upon Nehemiah's wall, but they are not directly related to the narrative of the text. Since this is a literary study, these archaeological questions will not be examined. For discussions of the archaeological evidence, see Yamauchi, "Archaeological Backgrounds of the Exilic and Postexilic Era, Part 4," 291–309; Finkelstein, "Archaeology and the List of Returnees in the Books of Ezra and Nehemiah," 7–16; Finkelstein, *Hasmonean Realities behind Ezra, Nehemiah, and Chronicles*; Avi-Yonah, "Walls of Nehemiah," 239–48; Williamson, "Nehemiah's Walls Revisited," 81–88; Finkelstein, "Jerusalem in the Persian (and Early Hellenistic) Period and the Wall of Nehemiah," 501–20; Ussishkin, "On Nehemiah's City Wall and the Size of Jerusalem during the Persian Period," 101–30; Burns, *Ezra, Nehemiah*, 58.

14. Pakkala, *Ezra the Scribe*, 83–88.

foreign wives in Ezra 9:2 and 10:2, which contain significant differences in word choice even though the event they are describing is the same.[15] In addition, the choice of the plural "people of the lands" in Ezra 9 versus "people of the land" in chapter ten indicate that there is at least one editorial seam between these chapters.[16] Though I am less concerned with the historical development of these editorial elements, the indications of editorial shaping and word choice are valuable for this work because I am arguing that this narrative was intentionally shaped to make it structurally similar to Neh 1–3. Also, this work is concerned only with the editorial phases of Ezra 9–10 and Neh 8 so it does not consider the connection with Neh 1–3.

Harkins studied the description of the penitential prayer in Ezra 9 and found many literary parallels between the actions of Ezra in Ezra 9–10 and the actions of Moses during the golden calf incident and Solomon during the temple dedication.[17] These details are found in the wording and hand gestures of the key actors (e.g., Ezra collapsing using a Hithpael of נפל which is found only in Ezra 10:1 and three times in Deut 9, where Moses collapses during the golden calf incident).[18]

Similarly, Mark Boda analyzed unique Deuteronomic and priestly language in the prayers of Neh 1 and Ezra 9 to show the background and authorship of the passages.[19] He also analyzed the rhetorical function of the prayers in their current literary settings and whether they were separate compositions that were brought into the narratives by an editor. Though this compositional argument is outside the scope of this work, the rhetorical function of the prayers and the connections with Deuteronomic language are helpful. The shared linguistic background of the two prayers helps to solidify the connection between the passages and show their shared purpose.

Csilla Saysell examined the relationship between Ezra 9–10 and the law. The second half of the book examines the interpretation through Jewish and Christian history, but the first half is more properly an exegesis of the text. Saysell focuses upon key themes within the text like holy seed, חרם, and abominations rather than examining each narrative movement in order. Each of these themes is traced from its origin in the Pentateuch

---

15. Pakkala, *Ezra the Scribe*, 83–84.
16. Pakkala, *Ezra the Scribe*, 82–135.
17. Harkins, "Pro-Social Role of Grief in Ezra's Penitential Prayer," 486–88.
18. Harkins, "Pro-Social Role of Grief in Ezra's Penitential Prayer," 486–88.
19. Boda, *Praying the Tradition*, 70; Goswell, *Study Commentary on Ezra-Nehemiah*, 204.

Introduction

through the rest of the Old Testament in order to shed light on the way that Ezra 9–10 is using these concepts.[20] This method elucidates important aspects of the narrative but does not analyze the order of events as they are portrayed in the text.

Literary Studies of Neh 1:1–3:32

Fewer literary studies have focused upon Neh 1–3. As noted above, some of the literary studies connect Nehemiah's return with the migrations of Sheshbazzar and Ezra.[21] More often, the studies focus on the integrity of the Nehemiah Memoir (Neh 1–7) and the redactional strata that may underlie it. Specifically, scholars focus upon whether certain texts, like Nehemiah's prayer or the builder list, are additions to the memoir or original.[22] The integrity of the Nehemiah Memoir is outside the scope of this work because the current text is treated as a literary unity. What is more significant from these studies is the linguistic and thematic shift between Neh 3:32 and 4:1 (MT 3:33), which signals a break in the narrative.

Additional studies focus upon the date formulas, interaction between Nehemiah and Artaxerxes, and whether Nehemiah was a eunuch.[23] The date formula is only marginally relevant to this study, but the interaction between Nehemiah and Artaxerxes is quite important for this literary analysis. There are many discussions about whether Nehemiah waited until a holiday to request a favor from the king or was suddenly overcome with emotion on a random day.[24] However, more significant for the immediate

---

20. Saysell, *"According to the Law,"* 123–25.

21. Campbell, "Structure, Themes, and Theology in Ezra-Nehemiah"; Williamson, *Ezra, Nehemiah*, xlix; Grabbe, *Ezra-Nehemiah*, 64–66; Kim, "Historiographic Characteristics of Ezra-Nehemiah."

22. See the lengthy discussion in Wright, *Rebuilding Identity*.

23. Yamauchi, "Was Nehemiah the Cupbearer a Eunuch?," 132–42; Yamauchi, "Archaeological Backgrounds of the Exilic and Postexilic Era, Part 4," 291–309; Williamson, *Ezra, Nehemiah*, 174; Blenkinsopp, *Ezra-Nehemiah*, 212; Boice, *Nehemiah*, 15; Van Wijk-Bos, *Ezra, Nehemiah, and Esther*, 54; Clines, *Ezra, Nehemiah, Esther*, 140.

24. For arguments that it was planned for a holiday because it was a custom to accept requests on special occasions, see Becking, *Ezra-Nehemiah*, 179; Williamson, *Ezra, Nehemiah*, 178; Schoville, *Ezra-Nehemiah*, 144; Larson and Dahlen, *Ezra, Nehemiah, Esther*, 144. For the argument that Nehemiah simply could not contain his sorrow, see Myers, *Ezra-Nehemiah*, 99; Clines, *Ezra, Nehemiah, Esther*, 141; Goswell, *Study Commentary on Ezra-Nehemiah*, 211; Steinmann, *Ezra and Nehemiah*, 399; Redditt, *Ezra-Nehemiah*, 234; Mangan, *1–2 Chronicles, Ezra, Nehemiah*, 181; Allen and Laniak, *Ezra, Nehemiah,*

literary context is the discussion of Nehemiah's request of Artaxerxes rather than Artaxerxes issuing a decree.[25]

Other literary studies of the passages connect the Nehemiah Memoir with Moses or Solomon. Clines and Goswell have identified the Mosaic language of Deut 30:1–5 in Neh 1:8–9.[26] These are similar to the studies of Deuteronomic language cited above, except that they focus specifically on Mosaic phrasing like "your (God's) servant."[27]

Parallels in Ezra-Nehemiah

Narrow verbal parallels have been drawn between Ezra 9–10 and Neh 1–3. For example, Goswell noted the use of תמעלו "act unfaithfully" in Neh 1:8 is the same description as Ezra 9–10.[28] Steinmann also notes that the Hithpael of ידה "to confess" is only used in Ezra 10:1, Neh 1:6; 9:2–3.[29]

Many other scholars note the similarity between Ezra's mourning in Ezra 9 and Nehemiah's mourning in Neh 1.[30] These studies also note the overlap of Deuteronomic language in both the penitential prayers. However, most of them do not draw any further comparisons between Ezra 10 and Neh 2–3.

Esther, 93.

25. Japhet, "Sheshbazzar and Zerubbabel—Against the Background of the Historical and Religious Tendencies of Ezra-Nehemiah," 75; Fleishman, "Nehemiah's Request on Behalf of Jerusalem," 241–66; Eskenazi, "Imagining the Other in the Construction of Judahite Identity in Ezra-Nehemiah," 251; Van Wijk-Bos, *Ezra, Nehemiah, and Esther*, 54–56; Clines, *Ezra, Nehemiah, Esther*, 141–43; Goswell, *Study Commentary on Ezra-Nehemiah*, 213–14.

26. Clines, "Nehemiah Memoir," 78; Goswell, *Study Commentary on Ezra-Nehemiah*, 206.

27. Baltzer, "Moses Servant of God and the Servants," 121–30; Polaski, "Nehemiah," 40–41; Smith, "Influence of Deuteronomy on Intercessory Prayers in Ezra and Nehemiah," 345–65; Goswell, *Study Commentary on Ezra-Nehemiah*, 205–7; Becking, *Ezra-Nehemiah*, 174.

28. Goswell, *Study Commentary on Ezra-Nehemiah*, 204.

29. Steinmann, *Ezra and Nehemiah*, 383.

30. Steinmann, *Ezra and Nehemiah*, 390; Dumbrell, "Malachi and the Ezra-Nehemiah Reforms," 42–52; Baltzer, "Moses Servant of God and the Servants," 121–30; Werline, *Penitential Prayer in Second Temple Judaism*, 54–55; Goswell, *Study Commentary on Ezra-Nehemiah*, 204.

Introduction

In broader structural analyses, many authors have seen parallels within Ezra, with Ezra 1–6 paralleling Ezra 7–10.[31] In this parallel, separating from foreign wives is building the holy community in Ezra 9–10 in the same way as the holy temple was built in Ezra 4–6.

A few other scholars have pointed to parallels between Ezra 1–6 and the beginning of Nehemiah. One challenge of this claim is that the number of paralleling chapters changes. So, for example, Goswell claims that Ezra 1–6 parallels Neh 1–6, whereas Mangan claims that Ezra 1–6 parallels Neh 1–7.[32] Grabbe even went as far as claiming Ezra 1–10 parallels Neh 1–10. He specifically singled out Ezra 9–10 and Neh 9–10 as having so many similarities that the Ezra account is a copy of Nehemiah.[33] These analyses often vary between content and structure parallels. For example, Grabbe points out that Ezra 9–10 has similar structural organization (recorded prayer, people gathering and repenting, resolution by separation) but then moves to the content of the prayer and the shared issue of mixed marriages.[34]

Most of the studies on the parallels between the beginning of Ezra and the beginning of Nehemiah have this same blurred boundary between literary structure and narrative content. In addition, most of these treat the text at a chapter level and draw broad parallels (like Ezra 1 and Neh 2 dealing with a king) but not detailed analyses (like the difference between Cyrus decreeing in Ezra 1 and Artaxerxes asking for Nehemiah's request in Neh 2).

Ezra-Nehemiah Thematic and Literary Unity Studies

Starting with a broad thematic analysis, Eskenazi's monograph, *In an Age of Prose: A Literary Approach to Ezra-Nehemiah*, has been as influential as much as it has been criticized.[35] Eskenazi sees an overarching narrative structure developing through Ezra-Nehemiah of potential (Ezra 1), process (Ezra 2–Neh 7), and completion (Neh 8–13).[36] Within the process section,

---

31. Steinmann, *Ezra and Nehemiah*, 69–71; Shepherd and Wright, *Ezra and Nehemiah*, 98; with the addition of Nehemiah 8, see Grabbe, *Ezra-Nehemiah*, 107.

32. Goswell, *Study Commentary on Ezra-Nehemiah*, 45; Mangan, *1–2 Chronicles, Ezra, Nehemiah*, 148.

33. Grabbe, *Ezra-Nehemiah*, 65, 175.

34. Grabbe, *Ezra-Nehemiah*, 175.

35. For a detailed critique of Eskenazi's work see Clines, "Force of the Text," 199–215.

36. Eskenazi, *In an Age of Prose*. For a more recent scholar arguing an almost identical

the "house of God" in Ezra is transformed into the "city of Jerusalem" in Nehemiah, and the sacral aspects of the wall building ceremonies indicate this widening of the sacred sphere.[37] Eskenazi's argument does not deal with the specific sequence of the narrative in Ezra 9–10 and Neh 1–3. Instead, thematic elements are drawn from the texts to support the overall framework. The purpose is to show the unity of Ezra-Nehemiah and, while this unity is convincing, the city of Jerusalem becoming equated with the house of God is suspect, even in the occurrences of the terms in Nehemiah which never appear to use the two synonymously.[38]

Outside of Eskenazi's argument that Jerusalem becomes the temple, the unity of Ezra-Nehemiah is almost universally accepted. Many scholars believe that Ezra and Nehemiah have a shared editorial process across both books based upon the literary overlap of structure and characters as well as the lack of historical attestation to two independent books.[39] However, this has been questioned by a few scholars, primarily VanderKam and Kraemer, who discount the literary arguments as superficial or evidence of later editing.[40] They also note that the early attestations of a single book are much later than the origin of the books themselves. So, this evidence does not necessarily indicate they were originally unified but that at some point between the writing of the text and the early Jewish and Christian writers, they came to be seen as a single, canonical work.[41]

Though these arguments primarily treat literary features throughout Ezra-Nehemiah or the attestations outside the text, they also touch upon the seam between Ezra and Nehemiah (specifically Neh 1:1 where the words of Nehemiah are introduced).[42] Though the unity of the books is not the primary question of a study on the literary structures in Ezra 9–10 and Neh 1:1–3:32, the editorial shaping and relationship between the Ezra Memoir and Nehemiah Memoir will be part of the discussion. Whether the books were originally a unity or originally separate is less valuable than

position, see Campbell, "Structure, Themes, and Theology in Ezra-Nehemiah," 394–411.

37. Eskenazi, *In an Age of Prose*.

38. Kraemer, "On the Relationship of the Books of Ezra and Nehemiah," 75; VanderKam, "Ezra-Nehemiah or Ezra and Nehemiah?," 73.

39. Tiemeyer, *Ezra-Nehemiah*, 40.

40. Kraemer, "On the Relationship of the Books of Ezra and Nehemiah," 73–92; VanderKam, "Ezra-Nehemiah or Ezra and Nehemiah?," 55–75.

41. Kraemer, "On the Relationship of the Books of Ezra and Nehemiah," 74; VanderKam, "Ezra-Nehemiah or Ezra and Nehemiah?," 61–62.

42. VanderKam, "Ezra-Nehemiah or Ezra and Nehemiah?," 61.

Introduction

their consideration as a unity in the current text and throughout much of the reception history.

Sociological Studies

The foreign wives crisis and Nehemiah's wall building are often analyzed through sociological methods to define the in-group versus the out-group and the relationship of the community to the Persian Empire.

The sociological discussions about the foreign wives crisis usually center around the identity of the foreign wives and the reasons why they are considered outsiders by the community.[43] Some scholars claim that the foreign wives were non-exiled Judeans, that is, people who had remained in Judah throughout the exile.[44] Others claim that it was an internal dispute within the exilic community, that is those who returned from exile, as to who belonged within the community.[45] A handful of scholars claim that an outside group of people came into the land during the Babylonian period and took over after the exile, so it is separation from this foreign ruling class that Ezra is targeting in the removal of foreign wives.[46]

However, other scholars have discussed the reasons behind the expulsion positing that the community had weak internal cohesion but strong external boundaries.[47] In this view, the exclusion of foreign women is a way for a community in jeopardy to maintain its existence and define its social boundaries.[48]

---

43. Koch claims that the list in Ezra 9:1 shows Ezra was intending to rebuild the nation of Israel. He specifically points out that Samaritans are not included in the list and, he hypothesizes, this was because Ezra saw them as the northern tribes of Israel. Koch, "Ezra and the Origins of Judaism," 193–94.

44. Wright, "New Model for the Composition of Ezra-Nehemiah," 343; Leuchter, "Exegesis of Jeremiah in and beyond Ezra 9–10," 62–80; Usue, "Is the Expulsion of Women as Foreigners in Ezra 9–10 Justifiably Covenantal?," 158–69; Becking, *Ezra, Nehemiah, and the Construction of Early Jewish Identity*, 58–73; Moffat, *Ezra's Social Drama*, 77–79; Eskenazi and Judd, "Marriage to a Stranger in Ezra 9–10," 266–85; Saysell, *"According to the Law,"* 45–49; Japhet, *From the Rivers of Babylon to the Highlands of Judah*, 110–12.

45. Van Wyk and Breytenbach, "Nature of the Conflict in Ezra-Nehemiah," 1254–63.

46. Myers, *Ezra-Nehemiah*, 77; Würthwein, "'Amm Ha'arez" im Alten Testament, 51–71.

47. Southwood, "Ethnic Affair?," 46–59; Janzen, *Witch-Hunts, Purity and Social Boundaries*, 105–15.

48. Southwood, *Ethnicity and the Mixed Marriage Crisis in Ezra 9–10*.

Separation of the People, Separation of the Land

This interpretation of the community in jeopardy has also been explored through concepts of wealth and power. Many scholars have claimed that excluding foreign women is an attempt to keep the wealth and power within the Judean community while others have posited that intermarriage may have been a way for the golah community to form alliances with the wealthy elite who were already living in the land.[49] Regardless of whether the golah community was the wealthy elite excommunicating their neighbors or an impoverished community attempting to marry outsiders to improve their status, the function of the separation from foreign wives is to maintain the external social boundary. Ezra was defining who belonged to the Judean community and purifying it from external influences.[50]

In Nehemiah, scholars typically focus upon building the wall as enforcing social boundaries or purifying Jerusalem.[51] The latter argument derives from Eskenazi's view of the house of God expanding to include the entire city of Jerusalem as described above.[52] Similar to Ezra 9–10, Nehemiah maintains the external social boundary between the Judean community and outsiders but instead of removing foreign wives, he builds a wall around Jerusalem. Even though Nehemiah's wall is seen as maintaining an external social boundary much like Ezra's expulsion of foreign wives, these

---

49. Van Wyk and Breytenbach, "Nature of the Conflict in Ezra-Nehemiah," 1260; Tollefson and Williamson, "Nehemiah as Cultural Revitalization," 52; Johnson, *Holy Seed Has Been Defiled*, 87.

50. Bertheau, *Bücher Esra, Nechemia und Ester*; Throntveit, *Ezra-Nehemiah*, 50–51; Clines, *Ezra, Nehemiah, Esther*, 116–17; Myers, *Ezra-Nehemiah*, 77; Rudolph, *Esra und Nehemia Samt 3. Esra*, 89; Williamson, *Ezra, Nehemiah*, 160–61; Ackroyd, *I & II Chronicles, Ezra, Nehemiah*, 261–63; Smith-Christopher, "Mixed Marriage Crisis in Ezra 9–10 and Nehemiah 13," 249; Janzen, "Sacrifice as Cultic Expression of the Law," 196; Redditt, *Ezra-Nehemiah*, 34; Esler, "Ezra-Nehemiah as a Narrative of (Re-Invented) Israelite Identity," 413–26; Moffat, *Ezra's Social Drama*; Janzen, "Scholars, Witches, Ideologues, and What the Text Said," 61; Oswald, "Foreign Marriages and Citizenship in Persian Period Judah," 1–17; Johnson, "Ethnicity in Persian Yehud," 177–86; Rothenbusch, "Question of Mixed Marriages between the Poles of Diaspora and Homeland," 65; Goswell, *Study Commentary on Ezra-Nehemiah*, 166.

51. Grabbe, "Law of Moses in the Ezra Tradition," 110; Esler, "Ezra-Nehemiah as a Narrative of (Re-Invented) Israelite Identity," 422; Wright, "New Model for the Composition of Ezra-Nehemiah," 334; Fried, "Who Wrote Ezra-Nehemiah – and Why Did They?," 75–97; Sapolu, "Reconciling Identities," 113–56; Knauf, "Bethel," 291–349; Lipschits, *Fall and Rise of Jerusalem*, 168–73.

52. Janzen, "Sacrifice as Cultic Expression of the Law," 185–208; Clauss, "Understanding the Mixed Marriages of Ezra-Nehemiah in the Light of Temple-Building and the Book's Concept of Jerusalem," 118–21; Harrington, "Holiness and Purity in Ezra-Nehemiah," 102–03; Goswell, *Study Commentary on Ezra-Nehemiah*, 198.

Introduction

same scholars understand the identity of the foreigners as different between the two texts. It is often noted that Ezra identifies women living within the province of Judah as foreign whereas the adversaries in Nehemiah appear to live outside of the territory in places like Samaria (cf. Neh 4).[53]

However, another common way scholars analyze the text is to examine the social symbolism of the wall. The reproach of the city and restoration of the wall is a symbol of the renewed strength of Judah.[54] This restoration of the political disgrace of the province through a new city wall is symbolically conquering the enemies of Judah, as shown in the interactions with the named adversaries of Sanballat the Horonite, Tobiah the Ammonite, and Geshem the Arab.[55] This is sometimes interpreted as a second conquest of the land but more often a cultural revitalization, that is using a sociological description rather than biblical typology.

METHODOLOGY

My methodology is text-driven but not content-driven. I want to analyze the way that the prominent characters are portrayed within the narrative (i.e., individual or group, speaking or silent, performing actions or being acted upon), the types of actions that they perform (i.e., recorded speech, geographic movement, interaction with other characters), and the types of literature within the narrative (i.e., name lists, item inventories, decrees, prayers). The goal is to analyze the narratives apart from their thematic similarity or dissimilarity and so show points of commonality that are not typically seen when examining narratives primarily on their thematic elements.

In order to accomplish this narrative structure analysis, I will start with thematically similar passages. I will analyze Ezra 9–10 and Neh 1–3 with thematically similar passages and then contrast their literary structure.

In the second chapter of this work, Ezra 1–2, 7–8, and Neh 1–3 are compared as migration narratives. Since the goal of this work is literary

---

53. Becking, *Ezra-Nehemiah*, 170; Vogt, *Studie zur nachexilischen Gemeinde in Esra-Nehemia*, 45; Knoppers, "Nehemiah and Sanballat," 305–31; Williamson, *Ezra, Nehemiah*, 171–72.

54. Wright, "Writing the Restoration," 27; Wright, "New Model for the Composition of Ezra-Nehemiah," 335.

55. Goswell, *Study Commentary on Ezra-Nehemiah*, 198, 217; Tollefson and Williamson, "Nehemiah as Cultural Revitalization."

structure, the major themes will not be discussed exhaustively. The focus will be the portrayal of the prominent character(s) and the primary concern. So, the first two narratives are dominated by the Persian king, both in terms of the amount of text because of their decrees and their influence by compelling the actions of the other characters, but Nehemiah dominates the third passage, again by the amount of text with his prayer, dialogue, and narration as well as his influence by compelling the actions of the other characters. Likewise, the primary concern in the two Ezra passages is the cult, with special emphasis on the temple and the cultic personnel, but Nehemiah's focus is upon the city with an emphasis on the city wall and the people as a whole.

These thematic contrasts lead into a discussion of the narrative structures of the passages in the next chapter. The elements of Ezra 1–2 and 7–8 overlap significantly and in the same order. Each has a Persian king making a decree which is recorded in the text, donations for the temple, the people rising to leave, an inventory of the temple donations when they arrive, and a list of returnees. However, Nehemiah contains none of these elements. Nehemiah appears to travel only with royal guards, brings no donations for the temple, has a dialogue with the king rather than receiving a decree, and has a list of wall builders not a list of returnees.

The fourth and fifth chapters follow the same pattern as the second and third chapters. Chapter four contains a thematic analysis of Ezra 9–10, Neh 9–10, and 13:23–28 focusing upon the prominent character(s) and the primary concern. Then chapter five compares the literary structures of the three passages, though in this case they are all quite divergent in their literary structure.

Chapters six and seven are the main argument of this work. In chapter six, the literary structures of Ezra 9–10 and Neh 1–3 are compared. Then, in chapter seven, the thematic overlap between these two passages is examined. The outline of this chapter follows the shared narrative movements identified in chapter six. In each section of the narrative, the connection between the people, the land, and exclusion of outsiders will be shown.

Besides the biblical text, I will examine modern scholarly works concerning the structure and theology of Ezra-Nehemiah. These will orient my interpretation of the text within the academic conversation as well as confirm (or challenge) my conclusions. I will address different methodologies throughout the chapters, including redactional theories, and compare them with my interpretations. Though my method will be to analyze the

Introduction

final form of the Hebrew text from a literary structure standpoint, other literary, sociological, and text critical methods can confirm or question the observations made from my method.

Chapter 2

Return Accounts
Ezra 1–2, 7–8, and Nehemiah 1–3

The return accounts of Sheshbazzar and Ezra have often been compared with Nehemiah's return to Jerusalem. In this chapter, I will discuss the primary thematic elements in the return migrations of Sheshbazzar, Ezra, and Nehemiah, and in the next chapter I will discuss the literary structures of these narratives. In this chapter, I will first explain where each literary unit begins and ends. The goal is to show that these are complete literary units within the broader narrative of Ezra-Nehemiah. Then, I will examine the prominent character in each passage. This is not necessarily the leader of the returnees but the catalyst in the narrative, whose actions or speech drive the other events in the literary unit. Finally, I will discuss the primary concerns of each migration narrative. By primary concerns, I mean the objects and people that the narrative and the prominent character are focused upon. These concerns will be shown by repeated references within the passage and the address of these items within reported speech or transcribed documents. I will argue that the return narratives of Sheshbazzar and Ezra share the same prominent character, the Persian king,[1] and primary concerns, the cultic personnel and temple, while Neh 1:1–3:32

---

1. Though I argue that Cyrus and Artaxerxes are the two predominant characters in the first two return migrations, I also use the conventional identification of them as the return migrations of Sheshbazzar and Ezra. This is not to claim that these two leaders are the predominant characters in their respective narratives but simply to align with the conventional names used by scholarship for the migrations.

focuses on entirely different themes (Nehemiah as the prominent character and concern for the wall and the people as a whole).

SHESHBAZZAR

The narrative movement of the return migration in Ezra 1–2 can be diagrammed as follows:

1. Cyrus issues a decree (1:1–4)
   A. God stirs and Cyrus writes (1:1)
   B. Transcription of the decree (1:2–4)
      i. Any of the people may leave (1:3)
      ii. People support the returnees (1:4)
2. Leaders rise up to go (1:5)
3. Offerings (1:6–11)
   A. From the people (1:6)
   B. From Cyrus (1:7–10)
   C. Given to Sheshbazzar and taken to Jerusalem (1:11)
4. List of returnees (2:1–67)
   A. Name list (2:1–61)
      i. Leaders (2:1–2a)
      ii. People (2:2b–35)
      iii. Priests (2:36–39)
      iv. Levites (2:40–58)
      v. Unclear ancestry people (2:59–60)
      vi. Unclear ancestry priests (2:61)
   B. Exclusion (2:62–63)
   C. Total numbers (2:64–67)
5. Amount of gold, silver, clothing given for the temple (2:68–69)
6. Israel lives in the cities (2:70)

There is a narrative break at the end of chapter two. This is indicated both by the closing formula and the introductory date. Chapter two ends with all Israel dwelling in their cities (2:70), and chapter three begins in the seventh month, when the sons of Israel were in the cities (3:1). The move forward in time from the statement of Israel being in the cities shows that this is a new section.[2] In fact, Lisbeth Fried argues that Ezra 1–2 have no place within the temple-building-story genre that comprises chapters 4–6. Instead, it functions as a prologue in the form of Hellenistic rhetorical composition. Though I do not agree with the overall structure proposed by Fried, the arguments for Ezra 1–2 being distinct subject matter is compelling and aligns with my argument for a narrative break between Ezra 2 and 3.[3]

Also, Jeshua and Zerubbabel become the prominent characters and Sheshbazzar is not mentioned (3:2). Though these two characters were mentioned in Ezra 2:2, they were simply among the leaders in the return list while Sheshbazzar was the leader orchestrating the return. In chapter three, they move from leaders in a list to the primary agents in the rebuilding of the temple.

The structural movements in the text which were outlined above will be discussed in more detail in the next chapter. However, two key thematic emphases will be discussed in this section: the focus on the king and the cultic emphasis.

Prominent Character: Cyrus

The narrative in Ezra 1 is dominated by the king, more specifically Yahweh working through the Persian king. As, Othniel Margalith notes:

> It is remarkable that the initiative of the Return did not lie with Zerubbabel but with Cyrus: Ezra i makes it abundantly clear that the king did not address his edict to any political or religious leader, but to the people as a whole, not merely permitting but actively encouraging their return, levying a (penal?) tax on those

---

2. Williamson, *Ezra, Nehemiah*, 38; Goswell, *Study Commentary on Ezra-Nehemiah*, 65.

3. Fried, "Ezra's Use of Documents in the Context of Hellenistic Rules of Rhetoric," 17.

who stayed behind (i 4, 6) and subsidizing the Temple from the royal treasury.[4]

The text opens by dating the events to the first year of King Cyrus (1:1). Goswell claims, "The placement of the decree of Cyrus at the head of the book, except for the one verse introduction (1:1), is the reader's first clue to its importance within the ensuing narrative. It is the decree issued by King Cyrus that initiates the movement of the book and sets out the plan of the first six chapters."[5] Then the return begins with God stirring Cyrus to make a decree in order to fulfill Jeremiah's prophecy.[6] The centrality of this proclamation is shown by its transcription in the text (1:2-4). As Robert Alter noted, Hebrew narrative is built around direct speech.[7] Though this is not a direct conversation, the insertion of this document indicates the value of this decree for the event. The switch into first person shows that this is intended to be read as a transcription or translation of Cyrus's words, and they are important enough to warrant copying into the narrative rather than summary.[8]

To be clear, I am not making a claim to the origin of this or any other document in Ezra-Nehemiah. The value of noting that this is an inserted document in this work is not in the Persian or Judean origin of the document but how it is portrayed within the text. The conversation surrounding whether the decrees in Ezra-Nehemiah were copied from original Persian

---

4. Margalith, "Political Background of Zerubbabel's Mission and the Samaritan Schism," 317; Laird, "Temple Building Account in Ezra 1-6," 97; Redditt, *Ezra-Nehemiah*, 68-69; Japhet, "Sheshbazzar and Zerubbabel," 71-80; Rudolph, *Esra und Nehemia Samt 3. Esra*, xxvii-xxx; Bickerman, *From Ezra to the Last of the Maccabees*, 30; Becking, *Ezra-Nehemiah*, 21; Goswell, *Study Commentary on Ezra-Nehemiah*, 65.

5. Goswell, *Study Commentary on Ezra-Nehemiah*, 54; Japhet, "Sheshbazzar and Zerubbabel - Against the Background of the Historical and Religious Tendencies of Ezra-Nehemiah," 73.

6. Though the text explicitly claims to fulfill the prophecy of Jeremiah, many scholars have noted a relationship to prophecies of Isaiah and specifically Isa 45. The question could be raised whether Cyrus is prominent in Ezra 1 in order to fulfill his role in Isa 45. Creating a link to Isaiah's prophecy could be a reason for the literary shaping of Ezra 1, but the text does not claim this. In addition, this study is more concerned with analyzing the shape of the narrative rather than identifying the possible intertextual reasons for the narrative shape.

7. Alter, *Art of Biblical Narrative*, 82; Van Wijk-Bos, *Ezra, Nehemiah, and Esther*, 17; Boda, "Prayer as Rhetoric in the Book of Nehemiah," 272-75.

8. Goswell, *Study Commentary on Ezra-Nehemiah*, 56; Hasler, "Cited Documents of Ezra-Nehemiah," 372-89.

documents or entirely fabricated by the editor of Ezra-Nehemiah is complex and not directly relevant to a literary study of the text. Therefore, when stating that documents are inserted into the narrative, I am speaking about the portrayal of the documents in the text, not making a historicity or authenticity claim.

The content of the decree is central in the text in two ways. First, the king identifies himself as the one appointed to build the temple (1:2). Cyrus claims, "Yahweh, the God of heaven ... has appointed me to build him a house in Jerusalem" (1:2).[9] The role of the Persian king within the religious and social ideology of Yehud is complicated.[10] However, this statement appears to be a clear indication that Cyrus and Yahweh are on the same side. Again, since this is a literary study, the text presents Cyrus and Yahweh as working together, but the actual conversion of Cyrus or any Yahwistic reverence on his part is doubtful. It was common practice for Persian kings to claim that they were supported by the gods of other nations they conquered and to claim that they were followers of the deity. However, it is unknown if the was the case for Cyrus and Yahweh but, from the standpoint of the narrative, Cyrus appears to be at least inspired by Yahweh, if not a follower of Yahweh.[11]

In addition to Yahweh stirring Cyrus's heart in verse 1, Cyrus makes the claim that Yahweh gave him rule over the entire earth and appointed him to build the temple. The language of the decree has been argued to be in line Persian propaganda and the inclusion of a Hebrew translation of Persian phrases could be an attempt to make the royal decree appear legitimate.[12] Becking sees some of these as non-Persian phrases, but "god of heaven" was used elsewhere in Persian literature at the time, so it could be diplomatic courtesy.[13] Williamson adds that the term "king of Persia" and the titles for God were not used by Persian kings.[14] However, even if

---

9. All translations are my own unless otherwise noted.

10. See discussions in Esler, "Ezra-Nehemiah as a Narrative of (Re-Invented) Israelite Identity," 413–26; Bedford, "Diaspora," 147–65; Cataldo, "Persian Policy and the Yehud Community during Nehemiah," 240–52.

11. For the use of divine appointments and worship practices in Persian literature see Williamson, *Ezra, Nehemiah*, 11–12; Becking, *Ezra-Nehemiah*, 28; Goswell, *Study Commentary on Ezra-Nehemiah*, 58–59; Clines, *Ezra, Nehemiah, Esther*, 36–37. Contra Burns, *Ezra, Nehemiah*, 19.

12. Myers, *Ezra-Nehemiah*, 8.

13. Becking, *Ezra-Nehemiah*, 26–28;

14. Williamson, *Ezra, Nehemiah*, 11.

these are not truly Persian phrases, Becking and Williamson agree that the author is attempting to portray these as legitimate words of the Persian king and thereby support the decree as an authentic Persian document (or at least an authentic translation of the document).

Regardless of the authenticity of the phrasing, the inclusion of the inspiration of Yahweh prior to the decree, and the subsequent actions of the people that follow the decree almost to the letter, indicates that the author of Ezra 1 is promoting Cyrus's appointment by Yahweh.[15] So, the introduction to the decree reinforces that it is not just Yahweh's actions but Yahweh working through Cyrus to bring about the divine plan.

The second way in which the decree functions as the central, driving force is that the actions of the people follow the commands in the decree.[16] Cyrus commands the people to go to Jerusalem to rebuild the temple (1:3) and the people surrounding them to donate gifts in addition to freewill offerings (1:5). The succeeding verses describe the events in this same order. The leaders rise up to leave (1:5), and the people living around them encouraged them with gifts in addition to freewill offerings (1:6). So, even though the primary actors in verses 5–6 are Jews or the people living around them, the catalyst is the decree, and the portrayal of the events reflects the commands in the decree of Cyrus.[17] In fact, Williamson claims that the narrator simply wrote up the response on the basis of the decree.[18] Christopher Lortie, examining Cyrus's commands "to go up" and "to build," claims,

> The עלה imperative was at the foreground of the narrative for most of 1:5–3:1, but 2:68–69 draws attention to the בנה imperative moments before the עלה imperative is completed by highlighting the freewill offerings which were designated for the temple rebuilding project being brought by the 'heads of families' (2:68).[19]

---

15. This reflects the Old Testament worldview. Becking, *Ezra-Nehemiah*, 21; Dumbrell, "Theological Intention of Ezra-Nehemiah," 66.

16. Goswell, *Study Commentary on Ezra-Nehemiah*, 61; Van Wijk-Bos, *Ezra, Nehemiah, and Esther*, 16. Eskenazi claims that Ezra 1:5–Neh 7 fulfills Cyrus's decree but also notes that Ezra 1:5–6 is a literal fulfilment of the decree. Eskenazi, "Imagining the Other in the Construction of Judahite Identity in Ezra-Nehemiah," 235; Grabbe, *Ezra-Nehemiah*, 10.

17. See the parallels in Steinmann, *Ezra and Nehemiah*, 142; Davies, *Ezra and Nehemiah*, 11; Becking, *Ezra-Nehemiah*, 31; Burns, *Ezra, Nehemiah*, 19.

18. Williamson, *Ezra, Nehemiah*, 15.

19. Lortie also argues that the commands to "go up" and "to build" in Cyrus's decree drive the entire narrative of Ezra 1–6. He argues that Ezra 1:5–3:1 is the "go up" section and 2:68–6:22 is the "build" section. Lortie, "These Are the Days of the Prophets,"

In verse 7, Cyrus returns as the primary agent by bringing out articles for the Jerusalem temple. These are passed to Sheshbazzar, counted, then brought to Jerusalem. So, immediately after the people fulfill the commands of Cyrus's decree, Cyrus again is the central actor in the narrative to the point that even Sheshbazzar's actions are based upon the primary action of Cyrus (the text states that he received the articles given by Cyrus and brought them to the place indicated by Cyrus).

In Ezra 2, the focus switches from Cyrus to the returnees. Though the primary characters are the returnees, specifically the leaders who controlled the status of unrecorded families and the donations to the temple (vv. 63–69), the entire chapter is predicated on the act of Cyrus. Even the mention of Nebuchadnezzar in Ezra 2:1 is an attempt to artificially connect the community with the pre-exilic nation of Israel, according to Becking, and so is a way of contrasting the negative state of the people under the previous king and the reversal of the same people's fortune under the new king, Cyrus.[20]

Ezra 1:11 states that Sheshbazzar brought the articles given by Cyrus to Jerusalem "with the exiles (גולה)" and chapter two begins with "and these are the people of the province who went up from the captivity of the exile (גולה) who were exiled (גלה) by Nebuchadnezzar." The list of returnees is not a new subject, but an extended definition of the exiles mentioned in Ezra 1:11 who returned after the decree of Cyrus in Ezra 1:2–4. Again, this is not a claim to the origin or authenticity of the list. The point here is the function of it and specifically its relationship to the exiles in Ezra 1:11 who were brought up by Sheshbazzar. The list is functioning like an appendix to the narrative of chapter one. These are the names of those who responded to Cyrus's decree and were brought up by Sheshbazzar (1:11).

Primary Concern: Cult

The religious emphasis and wording throughout Ezra-Nehemiah have led to scholars asserting that the books were written by a priest or a Levite.[21]

163n8. This confirms my analysis of this section, the decree is fulfilled by the actions of the people in chapters 1 and 2, though perhaps the command to build the temple is not ultimately completed but it is at least fulfilled in summary at the end of chapter two.

20. Becking, *Ezra-Nehemiah*, 41.

21. Williamson, *Ezra, Nehemiah*, xxxiv–xxxv; Williamson, "Composition of Ezra i–vi," 26–29; Throntveit, *Ezra-Nehemiah*, 8–10; Knoppers, "Hierodules, Priests, or Janitors?

Beyond the centrality of the cult generally, Ezra 1–2 contains significant cultic and priestly imagery.

Min has argued that priestly texts should be distinguished from Levitical texts on the basis of whether Levites are treated as equal with priests (Levitical text) or as a group with lesser status than priests (priestly text). He argues that with this distinction, Ezra-Nehemiah should be understood as Levitical and not priestly.[22] However, Fried has reassessed the portrayal of Levites in Ezra-Nehemiah and argued that the texts should be read as priestly.[23] My use of the term "priestly" and "priestly imagery" is not intended to argue for authorship based upon an ideological interpretation of Ezra-Nehemiah that turns upon the subservience of the Levites to the priests. Instead, these terms are intended to be a shorthand way of referring to temple or cultic personnel more generally. I am interested in whether the texts highlight cultic personnel or non-cultic personnel rather than how they portray the hierarchy of the cultic classes.

Temple

The text begins with the decree to build a temple in Jerusalem (1:2), and the response is that the leaders rise to go build the temple (1:5). It should be noted that the building project authorized by Cyrus is only the temple and not the city of Jerusalem or any other administrative building.[24] The focus upon rebuilding the temple is then reinforced in Ezra 2:68 when the people "arrive at the house of the Lord" in Jerusalem even though it is not built yet (2:68).[25]

Cyrus decrees a freewill offering for the house of God which is in Jerusalem (Ezra 1:4). Williamson notes that the term "freewill offering" in the decree of Cyrus (1:4) is a technical priestly term, so this phrasing would have originated with the Jews or specifically cultic personnel rather than Cyrus himself.[26] The designation that the freewill offering is for the house

---

The Levites in Chronicles and the History of the Israelite Priesthood," 49–72; Min, *Levitical Authorship of Ezra-Nehemiah*, 409.

22. Min, *Levitical Authorship of Ezra-Nehemiah*.
23. Fried, "Who Wrote Ezra-Nehemiah—and Why Did They?," 83n26.
24. See Steinmann, *Ezra and Nehemiah*, 84.
25. Steinmann, *Ezra and Nehemiah*, 84. Williamson argues this verse is a later addition. Williamson, *Ezra, Nehemiah*, 29–30.
26. Williamson, *Ezra, Nehemiah*, 15.

of God in Jerusalem also indicates that it is a technical cultic type of offering and not just random gifts given to the returning Judeans.

In addition, Cyrus gives articles from the first temple to Sheshbazzar to take to Jerusalem (1:7).[27] This appears to be especially significant to the author of Ezra because it is explained in detail. He provides their provenance as coming from the house of Yahweh that was plundered by Nebuchadnezzar (1:7). The author then explains that the articles are not given directly to Sheshbazzar but through Mithredath the treasurer (1:8). They are then counted out to Sheshbazzar, and the author provides the inventory list with the quantity and type of each article (1:9–11).[28] This focus on recording the number of items and their provenance becomes more prominent when the migration from Babylon to Jerusalem is treated with the summary phrase, "Sheshbazzar brought them [the temple articles] all up with the exiles who went up from Babylon to Jerusalem" (1:11). The amount of detail provided for the temple goods shows that the author is clearly more focused upon the number and acquisition of these items than detailing the migration journey itself. Becking claims that the text focuses on these cultic vessels because they symbolize continuity with the period before the Babylonian conquest. So, these are aniconic representations of the return of God to the temple in Jerusalem.[29] This aligns with the temple focus of the passage. The author is concerned with building the new temple and acquiring the temple utensils needed for it to function.

In addition to acquiring temple utensils from Cyrus, the leaders of the households donate gold, silver, and clothing to the temple when they arrive in Jerusalem (2:68–69). The narrative again focuses on the offerings by listing the quantity for each type of donation. The author emphasizes the utensils from the first temple while the people were still in Babylon and then describes additional donations for the functioning of the temple once the people have arrived. Clearly, the author is not just concerned about the

---

27. This has been seen as a fulfillment of Jeremiah's prophecy about the return of the temple vessels (Jer 28:1–17). However, this prophetic fulfillment is outside the scope of this work. See Steinmann, *Ezra and Nehemiah*, 144; Becking, *Ezra-Nehemiah*, 21–22.

28. For discussions of the origin of the list see Blenkinsopp, *Ezra-Nehemiah*, 79; Breneman, *Ezra, Nehemiah, Esther*, 73; Fensham, *Books of Ezra and Nehemiah*, 46–47; Kidner, *Ezra and Nehemiah*, 35–36; Myers, *Ezra-Nehemiah*, 9; Williamson, *Ezra, Nehemiah*, 7–8, 16; Steinmann, *Ezra and Nehemiah*, 144–45; Becking, *Ezra-Nehemiah*, 34–35.

29. Becking, "Silent Witness," 267–78; Fried, "Torah of God as God," 286; Ackroyd, *Studies in the Religious Tradition of the Old Testament*, 45–60.

building of the structure but the continued functioning of the temple and shows this through the lists of necessary income, utensils, and clothing.

Religious Officials

Besides the emphasis on the physical house and utensils for worship, priests and Levites are prominent in the narrative. The people who rise to leave Babylon are the heads of households and the priests and Levites (1:5).[30] Within the list of returnees, priests, Levites, the Nethinim, and the sons of Solomon's servants are listed separately (2:36–58).

The origin of the Nethinim is unclear, whether Israelites or foreigners, but in Ezra-Nehemiah they appear to be established cultic personnel somewhere below the priestly classes but above Solomon's servants because they are exempted from taxes and specifically sought after with the Levites by Ezra (Ezra 8). Most scholars view the Nethinim as foreigners dedicated to service in the temple.[31] They are normally assumed to have assisted the Levites by performing menial tasks in the temple.[32] There are also questions about the singers and gatekeepers. Most scholars view the singers and gatekeepers as Levites.[33] However, a few scholars follow Williamson who claims that the singers and gatekeepers were not Levites at this point. He believes the identification of singers and gatekeepers with the Levites is a later development.[34] An even more minority view is that singers, gatekeepers, and the Nethinim were all Levites.[35] Regardless of the Levitical status of singers, gatekeepers, and the Nethinim, their service within the temple sets them apart as cultic personnel. Even though they may not have been considered

---

30. Williamson claims that this division is common in Ezra-Nehemiah. Williamson, *Ezra, Nehemiah*, 15; Becking, *Ezra-Nehemiah*, 30, 40.

31. See Healey, "Nethinim," 1086; Lipiński, "נָתַן," 105–7; Botta, "Nethinim," 260–61; Schultz, "5987 נְתִין," 203–04. See also Puech's argument for the Nethinim being associated with Canaanite sanctuaries. Puech, "Tell El-Fûl Jar Inscription and the Nětînîm," 69–72.

32. Williamson, *Ezra, Nehemiah*, 35; Dyck, "Ezra 2 in Ideological Critical Perspective," 132.

33. Becking, *Ezra-Nehemiah*, 42–43; Goswell, *Study Commentary on Ezra-Nehemiah*, 75–76; Clines, *Ezra, Nehemiah, Esther*, 55–56; Myers, *Ezra-Nehemiah*, 19; Steinmann, *Ezra and Nehemiah*, 172; Allen and Laniak, *Ezra, Nehemiah, Esther*, 25; Thomas, *Ezra & Nehemiah*, 21–22.

34. Williamson, *Ezra, Nehemiah*, 35; Dyck, "Ezra 2 in Ideological Critical Perspective," 132.

35. Leuchter, "Levites in Exile," 583–90.

equal in status to priests or Levites, they were still considered different from lay Judeans, and so, in this work, they are treated as cultic classes.

All the laity are listed either by lineage or city, but the cultic personnel are designated by occupation. The Levites are even listed by function as singers and gatekeepers (2:41–42).[36] Undoubtedly, lineage plays a role in priesthood (sons of Aaron) and the Levites are from the tribe of Levi, but these groups are listed under the occupational headings, not just the lineage. None of the lay returnees are listed in this way, though occupations are found in other name lists (cf. Neh 3:8, 30; 11:9, 14, 24).

Williamson claims that this switch between family and location, as well as the switch between "son of" and "men of," indicates that this list was compiled from disparate sources.[37] However, Goswell claims this is simply stylistic and not indicative of sources.[38] A more interesting argument is presented by Dyck. He examines this interchange from an ideological standpoint and claims that these groups had the right kind of exilic connection, regardless of father's household lineage or location, but the excluded groups, Ezra 2:59–62, had lineages that did not fit in with the ideal of the community leaders. So, this switching between "son of" and "men of" and the exclusion of others is indicative of an internal struggle for identity and legitimacy within the community.[39] It is also important to note that this type of identification applies strictly to the lay people, as the cultic personnel are identified as priests, Levites, singers, gatekeepers, temple servants, and Nethinim. As Becking notes, the priests are not portrayed as "sons of Aaron," so the list is emphasizing their occupation rather than their lineage.[40] Therefore, the exilic connection for the laity is different from the connection for the cultic personnel who are identified by function rather that lineage or location.

---

36. For a list and percentages of these different groups see Steinmann, *Ezra and Nehemiah*, 167–73; Becking, *Ezra-Nehemiah*, 35; Shepherd and Wright, *Ezra and Nehemiah*, 26; Williamson, *Ezra, Nehemiah*, 15. Finkelstein claims that the numbers for these different locations are reflecting Hasmonian times based upon archaeological findings. Finkelstein, "Archaeology and the List of Returnees in the Books of Ezra and Nehemiah," 7–16; Finkelstein, *Hasmonean Realities behind Ezra, Nehemiah, and Chronicles*.

37. Williamson, *Ezra, Nehemiah*, 28; Becking, *Ezra-Nehemiah*, 41–42; Myers, *Ezra-Nehemiah*, 14–15.

38. Goswell, *Study Commentary on Ezra-Nehemiah*, 73.

39. Dyck, "Ezra 2 in Ideological Critical Perspective."

40. Becking, *Ezra-Nehemiah*, 41–42; Clines, *Ezra, Nehemiah, Esther*, 53.

The value of listing the priestly and Levitical returnees by their function rather than lineage or location is obvious. They are necessary for the function of the new temple just like the cultic vessels that were obtained by Sheshbazzar and listed in Ezra 1.[41]

Another indicator of the emphasis on cultic personnel is that for the people whose genealogical records could not be found, only the priests suffered repercussions (2:59–62). Becking claims that laity were denied access to the community but does not describe where he finds this in the text.[42] However, Williamson, among others, believes it is only the priests who were excluded, and this seems to fit the grammar of the text more closely.[43] Verse 62 claims that they were "considered unclean and excluded from the priesthood." If the exclusion included the laity, then it is difficult to understand the punishment of exclusion from the priesthood since they were not priests to begin with.

The lay people whose family could not be traced appear to be included in the community, but the priests without family records were considered unclean and excluded from the priesthood. To further the importance of the priesthood, the governor refrains from making a judgment on the questionable priests' status and requires them to wait until a priest could use the Urim and Thummim to decide what should be done (2:63).[44] The priests, therefore, are clearly the center of this pericope because the unrecorded priests are the only ones whose fate is mentioned (the outcome of the laity with unknown lineage is not described) and a priest is also the only one who can decide the questionable priests' relationship to the community (even the governor defers to the priests).

---

41. Goswell, *Study Commentary on Ezra-Nehemiah*, 75; Van Wijk-Bos, *Ezra, Nehemiah, and Esther*, 22; Esler, "Ezra-Nehemiah as a Narrative of (Re-Invented) Israelite Identity," 419.

42. Becking, *Ezra-Nehemiah*, 43; Clines, *Ezra, Nehemiah, Esther*, 58–59; Thiessen, "Function of a Conjunction," 65.

43. Williamson, *Ezra, Nehemiah*, 36–37; Goswell, *Study Commentary on Ezra-Nehemiah*, 76–77; Myers, *Ezra-Nehemiah*, 20; Burns, *Ezra, Nehemiah*, 22; Galling, "'Gōlā-List' According to Ezra 2 // Nehemiah 7," 152–53; Dyck, "Ezra 2 in Ideological Critical Perspective," 132; Eskenazi, "Imagining the Other in the Construction of Judahite Identity in Ezra-Nehemiah," 240.

44. Fried suggests that the Urim and Thummim might have been discovered even though the text does not mention it, because the sons of Hakkoz are mentioned as part of the community and priesthood in Neh 3:21 and 1 Chr 24:10. See Fried, "Did Second Temple High Priests Possess the Urim and Thummim?," 2–25; Yamauchi, "Reverse Order of Ezra/Nehemiah Reconsidered," 10–11; Steinmann, *Ezra and Nehemiah*, 316–17.

The final indication of cultic emphasis is the concluding statement that "the priests, Levites, some of the people, singers, gatekeepers, and the Nethinim lived in their cities, and all Israel in their cities" (Ezra 2:70). This verse lists cultic personnel in five different groups and relegates the rest of the community to "some of the people" and "all Israel." This is unlike Ezra 1:5 where the heads of households are mentioned with the priests and Levites as those arising to return. The section ends with the settlement of Israel, but with special emphasis upon the cultic personnel settling in their cities.

EZRA

The narrative movement of the return migration in Ezra 7–8 can be diagrammed as follows:

1. Introduction of Ezra (7:1–6)
2. Movement from Babylon to Jerusalem (7:7–10)
    A. Some sons of Israel migrated also (7:7)
    B. Desire to teach the Law (7:10)
3. The decree of Artaxerxes (7:11–26)
    A. transcription of the decree (7:12–26)
      i. Any of the people may leave (7:13)
      ii. Offerings (7:15–24)
        a. From Artaxerxes (7:15)
        b. From the people (7:16)
        c. Given to Ezra for the temple (7:17–20)
        d. From other treasurers (7:21–23)
      iii. No taxes on religious personnel (7:24)
      iv. Authority given to Ezra (7:25–26)
4. Blessing to God for decree (7:27–28a)
5. Leaders rise up to go (7:28b)
6. List of returnees (8:1–14)
7. Gathering of specialized temple personnel (8:15–20)
8. Fasting for the journey (8:21–23)

9. Weighing gold and silver offerings for the temple (8:24–30)

10. Moving to Jerusalem and remaining there three days (8:31–32)

11. Weighing of offerings for the temple (8:33–34)

12. Returnees sacrifice, deliver edicts, and support the temple (8:35–36)

This narrative section begins with a date formula "and after these things, in the reign of King Artaxerxes of Persia," which signals a new literary movement in the narrative (7:1). As Dwight R. Daniels notes, "after these things" in Ezra 7:1 is considered a redactional link by many commentators.[45] Steinmann observes that the last date given is in Ezra 6:19, and so the gap between the Passover date and the beginning of the return migration, according to the text, is fifty-seven years.[46] Besides movement in time, the first verse also introduces a new character, Ezra, and gives an extended genealogy which indicates that he will become the prominent character in this new section (7:1–5).[47] The new scene is also placed in a new location. Ezra 6 ended in Jerusalem during the Feast of Unleavened Bread, but Ezra is coming up from Babylon (7:6), and even after the date of arrival in Jerusalem is mentioned (7:8), the rest of the events in Ezra 7–8 primarily take place in Babylon or on the way to Jerusalem. Pakkala claims, "There seems to be no connecting element between Ezra 6 and 7. Ezra 6.19–22 describes how the community of the returnees from the exile celebrated the Passover in Jerusalem after the temple had been built, whereas Ezra 7.1 jumps to Babylon and begins to describe the journey of a scribe called Ezra."[48]

The date formula, new character, and new location indicate a narrative break between Ezra 6 and 7, and another movement in time and change in characters indicates a new section of narrative starting in Ezra 9. Ezra 9 begins with "and when these things were finished," which indicates a break in the series of events. The chapter also begins with the leaders approaching Ezra with a concern that is presented in recorded speech. In Ezra 8, only Ezra's speech was recorded, and there are only two recorded speeches (8:22,

---

45. Daniels, "Composition of the Ezra-Nehemiah Narrative," 312; Bertholet, *Bücher Esra und Nehemia*, 30; Williamson, *Ezra, Nehemiah*, 91; Pakkala, *Ezra the Scribe*, 23; Pakkala, "Original Independence of the Ezra Story in Ezra 7–10 and Neh 8," 20; Burns, *Ezra, Nehemiah*; Japhet, *From the Rivers of Babylon to the Highlands of Judah*, 246.

46. Steinmann, *Ezra and Nehemiah*, 286; Van Wijk-Bos, *Ezra, Nehemiah, and Esther*, 34; Goswell, *Study Commentary on Ezra-Nehemiah*, 137.

47. For the syntactic function of ויהי see Harmelink, "Exploring the Syntactic, Semantic, and Pragmatic Uses of וַיְהִי in Biblical Hebrew," 285–86, 445.

48. Pakkala, "Disunity of Ezra-Nehemiah," 205.

28–29). The speech also functions differently between Ezra 8 and Ezra 9. In Ezra 8, the recorded speech echoes the events surrounding it: Ezra was ashamed to ask for guards because of the recorded speech (which was spoken before Artaxerxes), and the recorded charge to the priests with the temple donations. However, Ezra 9:1 does not use direct speech to support the narrative actions but to initiate the actions. Ezra's actions are in direct response to the speech in Ezra 9:1. So, Ezra 9 is demarcated from Ezra 8 by a new time indicator, new characters being introduced and speaking, and the use of recorded speech to drive the events of the narrative. Wright also observes that Ezra 7–8 is in tension with Ezra 9–10 because the holiness of the temple and personnel is pushed into the background in the latter chapters while the priests become the center of scandal.[49]

The structural organization of the text will be discussed in more detail in the next chapter. However, two key thematic emphases will be discussed in this section: the focus on the king and the cultic emphasis.

Prominent Character: Artaxerxes

Ezra 7:11 introduces the decree of Artaxerxes. The transcript of the decree dominates the chapter (7:12–26), and even after the decree, the author reflects upon the decree as a blessing of God (7:27–28). Goswell also notes that both introductions of Ezra (7:1–6 and 7:7–10) begin with the mention of Artaxerxes.[50] Immediately after the transcription, the author (presumably Ezra) claims that this was put into the heart of Artaxerxes by God, and then claims it is to "adorn the house of the Lord," which is interesting given that Ezra is returning to teach the Law, not to build or furnish the temple (7:10).

Eskenazi observes that Ezra 7:6 states, "the king granted him (Ezra) all that he requested." So, this is significantly distinct from the decree of Cyrus in Ezra 1.[51] However, this statement sums up Ezra's relationship to the king, and God, but it does not introduce the decree. The forward to the decree (Ezra 7:1–10) is different from Ezra 1, but the introductory clause to the

---

49. Wright, "Seeking, Finding and Writing in Ezra–Nehemiah," 285.
50. Goswell, *Study Commentary on Ezra-Nehemiah*, 137.
51. Eskenazi, "Imagining the Other in the Construction of Judahite Identity in Ezra-Nehemiah," 244; Clines, *Ezra, Nehemiah, Esther*, 100; Goswell, *Study Commentary on Ezra-Nehemiah*, 141–42; Steinmann, *Ezra and Nehemiah*, 289; Thomas, *Ezra & Nehemiah*, 116.

decree and the decree itself do not portray a dialogue between Ezra and the king, nor does it portray the king writing in response to a request by Ezra. In fact, Ezra's response to the decree credits God with putting the thing in the king's heart rather than thanking God for the king fulfilling Ezra's request (Ezra 7:27). So, Ezra is decidedly more prominent in the narrative than Sheshbazzar in chapter one, but he is not the primary force driving the narrative—that is Artaxerxes's decree.

In addition to the value placed upon the decree by the comments at the end of the chapter, within the decree itself are indications of the importance of Artaxerxes and his commands for the narrative.[52] The decree shows Artaxerxes's power to command. He decrees the return migration (7:13), the use of the gifts (7:14–19), the provisions by the treasurers beyond the River (7:21–22), and tax exemptions (7:24). Also, the purpose for Artaxerxes sending Ezra is centered upon himself: to protect the king and his sons from the wrath of God (7:23).[53] Finally, Artaxerxes shows his control by delegating power to Ezra both in civil and religious matters (7:25–26).

All the claims to power that Artaxerxes makes in his decree are borne out in chapter 8. Artaxerxes gives Ezra the power to appoint magistrates and judges and teach the Law (7:25–26). He also introduces the letter by speaking directly to Ezra and stating that anyone who wishes to go to Jerusalem may go "with you" (7:13). Ezra 7:28 echoes this by claiming "I gathered leaders from Israel to go up with me," and Ezra 8:1 provides "the genealogy of those who went up with me." The emphasis is clearly on the king sending Ezra and the community following.

After the list of returnees in Ezra 8, Ezra becomes the primary speaker. However, his actions are exercising the power that was given to him by Artaxerxes. When Ezra recognized that there were no Levites in his group,

---

52. Japhet, "Sheshbazzar and Zerubbabel," 74. For an overview of the discussion of the authenticity of the decree see Blenkinsopp, "Footnotes to the Rescript of Artaxerxes (Ezra 7:11–26)," 150–58; Clines, *Ezra, Nehemiah, Esther*, 102; Becking, *Ezra, Nehemiah, and the Construction of Early Jewish Identity*, 50–52; Becking, *Ezra-Nehemiah*, 108–12; Hoglund, *Achaemenid Imperial Administration in Syria-Palestine and the Missions of Ezra and Nehemiah*, 227; Steinmann, *Ezra and Nehemiah*, 296–97; Blenkinsopp, *Ezra-Nehemiah*, 147; Breneman, *Ezra, Nehemiah, Esther*, 132; Fensham, *Books of Ezra and Nehemiah*, 103–4; Myers, *Ezra-Nehemiah*, 61–62; Williamson, *Ezra, Nehemiah*, 98–99.

53. Kiel notes that the dual nature of Artaxerxes command to teach the Law of God and law of the king shows the king as the agent of the supreme deity and his religious and political commission to Ezra. Kiel, "Reinventing Mosaic Torah in Ezra-Nehemiah in the Light of the Law (Dāta) of Ahura Mazda and Zarathustra," 329; Conklin, "Decrees of God and of Kings in the Aramaic Correspondence of Ezra," 86.

he sent for them so that he fulfilled the command of Artaxerxes that Levites be included in return migration (Ezra 7:13; 8:15-20).[54] Artaxerxes gave him the authority to appoint leaders (7:25-26) and Ezra appoints twelve leading priests (8:24). Artaxerxes commanded Ezra to bring the offerings and utensils to the temple and do what seemed right to him and his God with it (7:14-19), and Ezra describes counting the offerings and utensils to the leaders before going to Jerusalem and then inventorying them again with the priests in Jerusalem (8:25-30, 33-34). The decree even commands them to use the offerings to buy sacrificial animals and offer them on the altar (7:17) and Ezra describes the exiles sacrificing immediately after counting out the offerings to the priests (8:35). Finally, Ezra delivers the edicts of the king to the governors, and they provide support for the house of God (8:36). Artaxerxes commanded the treasurers beyond the River to support the house of God in any way that Ezra required (7:21-22).[55]

The fulfillment of each command in the decree shows that even though the primary actor in chapter eight is Ezra, he is performing the duties of the royal instructions he has been given. In this way, the decree of Artaxerxes drives the narrative even when Ezra is the individual performing the actions.

Primary Concern: Cult

Though most discussions of the mission of Ezra are usually centered around the reading of the Law, in chapters 7-8 teaching the Law does not appear central.[56] Teaching the Law is the only command from the decree (7:25) that is not fulfilled in chapter 8. Instead, the temple and the religious officials are the primary concerns of Ezra 7-8.[57]

---

54. Steinmann, *Ezra and Nehemiah*, 280.

55. See Redditt, *Ezra-Nehemiah*, 174.

56. Blenkinsopp, "Was the Pentateuch the Civic and Religious Constitution of the Jewish Ethnos in the Persian Period?," 41-62; Grabbe, "Law of Moses in the Ezra Tradition," 91-114; Goswell, *Study Commentary on Ezra-Nehemiah*, 142.

57. Lisbeth Fried claims that Ezra was only given authority to appoint judges and magistrates (7:25). In the Persian empire, only Persian officials could enforce laws, whether cultic or administrative, and so Ezra could not do this. However, Nehemiah, as the provincial governor, could enforce the sabbath and marriage laws even without appeal to the Law of Moses because he had the authority vested by the Persian king that Ezra did not. The political reasons behind the omission of the Law in Ezra 7-8 lie outside the scope of this analysis, but Fried's work highlights the fact that enforcement

Pakkala and many other scholars argue that Neh 8 originally preceded Ezra 10, and so the reading of the Law would have taken place before the separation from foreign wives.[58] However, I am treating the current form of the book rather than reconstructions of earlier editions. As the text is arranged currently, any reading of the Law in Ezra 7–10 is unknown, and so it is the one piece of Artaxerxes's decree that is not explicitly fulfilled according to the narrative.

Temple

Ezra desired to go to Jerusalem to teach the Law in Israel (7:10), but the decree of Artaxerxes commands Ezra and his company to inquire of God and more specifically to bring articles for the temple. Much of the decree is concerned with the functioning of the temple and the Law appears to be important primarily as a guide to proper temple functioning so that the wrath of God does not fall upon the king (7:14, 23). The temple is presented in two ways in these chapters: function and location.

The function of the temple is shown by the emphasis placed upon cultic objects and sacrifices. Not only does Artaxerxes give gold and silver to the temple, but he also requires Ezra to buy bulls, rams, lambs, grain offerings, and drink offerings (7:16–17). In addition, Artaxerxes provides utensils that are to be used in the service and access to the royal treasury for any remaining needs for the temple (7:19–20). It is notable that these articles are donated by Artaxerxes rather than being returned from the pre-exilic temple like the utensils in Ezra 1.[59] This distinction is minor though, and Artaxerxes's donations may perhaps be considered a matter of pragmatics rather than differing ideologies (the utensils from the pre-exilic temple were already taken to Jerusalem so any additional utensils must be newly crafted).

---

and teaching of the Law primarily takes place within the book of Nehemiah not Ezra. Fried, "'You Shall Appoint Judges,'" 63–90. However, Heltzer argues for the likelihood Ezra's imperial authority. Heltzer, "Right of Ezra to Demand Obedience to 'The Laws of the King' from Gentiles of the V Satrapy (Ez 7:25–26)," 192–96; Clines, *Ezra, Nehemiah, Esther*, 105–6.

58. Pakkala, *Ezra the Scribe*, 167–77; Pakkala, "Exile and the Exiles in the Ezra Tradition," 93. See also Goswell, *Study Commentary on Ezra-Nehemiah*, 144; Grabbe, "What Was Ezra's Mission?," 286–99; Janzen, "'Mission' of Ezra and the Persian-Period Temple Community," 619–43.

59. Fried, "Torah of God as God," 286.

The treasurers in the other provinces are also commanded to provide for the temple with silver, wheat, wine, oil, and salt (7:21-22). Artaxerxes provides specific quantity limits for each item that should be donated by the treasurers beyond the River, which highlights the emphasis that the text is placing on these donations for the temple.

This emphasis on providing cultic objects and continuing the sacrificial system in Artaxerxes's decree is mirrored in Ezra's actions. Ezra not only weighs out the silver, gold, and utensils to the priests on the way to Jerusalem, he tells them that the utensils are holy, and the freewill offering is dedicated to God (8:24-28). The value of these items is also shown by the insertion of Ezra's direct speech to the twelve priests instructing them to keep watch over these items until they give them to the priest at the temple (8:28-29). The designation of the items as holy and the presentation of Ezra's speech shows the importance of these items within the narrative.

In addition, the first recorded act when the people arrive in Jerusalem is their presentation of these utensils to Meremoth in the temple (8:33-34). This is highlighted in the text, not by direct speech but by detailed record. It is the fourth day in Jerusalem, and the text lists all four people that were there, their genealogy, and whether they were priests or Levites. The author also begins by claiming that the silver, gold, and utensils were weighed out in the house, and, after naming the people who received them, reiterates that "everything was counted and weighed, and all the weight was recorded at that time" (8:34). This shows the chain of custody for the items and the witnesses to the transaction; it also specifies that inventory was recorded at the time of the transaction.

The exiles then make sacrifices at the temple, and this was recorded in detail as well (8:35). The quantity of each animal and the type of offering, burnt offering, is listed. The text focuses on the functioning of the temple, and this mirrors the decree of Artaxerxes to buy bulls, rams, and lambs to make sacrifices.

The pericope ends with the governors beyond the River supporting the temple (8:36). The edicts of the king are delivered to the governors who send support, and this again reflects the decree from chapter seven. In fact, a second decree formula is found in 7:21, "I, King Artaxerxes issue a decree to all the treasurers beyond the River," and this could be the substance of the edicts that were delivered to the governors in 8:36. Regardless of whether this is the precise document that was delivered, the command to support the functioning of the temple in Ezra 7:21-24 is what the people gave to the governors in Ezra 8:36. This again emphasizes the temple as a primary concern in the narrative.

The second way in which the temple is presented in the text is location. Frequently the temple is referred to as "the house of God which is in Jerusalem" (7:15–17, 19, 27). Though often the location that the returnees are traveling to is Jerusalem, when the people arrive, all the activities take place within the temple (depositing offerings and sacrificing, 8:29, 30, 33–35). So, the temple is in the foreground of the narrative, whereas Jerusalem is in the background, primarily as defining the location where the temple is located.

Religious Officials

The function and location of the temple are important themes in Ezra 7–8, but the religious personnel are also prominent. The introduction of Ezra traces his lineage to Aaron the chief priest (7:1–5). The text also emphasizes Ezra's priestly status by continuously calling him "priest," "scribe," "skilled in the Law," or all three (7:6, 11, 12, 21).

In addition to Ezra's portrayal as a religious leader, the people returning to Jerusalem are divided between religious and lay people with a special emphasis on the religious leaders. In Ezra 7:7, the returnees are described as "some of the sons of Israel, some of the priests, the Levites, the singers, the gatekeepers, and the temple servants." The only leadership mentioned are the temple personnel. In fact, the "sons of Israel" has a partitive מן indicating that is an undefined "some."[60] This does not indicate that these are heads of households or community leaders but simply some subset of Israelites generally. By contrast, the priests, Levites, and temple servants are listed specifically, and the Levites are even divided further into singers and gatekeepers. This same formulation with מן is used in Ezra 7:13 where Artaxerxes addresses "some of the people of Israel, the priests, and the Levites." This again does not define the non-cultic personnel as leaders or anything other than Israelites, but it highlights the priests and the Levites as special groups.

Besides the wording of the decree singling out the cultic personnel, Artaxerxes also provides a special tax exemption for them (7:24). The tax was forbidden on the priests, Levites, singers, doorkeepers, Nethinim, and

---

60. Fuller and Choi, *Invitation to Biblical Hebrew Syntax*, §12d, 78; Van der Merwe et al., *Biblical Hebrew Reference Grammar*, 362.

servants of the temple. This type of exemption appears to have taken place elsewhere in the Persian empire, as has been attested in Greek witnesses, so it would not be unusual for this to be the case in Jerusalem.[61] Grabbe disputes the historicity of this tax exemption because it only took place in the Persian homeland with major deities, and so it is unlikely that a minor city on the edge of the empire would be given this special status.[62] However, even if it is unlikely that the Persians saw the Jerusalem Temple as significant, this interpretation fits well with the ideology of the text. The narrative is clearly portraying Ezra, Artaxerxes's decree, and the migration as historically significant, so it is logical that tax exemptions for significant temples would apply to the most significant temple from the viewpoint of the book of Ezra, the Jerusalem Temple. The insertion of this tax exemption command after the commands for the treasurers to supply temple goods shows that both the physical temple and the cultic personnel are central in the narrative and the decree.

The list of returnees in Ezra 8 places the priests at the beginning.[63] The naming of two priests from the two sons of Aaron and Hattush as the son of David shows the importance of these groups in the text.[64] After the priests and the royal descendent, twelve families are listed by their genealogies (8:3–14). However, immediately after the list of returnees, Ezra realizes that only lay people and priests were with him (8:15). Interestingly, though Hattush is listed as Davidic, Ezra does not list royalty as one of the groups that were with him. This again demonstrates the focus upon cultic personnel as does the group that Ezra finds lacking: the Levites. Ezra must correct the lack of Levites and so sends leaders to Casiphia to bring back Levites and temple servants (8:16–20). Koch and van Wijk-Bos claim that the Levites were necessary because Ezra wanted to recreate the exodus. There were already Levites in the land (Ezra 10:23), but if Ezra is following the pattern of the exodus, then Levites are necessary (Num 10:13–28). This highlights the importance of cultic personnel in the narrative even more. Instead of just being essential for service in the temple, they are also essential for the exodus procession.[65]

---

61. Becking, *Ezra-Nehemiah*, 115.

62. Grabbe, "Law of Moses in the Ezra Tradition," 110.

63. Clines believes this is because the list was compiled by Ezra the priest. Clines, *Ezra, Nehemiah, Esther*, 108.

64. Steinmann, *Ezra and Nehemiah*, 304.

65. Koch, "Ezra and the Origins of Judaism," 187; Van Wijk-Bos, *Ezra, Nehemiah,*

After adding Levites to their company, Ezra designates twelve leading priests to carry the cultic vessels and lists them by name (8:24–25). However, the narrative highlights these priests even more by having Ezra call them holy in a recorded speech (8:28). The priests are holy to Yahweh just like the utensils for the temple, and this is significant enough for the author that he records Ezra's instructions directly.[66]

Once the exiles arrive in Jerusalem, the priests and the Levites who received the items are named (8:33). This is written like an inventory or an account that would be sent to Ezra's superior to verify that the transaction occurred.[67] It is significant, though, that the only named witnesses to the transaction are priests and Levites. This is significant because the direct speech of Ezra says that the items would be delivered to the "leading priests, the Levites, and the heads of the fathers' households of Israel in Jerusalem, in the chambers of the house of Yahweh" (8:29). Ezra specifically mentions that the heads of the fathers' households of Israel will be in the temple to receive the offerings but then they are not mentioned when the event occurs. Whether additional unnamed individuals received the donations in the temple is purely speculation, but the way that the event is portrayed in Ezra 8:33, the only significant individuals are the priests and the Levites.

COMBINED SHESHBAZZAR AND EZRA RETURN MOTIFS

To show the distinction between the return of Nehemiah and the returns of Sheshbazzar and Ezra, the latter two must be compared. In this section the thematic emphases in the migrations of Sheshbazzar and Ezra will be compared.

Prominent Character: The King

The narratives of Ezra and Sheshbazzar begin with the reign of the Persian king (1:1; 7:1).[68] The name and year of the king's reign is given at the beginning of the narrative, though the full date formula in Ezra's migration is split between 7:1, the name of the king, and 7:7–9, the year of his reign.

and Esther, 38–39.

66. Clines, *Ezra, Nehemiah, Esther*, 112–13; Goswell, *Study Commentary on Ezra-Nehemiah*, 159; Becking, *Ezra-Nehemiah*, 129; Steinmann, *Ezra and Nehemiah*, 313–14.

67. Clines, *Ezra, Nehemiah, Esther*, 114.

68. Goswell, *Study Commentary on Ezra-Nehemiah*, 55; Eskenazi, *In an Age of Prose*.

Separation of the People, Separation of the Land

The return migration is centered upon a royal decree in both texts and a transcription of the decree in the first person is presented in Ezra 1 and 7. In Ezra 1, the introduction to the decree, and Cyrus himself within the decree, claims that he was appointed and inspired by Yahweh to build the temple. The decree in chapter seven is much longer and Artaxerxes does not explicitly claim to be inspired or appointed by God.[69] However, Ezra's reflection after the decree states, "Blessed be Yahweh ... who put something like this in the king's heart to glorify the house of Yahweh which is in Jerusalem" (7:27). Both texts, then, record the royal decree and claim that Yahweh inspired the king to either build or adorn the temple.[70] Goswell notes that both decrees have a single Hebrew verse introduction and can be divided into three parts or commands.[71]

Besides the transcriptions of the decrees and the inspiration of Yahweh, the kings' decrees are centralized in their respective narratives through the events that follow. The actions of the returnees follow the instructions of each decree. The decrees name the people of Israel, the priests, and the Levites and the lists of returnees follow this categorization.[72] The decree of Cyrus commands donations to be given from his treasury and the people surrounding, and this is recorded as being given to Sheshbazzar (1:7–11). Additional gifts for the temple are even recorded in Ezra 2:68–69. In the same way, the decree of Artaxerxes commands gifts from the king, his counselors, and the treasurers beyond the River, and chapter eight records the donations given by the king and his counselors and the support received from the governors beyond the River (8:25–27, 36). The decree to build the temple and the decree to make sacrifices are also followed by the returnees (2:68; 8:35).

The seam between the chapters also focuses on the decree of the king in both narratives. Cyrus commands the people to go up and rebuild (1:3), and this same terminology is used for the leaders who rise to go up to Jerusalem (1:5). The parallel phrasing in these two verses has been noted often.[73] However, verse 11 refers to the people who went up to Jerusalem as "exiles,"

---

69. Goswell, *Study Commentary on Ezra-Nehemiah*, 141.

70. Venema, *Reading Scripture in the Old Testament*, 143; Becking, *Ezra, Nehemiah, and the Construction of Early Jewish Identity*, 34–36.

71. Goswell, *Study Commentary on Ezra-Nehemiah*, 144.

72. Redditt, *Ezra-Nehemiah*, 171.

73. Goswell, *Study Commentary on Ezra-Nehemiah*, 61; Davies, *Ezra and Nehemiah*, 11.

which is then reiterated in 2:1 as "those who came up out of the exile." In this way, the list of returnees in chapter two is an expansion of those mentioned in chapter one who are responding to the decree of Cyrus. The returnee list in Ezra 8 functions similarly. Artaxerxes decrees that the people "may go with you" (speaking to Ezra), and Ezra claims that he gathered the heads of Israel "to go up with me" (7:28). Not only is Ezra reflecting the phrase used in the decree; he clearly indicates that the decree of Artaxerxes encouraged him to do this. The genealogy then is an expansion of this, as it reiterates this phrasing, "these are the heads . . . those who went up with me" (8:1). This uses similar phrasing as the last verse of chapter seven and indicates that this is adding detail to the action described in the previous chapter: Artaxerxes commands Ezra to bring people to go up with him, Ezra gathered people to go up, and these are the people that he gathered. Just like in the Sheshbazzar narrative, the decree is given, the response to the decree is given in summary, and then the names of the people involved in the response are listed.

Primary Concern: Cult

Temple

In addition to a shared focus upon the Persian king. Both Ezra's return and Sheshbazzar's return is centered on the temple. The most prominent of this shared focus is the cultic vessels.[74] Not only do both leaders receive vessels for the temple from the Persian king; the precise weight of the items and the chain of custody is recorded within each narrative (1:7–11; 8:26–34). In addition to the cultic vessels from the kings, they both receive further donations for the temple from fellow Israelites and others within the Persian empire (1:6; 2:68–69; 8:25, 36).

Cyrus focuses on the rebuilding of the temple in his decree, and the ending of chapter two reiterates this emphasis with the laying of the foundation. Artaxerxes, however, does not mention building the temple but focuses on the function of the temple. All the donations are intended to reinstate the cultic practices within the temple building or, as Ezra described it, to "glorify the house of Yahweh" (7:27). This intention of reinstating the cult is fulfilled at the end of chapter eight when the people make sacrifices and the governors make donations to support the temple. Though one passage

---

74. Goswell, *Study Commentary on Ezra-Nehemiah*, 147.

is focused on building the temple and the other on reinstating the worship practices within the temple, both narratives highlight the place and activity of worship as a central theme.

The final shared aspect of the temple in the return migrations is the location. In both texts, the phrase "the house of Yahweh which is in Jerusalem" is used, and Yahweh is also described as "the God who is in Jerusalem" (1:3, 5; 2:68; 7:17, 19, 27). This emphasis on the location of the temple indicates that Sheshbazzar and Ezra are focused upon restoring the physical temple in Jerusalem and reinstating the cultic practices with the donations and temple utensils given to them by the Persian king.

Becking follows Antonius Gunneweg by claiming the exodus references are too general or contradictory in Ezra 1–2. Instead, he claims that the author is pointing to a restoration of pre-exilic institutions.[75] The cultic focus fits well within this framework because the cult is the primary institution that is being restored. However, many other scholars do find exodus and pilgrimage imagery within the return migrations of Sheshbazzar and Ezra and specifically point to the cultic and temple emphasis to support this interpretation. Aaron J. Koller notes the cultic vessels along with significant dates for the migration as evidence of Ezra's blending of exodus and Jerusalem pilgrimage imagery. However, he does not address these same features in Sheshbazzar's migration nor the lack of these exodus and pilgrimage features in Nehemiah's migration.[76] By contrast, Melody Knowles discusses the pilgrimage imagery in the returns of Sheshbazzar and Ezra but notes that Nehemiah's return is a "more secular" account which lacks these themes.[77]

Religious Officials

The emphasis on cultic personnel is found in both Sheshbazzar's migration and Ezra's migration. The people are divided between religious officials, priests and Levites, and the rest of Israel with the Levites further delineated

75. Gunneweg, *Nehemia*, 57; Becking, "Does Ezra Present the Return from Exile as a Second Exodus?," 65–73.

76. Koller, *Esther in Ancient Jewish Thought*, 21; Koch, "Ezra and the Origins of Judaism," 184. For pilgrimage imagery in Ezra 8, see Goswell, *Study Commentary on Ezra-Nehemiah*, 153. For exodus imagery in Ezra 1–2 and 8, see Hamilton, *Exalting Jesus in Ezra and Nehemiah*, 8–15, 72; Redditt, *Ezra-Nehemiah*, 65.

77. Knowles, "Pilgrimage Imagery in the Returns in Ezra," 57–74. See also Dozeman, "Geography and History in Herodotus and in Ezra-Nehemiah," 462–63.

by function in the decree of each king. The Nethinim, singers, and gatekeepers are special classes of Levites and additional cultic personnel that are listed separately in each account. In addition, in Ezra 8, the descendants of Aaron are listed and the leading priests and Levites in the temple are named. Both passages emphasize the cultic personnel in the decree and in the later activities of the returnees, but the Ezra return focuses more heavily upon the priests and the activities of individual priests (including Ezra himself) than the Sheshbazzar account.

NEHEMIAH

The narrative movement of the return migration in Neh 1–3:32 can be diagrammed as follows:

1. Introductory formula (1:1)

2. Judeans return to Susa (1:2–3)

    A. Nehemiah questions Judean returnees (1:2)

    B. Bad news in reported speech (1:3)

3. Nehemiah mourns (1:4–11)

    A. Fasted and prayed (1:4)

    B. Penitential prayer in reported speech (1:5–11a)

    C. Nehemiah's position (1:11c)

4. Nehemiah before the king in reported speech (2:1–8)

    A. Nehemiah describes the state of Jerusalem (2:1–3)

    B. Nehemiah requests to rebuild (2:4–5)

    C. Artaxerxes grants the request (2:6–8)

5. Move to the provinces beyond the River (2:9–10)

    A. Letters sent to officials (2:9)

    B. Displeased outsiders (2:10)

6. Arrival and assessment (2:11–16)

    A. Arrival and stay (2:11)

    B. Small group of leaders convened by Nehemiah (2:12)

    C. Nehemiah's survey (2:13–15)

D. Officials excluded (2:16)

7. Plan of action (2:17–20)

   A. Assessment and plan in reported speech (2:17)

   B. Reported response of agreement (2:18)

   C. Strife and response in reported speech (2:19–20)

8. List of people resolving the problem (3:1–32)

The break in the narrative at Neh 4:1 (MT 3:33) is indicated by the closure of 3:32, the change in prominent characters, and the time formula in 4:1. The list of builders concludes with the merchants finishing repairs at the Sheep Gate (3:32). Eliashib and his brothers started rebuilding at the Sheep Gate in Neh 3:1, so this finishes the circuit around the city.

Many scholars have noted the historical and narrative disruption caused by the builder list. First, chapter three is no longer in the first person, nor does it mention Nehemiah at all, unlike the previous two chapters and the following chapter, which make frequent reference to Nehemiah's actions in the first person.[78] In addition, the list appears to conclude with the wall fully built but in subsequent chapters, it is incomplete. For example, Neh 4:6 (MT 3:38) it is only built to half its height and in 6:1 the doors are not set in the gates yet.[79] For this reason the text is often understood as an embedded document, and Mordechai Cogan even argues that the builder list is an embedded document written by multiple scribes. This accounts for the varying style within the list (interchange between "after him/them" and "beside him/them"), as well as the disjunction with the incompleteness of the building after the name list.[80] Regardless of the origin of the name list, the completion of the wall and lack of first-person narrative clearly separates this list from Neh 4:1 (MT 3:33).

---

78. Cogan, "Raising the Walls of Jerusalem (Nehemiah 3:1–32)," 85; Blenkinsopp, "Nehemiah Autobiographical Memoir," 199–212; Clines, *Ezra, Nehemiah, Esther*, 149; Becking, *Ezra-Nehemiah*, 194–96.

79. Cogan, "Raising the Walls of Jerusalem (Nehemiah 3:1–32)," 85. See also Williamson, *Ezra, Nehemiah*, 202; Galling, *Bücher der Chronik, Esra, Nehemia*, 222; Rudolph, *Esra und Nehemía Samt 3. Esra*, 113; Kellermann, *Nehemia*, 14–15; Myers, *Ezra-Nehemiah*, 112; Blenkinsopp, *Ezra-Nehemiah*, 231; Clines, *Ezra, Nehemiah, Esther*, 148; Gunneweg, *Nehemia*, 75; Bartlett, "Nehemiah's Wall," 77–78.

80. Cogan, "Raising the Walls of Jerusalem (Nehemiah 3:1–32)," 92; Mitchell, "Wall of Jerusalem According to the Book of Nehemiah," 88–89; Wright, "New Model for the Composition of Ezra-Nehemiah," 337–38.

Oded Lipschits argues that this is not a list of builders but a list of financiers for the building of the wall. However, he also notes that it is an embedded document that is not original to the Nehemiah narrative. The argument for the list as builders or financiers is secondary to the narrative break argument that I am making since both views interpret it as an embedded document that disrupts the narrative flow.[81] The primary purpose of this discussion is to show that this is often claimed to be an embedded document.

The second indication of a new segment is the introduction of Sanballat in 4:1 (MT 3:33). In chapters one and two, the prominent character is Nehemiah, with all other characters reacting to Nehemiah's words or actions. Sanballat is introduced twice in chapter two but in both cases as a reaction to the deeds of Nehemiah and with other non-Israelite adversaries (2:10, 19). However, starting in chapter four, Sanballat has a central role in the narrative. Instead of being displeased or questioning the actions of Nehemiah, Sanballat and Tobiah have recorded speeches calling for action. Rice claims that Neh 4:1 is the oldest of the שמע reports (narratives that begin with the adversaries "hearing") and probably originally followed an earlier form of "2:17–18 before the insertion of the שמע-report in 2:19–20 and the builders' register in 3:1–32."[82] Though I do not follow this compositional framework, the sharp contrast observed by Rice supports my division of the text at Neh 3:32.

The adversaries are no longer supporting characters interacting with the prominent character of Nehemiah in chapter four; they are treated as prominent characters addressing background characters (brothers and wealthy people of Samaria). The text even implies that the location has changed because they are not speaking in front of the people of Jerusalem but the people of Samaria (4:2). The reason the location is "implied" in Neh 4:2 is because the text does not explicitly state where Sanballat is located. He is speaking to the people of Samaria but, unlike Neh 1:2; 2:9, 11, the narrator does not explicitly state that he is standing in the city of Samaria. In addition, Sanballat and the Samaritans are conspiring to come to Jerusalem to fight against it, which also strongly suggests that they are not in Jerusalem or at least not while they are conspiring (4:8).

The third indication of a new segment in the narrative is the time formula in 4:1 (MT 3:33). The verse begins, "And it was when Sanballat heard."

---

81. Lipschits, "Nehemiah 3," 73–99.
82. Rice, "Diachronic Composition of the Shema-Reports in Nehemiah 1–6," 97–98.

The temporal clause moves the narrative forward.[83] Following the closure of the previous verse and with the focus on a new prominent character, this indicates a new segment.[84] The temporal reference reorients the narrative, and the new prominent character and setting (most likely in Samaria) indicates that this is a shift in the narrative. The time reference is now centered upon the action of Sanballat hearing the news of the actions in the previous verses. Sanballat reacts to this receipt of information, and this begins a series of hostile actions between the Judeans and non-Judeans throughout the rest of chapter four.

Based upon the changes in the narrative, the segment should end with 3:32. After this verse, the narrative moves from the list of Judeans rebuilding the wall in Jerusalem to Sanballat and the adversaries working outside of Jerusalem. The temporal reference helps to push the narrative into a new section by creating a new temporal marker: "when Sanballat heard." These three movements in the text make this a clear break in the narrative.

Prominent Character: Nehemiah

Nehemiah's return migration begins by identifying the text as his words (Neh 1:1). The focus continues with Nehemiah discussing the state of Jerusalem with his brother and other men from Judah (1:2). The focus on Nehemiah is evident in these introductory verses not only because Nehemiah is the first character identified but also because he is the initiator of the conversation. The men from Judah came, and Nehemiah asked them about the state of the people and city of Jerusalem. So, it is Nehemiah's question that begins the dialogue and introduces the entire dilemma being solved by Nehemiah's migration.

The focus remains upon Nehemiah throughout chapter one. Though the first reported speech is by the men from Judah, the penitential prayer of Nehemiah takes up most of the chapter.[85] The ending of the prayer also

---

83. Harmelink, "Exploring the Syntactic, Semantic, and Pragmatic Uses of וַיְהִי in Biblical Hebrew," 445.

84. Harmelink, "Exploring the Syntactic, Semantic, and Pragmatic Uses of וַיְהִי in Biblical Hebrew," 403.

85. The people turning to God and being returned to the land and the land itself being restored can be found in other Old Testament texts (1 Kgs 8:33–34, 46–52; Deut 4:25–31). The description of the ruined state of Jerusalem followed by Nehemiah's prayer of repentance might reflect this tradition. However, the historical or broad theological background is outside of the focus of this work. Instead of comparisons to other books

hints at what is coming at the beginning of the next chapter. After describing the sins and resulting exile of Israel, Nehemiah prays that God will give him compassion before "this man" (1:11). Van Wijk-Bos notes that the king is noticeably absent in the first chapter, both in the date formula and in the plea for God's favor.[86] Goswell goes so far as to claim "this man" is a term of contempt, but this is not self-evident in the wording of the text, so this negative interpretation is likely more than the narrative is intending.[87] The end of the verse then states that Nehemiah was the cupbearer to the king (though the king is still unnamed).[88] In chapter two, the king is Artaxerxes, and he does grant the desire of Nehemiah (2:8). Even this granting of Nehemiah's request is because the "hand of my God was on me," which points to Nehemiah asking for God to make him successful before the king in his prayer in chapter one.

The hand of God imagery is also found in 1:10, where Nehemiah claims that God redeems his people by his strong hand. This further links the prayer of chapter one with Nehemiah's assessment in 2:8. The reflection of God's providence in 2:8 could also link with Nehemiah's prayer in 2:4, but there is no explicit request for God's favor with the king nor the hand of God imagery in that passage.

The interaction between Nehemiah and Artaxerxes in Neh 2:1–8 sets the rest of the events in motion and solidifies Nehemiah as the primary actor. Though Nehemiah's responses are respectful and his reaction to the king's question is fear, his speech drives the narrative. The recorded speech of the king asks why Nehemiah is sad, what he would request, and how long he will be gone (2:2, 4, 6). By contrast, Nehemiah's recorded speech contains all the elements that will be fulfilled through the actions in the rest of the chapter. He claims the city is burned and desolate (2:3), the extent of which he assesses upon his arrival in Jerusalem (2:13). He asks to rebuild the city (2:5), which he then recruits people to do (2:17–18). Finally, Nehemiah

of the Old Testament, my goal is to describe the literary structure of Neh 1–3 and the explicit theological statements within the passage.

86. Van Wijk-Bos, *Ezra, Nehemiah, and Esther*, 53.

87. Goswell, *Study Commentary on Ezra-Nehemiah*, 208.

88. Cupbearers were often close confidantes to the king, which may explain Nehemiah's ability to speak quite openly to the king in Neh 2. For a discussion of the position of cupbearer, see Yamauchi, "Was Nehemiah the Cupbearer a Eunuch?," 132–42; Yamauchi, "Archaeological Backgrounds of the Exilic and Postexilic Era, Part 4," 291–309; Williamson, *Ezra, Nehemiah*, 174; Blenkinsopp, *Ezra-Nehemiah*, 212; Boice, *Nehemiah*, 15; Van Wijk-Bos, *Ezra, Nehemiah, and Esther*, 54; Clines, *Ezra, Nehemiah, Esther*, 140.

requests letters in order to pass through the provinces and obtain supplies for the rebuilding (2:7–8), which he delivers during his travel to Jerusalem (2:9). So, the recorded speech of the king is reactionary. He is responding to the demeanor of Nehemiah or the proposals of Nehemiah but not recommending or commanding any actions. The portrayal of the king as reacting and approving Nehemiah's plans places Nehemiah as the central character in the narrative again.[89]

Andrew Dyck argues that Artaxerxes is the governing discourse participant even though Nehemiah dominates the conversation by having more recorded speech. He notes that Nehemiah has sixteen clauses in recorded speech that range from commands to questions, while Artaxerxes only has six clauses and they are all questions.[90] However, the subjugating introductions to his speeches ("may the king live forever") and the first-person descriptions of Nehemiah's reactions between the speeches indicate that Artaxerxes is the one controlling the discourse.[91] Artaxerxes controlling the outcome of the dialogue is unsurprising given his position as ruler and Nehemiah as his subject. On the other hand, it is notable that Nehemiah dominates the conversation both in quantity of speech and in the use of statements (versus questions). This is not a command from Artaxerxes to Nehemiah but a request by Nehemiah that is fulfilled by Artaxerxes. Artaxerxes maintains the power dynamic of a king to his subject, but he does not dominate the dialogue and, in fact, does not make any commands or decrees at all.

Polaski notes that Ezra's portrayal of Artaxerxes uses writing in a powerful way, but Nehemiah's narrative has the king only loosely connected to scribal and bureaucratic writing. This minimalizing of imperial writing in Nehemiah's account even extends to the record of the letters being delivered to the provincial authorities outside of Yehud. In fact, no letters are recorded as being delivered to Jerusalem.[92]

---

89. Japhet, "Sheshbazzar and Zerubbabel," 75. See Fleishman's discussion of Nehemiah's political and religious actions in comparison to Zoroastrian principles of persuasive acts, which shows Nehemiah's calculation in presenting his request, Fleishman, "Nehemiah's Request on Behalf of Jerusalem," 241–66. See also Eskenazi, "Imagining the Other in the Construction of Judahite Identity in Ezra-Nehemiah," 251; Van Wijk-Bos, *Ezra, Nehemiah, and Esther*, 54–56; Clines, *Ezra, Nehemiah, Esther*, 141–43; Goswell, *Study Commentary on Ezra-Nehemiah*, 213–14.

90. Dyck, "'My Sad Face,'"183.

91. Dyck, "'My Sad Face,'" 186.

92. Polaski, "Nehemiah," 42–44; Eskenazi, "Imagining the Other in the Construction

Return Accounts

The events following Nehemiah's conversation with Artaxerxes highlight the focus on Nehemiah. Nehemiah is the subject of almost every verb in 2:9–18. Nehemiah went to the governors and gave them the letters (2:9). He came to Jerusalem, and he arose for the night ride (2:12). The examination of the wall and challenge of riding around it is presented in the first-person singular so that only Nehemiah is the subject (2:13–15). Even when the officials are the subject of the verb (they did not know where he had gone), it is followed by Nehemiah as the subject (he had not told them) (2:16). Finally, Nehemiah addresses the leaders about the situation, and he devises the plan to rebuild (2:17–18). Nehemiah is the character performing all the actions. As Clines notes on Neh 2:16, "his [Nehemiah's] repeated insistence that no one knew of his plans is perhaps intended to stress that the rebuilding of Jerusalem's walls was entirely due to his initiative."[93]

Besides being the subject of almost every sentence in the second half of Neh 2, there are only three other people named, and they are detractors responding to Nehemiah. Sanballat and Tobiah are mentioned as hearing about Nehemiah and being displeased (2:10), and Geshem is with them in their criticism of Nehemiah's plan to rebuild the city in 2:19. The other characters are nameless figures listed by their position (governors, officers, and horsemen in 2:9; a few men in 2:12; officials, Jews, priests, nobles, and the rest in 2:16). Even though three opponents are mentioned by name, they only serve to emphasize Nehemiah's actions. They are depicted as hearing and reacting to Nehemiah's arrival and building plan but do not take their own separate actions or change the flow of the narrative. This is unlike Neh 4 (MT 3:33–4) where Sanballat and Tobiah have extended speeches and devise their own plans for disrupting the work to which Nehemiah reacts by placing soldiers along the wall.

Nehemiah 3 is also based upon the speech of Nehemiah. In 2:18, Nehemiah tells the leaders about God's plan and the king's permission, and they respond, "Let us arise and build" and begin to work. This is echoed in 3:1 where the high priest and his brothers "arose . . . and built" their section of the wall. This phrase is also in Nehemiah's response to Sanballat, Tobiah, and Geshem (2:20). However, Nehemiah's recorded speech is directed at the outsiders who are excluded. Unlike 2:17–18, this speech is not a command to the Judean leaders to arise and build. The list in chapter three, then, is

---

of Judahite Identity in Ezra-Nehemiah," 251.

93. Clines, *Ezra, Nehemiah, Esther*, 147.

detailing the actions presented in 2:18, all of which is preceded by the plan that Nehemiah presented to the king and the Judean leaders (2:5, 18).

Primary Concern: City

Fortifications

The most obvious example of the focus on fortifying the city of Jerusalem is Neh 3. The entire chapter is a description of the people involved in building the wall and the sections that they built. However, this emphasis on the fortification of Jerusalem is found in repeated references to the gates, wall, and city in chapters one and two.

In Neh 1:2, Nehemiah asks the men from Judah about the people but also about the city of Jerusalem. The reply is that the "wall of Jerusalem is broken down and its gates burned with fire" (1:3). This phrasing recurs in the conversation with Artaxerxes ("the city . . . is desolate and its gates consumed with fire" [2:3]), the description of Nehemiah's night ride ("walls of Jerusalem which were broken down and its gates which were consumed with fire" [2:13]), and Nehemiah's speech to the leaders ("Jerusalem is desolate, and its gates burned with fire" [2:17]). All the phrasing reflects the initial assessment by the people who gave the report to Nehemiah. Not only was the initial report the catalyst for the penitential prayer and the request to Artaxerxes, but the damage is also reported by Nehemiah in the narrative and reported speech in way that reflects the original description by the men from Judah.

The burnt and broken-down state of the city wall was the catalyst for Nehemiah's prayer and migration, but the goal was rebuilding. Starting with Neh 2:5, the goal of rebuilding the wall is presented. The conclusion of this goal is found in the statement by the leaders that they will rebuild and the detailed description of the rebuilding process (2:18; 3:1–32). However, rebuilding the gates and city wall is also the topic of one of Nehemiah's letters (2:8). In fact, this seems to be the most important letter that Nehemiah requests. It is not only highlighted by being presented in reported speech, but Asaph is mentioned by name with his position, keeper of the king's forest, and the precise purpose of the materials is stated, wood for the gates of the fortress by the temple, the wall of the city, and the house in which Nehemiah will reside. The other letters are for the governors so that Nehemiah can pass through their provinces, but none of the governors are named, nor the precise provinces in which they are stationed.

People

The main characters in Neh 1–2 are often described in general terms. The people who tell Nehemiah about the state of Jerusalem are described as "Hanani, one of my brothers, and some men from Judah" (1:2). Outside of Nehemiah's brother, the others are not mentioned by name, title, or lineage. Nehemiah's question and the men's report are equally broad, referencing "the remnant" and "the Jews" (1:2–3).

The penitential prayer calls the people "sons of Israel," "your [God's] people," and "your [God's] servants" (1:6, 10–11). The category "sons of Israel" is also used in Neh 2:10 to describe the people whose welfare Nehemiah is seeking. In Neh 2:12, Nehemiah takes "a few men" with him on his night ride around the city. None of these references further define social or religious groups within the Israelite community, nor do they name or give the status of any individuals within the community.

Outside of Nehemiah's brother, the only place in Neh 1–2 where Judean groups are named is 2:16. This mentions officials, Jews, priests, nobles, and the rest who did the work. The term "officials" (סגן) is mentioned twice, but the first use might indicate a broad term encompassing the other, more specific titles and possibly even Persian leaders.[94] Even here, the leaders are mentioned with "the rest" and only by their titles, not by their names. This indicates that there are multiple social strata in Yehud, but particular social groups (like priests or officials) are not the focus of this return migration.

Contrary to the broad categories used for Jews, Nehemiah's adversaries are named explicitly. Sanballat the Horonite and Tobiah the Ammonite are mentioned twice, and Geshem the Arab is named once (2:10, 19). The name and lineage of Nehemiah's adversaries makes the quarrel vivid and personal. It appears that Nehemiah is competing with his adversaries individually and the rest of the Judean community is relegated to the background of the narrative.

The quarrel between Nehemiah and his adversaries is over the people of Israel. It is important to note that Sanballat and Tobiah were angry not because Nehemiah was building the wall but because "a man was seeking the well-being of the sons of Israel" (2:10). Even in the second appearance

---

94. Steinmann, *Ezra and Nehemiah*, 409.

of the adversaries, they do not mention the wall directly. In Nehemiah's response to their question of what the Israelites are doing, he says they are building (though again not mentioning "the wall") and tells the adversaries, "you have no portion, right, or memorial in Jerusalem" (2:20). Though seeking the welfare of the sons of Israel and rising up to build most likely indicate building the wall, it is indirect. The emphasis in both passages is on the people of Israel and specifically those living in Jerusalem. The point Nehemiah seems to be making is that Sanballat, Tobiah, and Geshem are not part of the sons of Israel living in Jerusalem. So, the disagreement between the major characters centers around the people of Israel and who is part of the community in Jerusalem.

Nehemiah 3 is the first in-depth mention of genealogy, location, and occupation in this narrative. Most of the people involved in building are listed by genealogy, but some of them are listed by occupation (3:8, 29, 31, 32) and others by city (3:2, 5, 7, 13, 27). The most interesting comparison, though, is the cultic and civil personnel. The list begins with Eliashib the high priest and his brothers but quickly moves non-cultic individuals and city populations (3:1). Religious personnel are then mentioned in general terms as priests (3:22, 28), Nethinim (3:26), and the most explicit detail, "the Levites under Rehum the son of Bani" (3:17). However, civil officials are frequently mentioned by name: Rephaiah the official of half the district of Jerusalem (3:9), Shallum the official of half the district of Jerusalem (3:12), Malchijah the official of the district of Beth-Haccerem (3:14), Shallum the official of the district of Mizpah (3:15), Nehemiah the official of half the district of Beth-zur (3:16), Hashabiah the official of half the district of Keilah (3:17), Bavvai the official of half the district of Keilah (3:18), Ezer the official of Mizpah (3:19). The term for "official" in this list is שר which is a different title than the "officials" (סגן) that Nehemiah spoke to in 2:16.[95] Regardless of the distinction between the titles for the officials, the list of builders is diverse and a significant emphasis is placed upon non-cultic leaders and apparently common people known only by their lineage or occupation. None of the individuals are portrayed as directing or organizing the building project except Nehemiah in the previous chapter and the list is organized by location along the wall rather than social group or genealogical affiliation.

---

95. For a more detailed examination of the administrative titles and districts in this name list see Demsky, "'Pelekh' in Nehemiah 3," 242–44.

COMPARISON OF NEHEMIAH TO SHESHBAZZAR AND EZRA

Since the migration narratives of Sheshbazzar and Ezra have already been discussed, their themes will be treated as a single pattern in this section. The goal is to compare the largely overlapping themes of migrations of Sheshbazzar and Ezra to the themes in Nehemiah's return. In the same method as the previous two sections, the focus on the prominent character and the primary concerns of the narratives will be discussed.

Prominent Character

The return migrations of Sheshbazzar and Ezra are initiated by a decree of the king. Both narratives show that the king's decree is central because the commands of the decree are fulfilled through the actions of the returnees immediately after the transcriptions of the decrees in the narratives.

By contrast, Nehemiah's return begins with Nehemiah's concern for the city of Jerusalem and his penitential prayer. Goswell notes that Nehemiah's prayer is at the head of the narrative which is the location of the royal decrees in the previous migrations.[96] The centrality of Nehemiah's speech is also shown by the fulfillment of his requests to the king in Neh 2–3. It is in the form of a conversation rather than a decree and the plans for a migration and rebuilding are coming from the mouth of Nehemiah, not Artaxerxes.[97]

---

96. Goswell, *Study Commentary on Ezra-Nehemiah*, 197.

97. In an article comparing Chronicles' emphasis on the Davidic dynasty to speeches in Ezra-Nehemiah, Mason notes that Cyrus's decree (Ezra 1) functions like David providing utensils and building plans for the temple. He also claims that Artaxerxes gives authority to Ezra to appoint judges and magistrates, which is reminiscent of David's appointment of judges, priests, and leaders. However, he shows that Nehemiah's speech reflects Davidide history as he commands the people to arise and strengthen their hands just as David charged Solomon and David, Hezekiah, and Manasseh built the walls of Jerusalem. Though the comparison with Chronicles is outside this scope of this study, this again shows that the focus is upon the Persian kings in Ezra 1–2 and 7–8 but on Nehemiah in Neh 1–3. Mason, "Some Chronistic Themes in the 'Speeches' in Ezra and Nehemiah," 72–73. Joseph Blenkinsopp notes that Nehemiah's mission is a case of imperial authorization, but Ezra's is not because it is not presented as a response to a request by a Jewish individual or community. Blenkinsopp, "Was the Pentateuch the Civic and Religious Constitution of the Jewish Ethnos in the Persian Period?," 54; Margalith, "Political Role of Ezra as Persian Governor," 110.

Also, Wright notes, "Although Nehemiah is granted permission to build, he does not

Ezra 1 and Ezra 7 begin with a date formula stating the name of the Persian king and the year of his reign. However, Nehemiah begins with "the words of Nehemiah" and then states that it was in the month Chislev in the twentieth year (1:1). This has often been interpreted as a corruption in the text or an editor dating the Nehemiah Memoir with the last king mentioned at the end of Ezra (and subsequently in Neh 2).[98] The argument for a corruption in the text is hypothetical, and, though it is possible, it is unprovable at this point. In the same way, omitting the king's name makes the narrative appear to follow Ezra directly, but whether this was an intentional device on the part of an editor or author is only speculation. Steinmann proposes that Nehemiah was reckoning from another important event like his twentieth year of service in the Persian court, but this still is speculative.[99] What is obvious, though, is that Nehemiah is fronted. In chapter one, only Nehemiah and Hanani are mentioned by name (Moses is mentioned in the prayer, not in the mainline narrative), and Hanani is named in relation to Nehemiah, as his brother. Unlike the other two migrations where the king's name, year of his reign, and decree are mentioned at the beginning, Nehemiah begins with the story of Nehemiah, his speech, and his occupation and does not even name the Persian king until chapter two. So, regardless of the origin of the missing date formula, the present form of the text is clearly focused upon the character and actions of Nehemiah over the Persian king.

Primary Concern

Location

The cultic emphasis of the migrations in Ezra have been noted. Sheshbazzar and Ezra were given donations by the Persian king and other

---

come to Judah with an imperial decree comparable to those recorded elsewhere in Ezra-Nehemiah. The success of his project depended ultimately on his own pith and pluck." Wright, "Commensal Politics in Ancient Western Asia," 350; Wright, "New Model for the Composition of Ezra-Nehemiah," 344; Grabbe, "Law of Moses in the Ezra Tradition," 110; Goswell, *Study Commentary on Ezra-Nehemiah*, 214.

98. Breneman, *Ezra, Nehemiah, Esther*, 169; Fensham, *Books of Ezra and Nehemiah*, 150; Kidner, *Ezra and Nehemiah*, 77; Myers, *Ezra-Nehemiah*, 92; Williamson, *Ezra, Nehemiah*, 169–70; Blenkinsopp, *Ezra-Nehemiah*, 205; Allen and Laniak, *Ezra, Nehemiah, Esther*, 91; Redditt, *Ezra-Nehemiah*, 227.

99. Steinmann, *Ezra and Nehemiah*, 386.

individuals for the temple as well as utensils for cultic worship. However, Nehemiah does not record any donations by the king or by other individuals. The only items that Nehemiah received from Artaxerxes were letters that allowed him to pass through other territories and one letter that allowed him to obtain building supplies (2:7–8). Artaxerxes also gave letters to Ezra, but they were not for building supplies (7:21–23). These were items needed for worship at the temple, and the way that the decree was fulfilled in Ezra 8:36 seems to imply that this was continued support for the temple functioning, not just a one-time gift of necessary supplies. So, the lack of monetary support and cultic vessels is notable in the Nehemiah migration. Wright also notes the difference in wording between Nehemiah's going to Jerusalem (בוא Neh 2:11) and Ezra's and Sheshbazzar's going up to Jerusalem (עלה Ezra :11; 2:1; 7:7, 28; 8:1).[100] This linguistic shift points to a cultic procession in the first two migrations, using the common phrase "going up to Jerusalem," but a simple movement from Susa to Jerusalem in Nehemiah's migration.

In addition to the lack of items for the temple and cultic "going up" terminology, Nehemiah rarely mentions the building itself. Whereas Cyrus and Artaxerxes frequently mention the house of God and the city where God dwells, Nehemiah describes Jerusalem as the place of his fathers' tombs when he is speaking to Artaxerxes (2:3, 5). In fact, when he describes his plans, Nehemiah uses the temple (just called "the house" in 2:8) only as a spatial referent ("the gates of the citadel which is by the temple" [2:8]). As Kraemer observes, the mention of the temple in Neh 2:8 is one of only two in the book of Nehemiah (the other is 6:10), and both are only passing references. In addition, the mention in Neh 2:8 is not found in the Septuagint.[101] This is distinct from the phrasing in Sheshbazzar's and Ezra's migration where Jerusalem is frequently the spatial modifier for the house of God ("the house of God which is in Jerusalem" [1:2, 4, 5; 2:68; 7:15, 16, 17, 19, 27]). It appears, then, that the narratives of Sheshbazzar and Ezra are focused upon the temple to the exclusion of the city, but the Nehemiah migration is focused upon the city to the exclusion of the temple.[102]

---

100. Wright, "New Model for the Composition of Ezra-Nehemiah," 342n24.

101. Kraemer, "On the Relationship of the Books of Ezra and Nehemiah," 80.

102. Donna Laird notes the parallels between the destruction of Jericho's walls in Josh 6 and Nehemiah's building of Jerusalem's walls. This holy war imagery in Nehemiah is not found in the return migrations of Ezra and Sheshbazzar. Laird, "Political Strategy in the Narrative of Ezra-Nehemiah," 276–85; Davies, *Ezra and Nehemiah*, 92–93.

The functioning of the temple is also an important element of the narrative for Sheshbazzar and Ezra. Not only do the texts mention donations for the temple and the location of the temple, they both indicate that cultic activities were taking place. Ezra 2 mentions holy meals and cultic garments (2:63, 69). This implies that at least some level of cultic activity was happening even though sacrifices and festival observances are not mentioned until the next chapter. The decree of Artaxerxes in Ezra 7 describes temple function much more explicitly by commanding sacrifices to resume and making donations to ensure this will happen (7:17). The passage then concludes with the people sacrificing burnt offerings (8:35). Nehemiah, on the other hand, does not mention cultic activity at all. Not only does he not mention the state of the temple building in Neh 1:1–3:32, he does not mention any cultic activities. Sacrifices, donations, and feasting are all absent in this passage, even though they are one of the prominent features for the other two returns.

People

Ezra and Sheshbazzar focus upon priests, Levites, and other cultic personnel. The narratives mention heads of households and other families, but priests, Levites, and other cultic personnel are always specifically named. The religious leaders are treated as groups separate from the other people of Israel and worthy of special mention.

The Nehemiah narrative is concerned with the sons of Israel as a whole. In fact, Kraemer uses this cultic versus laity emphasis to argue for Ezra and Nehemiah being originally separate.[103] Pakkala claims, "Priestly and Levitical additions are met throughout the book of Ezra, but they are missing in the NM. In fact, priestly issues are almost non-existent in the NM, especially in comparison with the book of Ezra."[104] Though priests, Levites, and cultic personnel are mentioned, they are given only minor attention. Even when the priests and Levites are mentioned, it is with other officials and people of Israel and the priests are not prioritized by being named or mentioned first (2:16). Though, the list of builders begins with the high priest, the rest of the priests, Levites, and Nethinim are unnamed in contrast to the name, genealogy, and position of civil officials and many other people of the Judean community. Mitchell claims that the priests and

---

103. Kraemer, "On the Relationship of the Books of Ezra and Nehemiah," 77–80.

104. Pakkala, "Original Independence of the Ezra Story in Ezra 7–10 and Neh 8," 17.

Levites being named specifically in the builder list is an indication that it is a different source because this is at odds with the downplaying of the role of priests in the rest of the Nehemiah Memoir.[105] This source critical assertion may not be entirely convincing, but Mitchell's observation that naming cultic personnel is uncharacteristic of the Nehemiah narrative supports the distinction between the cultic emphasis of Ezra and the non-cultic emphasis in Nehemiah.

To further display this difference, the cultic personnel are so important to the Ezra migration that Ezra notes in detail the special request he had to make to have Levites in his return party (8:15–20). The Sheshbazzar migration describes priests whose ancestry was unknown and the judgment that they cannot eat holy food until the Urim and Thummim have been consulted by a priest (Ezra 2:61–63). Nehemiah has an exclusionary conversation as well but not with the cultic personnel. Nehemiah excludes Sanballat, Tobiah, and Geshem from the community, but they are described as Horonite, Ammonite, and Arab (2:19–20), which is to say non-Israelite. So, whereas the first two migrations are concerned with fulfilling cultic roles, Nehemiah is concerned with the role of Israel and who is a part of the community in Jerusalem (2:20).

CONCLUSION

In summary, the return migrations of Sheshbazzar and Ezra share many thematic similarities. The Persian king is the central character, and his decree is the catalyst for the events in the narrative. The primary foci of the passages are the temple and the cultic personnel. Nehemiah stands in sharp contrast with this pattern. The Nehemiah passage focuses on Nehemiah as the prominent character, and his recorded speech is the pattern that the narrated events follow. The two foci of the passage are the city of Jerusalem and the sons of Israel, and there is a notable lack of cultic concern.

---

105. Mitchell, "Wall of Jerusalem According to the Book of Nehemiah," 89.

Chapter 3

The Literary Structure of the Return Migrations

THE PREVIOUS CHAPTER FOCUSED upon thematic elements of the return migrations. This chapter will explore their literary structures. First the structural patterns in the migrations of Sheshbazzar and Ezra will be discussed individually and then compared. Finally, the structural pattern of Nehemiah will be examined and contrasted with the previous two migrations.

SHESHBAZZAR

1. Cyrus issues a decree (1:1–4)
    A. God stirs and Cyrus writes (1:1)
    B. Transcription of the decree (1:2–4)
        i. Any of the people may leave (1:3)
        ii. People support the returnees (1:4)
2. Leaders rise up to go (1:5)
3. Offerings (1:6–11)
    A. From the people (1:6)
    B. From Cyrus (1:7–10)
    C. Given to Sheshbazzar and taken to Jerusalem (1:11)

The Literary Structure of the Return Migrations

4. List of returnees (2:1–67)

   A. Name list (2:1–61)

   i. Leaders (2:1–2a)

   ii. People (2:2b–35)

   iii. Priests (2:36–39)

   iv. Levites (2:40–58)

   v. Unclear ancestry people (2:59–60)

   vi. Unclear ancestry priests (2:61)

   B. Exclusion (2:62–63)

   C. Total numbers (2:64–67)

5. Amount of gold, silver, clothing given for the temple (2:68–69)
6. Israel lives in the cities (2:70)

Cyrus Issues a Decree (1:1–4)

The book of Ezra begins with background information written in the third person. Ezra 1:1 starts with an introductory formula: "In the first year of Cyrus king of Persia." This is followed by an infinitive construct, usually translated as a purpose clause, "to fulfill the word of Yahweh by the mouth of Jeremiah," and the main clause, "Yahweh stirred up the spirit of Cyrus king of Persia." The result is that "he made a proclamation throughout all his kingdom and also in writing" (1:1). This verse serves as an introduction to the transcribed proclamation and the final word is the infinitive construct of אמר, which is a common way of introducing recorded speech.[1]

Ezra 1:2–4 is the transcription of the decree written in first person with Cyrus as the speaker/writer. Within the document itself, Cyrus identifies himself as king of Persia and introduces his words. The letter contains three sections, not counting the introductory line in the third person "thus says Cyrus king of Persia" (1:2). In the first section of the letter, Cyrus describes his appointment and commission by God to rule over the world and build a temple in Jerusalem. In the second section, Cyrus calls to the people of Israel, who he initially calls "his (God's) people," to go up to Jerusalem and rebuild the temple (1:3). The third section focuses upon the people

---

1. Miller, *Representation of Speech in Biblical Hebrew Narrative*, §4.3, 163–212.

living around the potential returnees giving donations (1:4). These three sections of the letter also feature a repetition of בית, כל, and בירושלם: "All the kingdoms of the earth" and "house in Jerusalem" (1:2), "from all his people" and "house of Yahweh ... in Jerusalem" (1:3), and "every survivor" and "house of God which is in Jerusalem" (1:4).[2]

Leaders Rise up to Go (1:5)

The second movement of the text in Ezra 1 reflects the decree of Cyrus. Ezra 1:5 changes from the jussives and *yiqtol* verbs in verses 3–4 to a *wayyiqtol* verb with "heads of fathers' households of Judah and Benjamin and the priests and the Levites" as the subject. This verse also reflects verse 3 by utilizing the same verbs עלה and בנה but as infinitive constructs rather than jussives.

Becking considers Ezra 1 to be split into three sections: the edict of Cyrus (1:1–4), the reaction of the heads (1:5–8), and the return of the temple vessels (1:9–11).[3] However, his second section does not account for the change of subject between verse 5 and verse 6. The heads of Israel react in verse 5, but then it is the people around the returnees that are encouraging them in verse 6, so this should be considered a different section. In addition, this follows the pattern of the decree, which divides the rising up of leaders from the offerings of the surrounding people.

The mirroring of verbs and the phrase "house of Yahweh which is in Jerusalem" in verse 5 shows that this is a direct fulfillment of the decree and is structurally parallel to verse 3.[4] Verse 6 also begins with כל, which grammatically patterns the actions after the wording of the decree.[5]

---

2. Goswell, *Study Commentary on Ezra-Nehemiah*, 59–60.

3. Becking, *Ezra-Nehemiah*, 23.

4. This emphasis upon "Jerusalem, which is in Judah" was claimed to be bureaucratic pedantry by Williamson but has been argued to be polemic by many others. For Becking, it is an "inner-Yahwistic polemic . . . [against] temples for Yahweh in Samaria/Gerizim, Maqqedah and Lakish." Williamson, *Ezra, Nehemiah*, 12; Clines, *Ezra, Nehemiah, Esther*, 37. Contra Becking, *Ezra-Nehemiah*, 28; Steinmann, *Ezra and Nehemiah*, 135. For this study of the structure, the polemic or bureaucratic nature of the designation is less important than the repeated use of the phrase in the edict and the responses to it.

5. Goswell, *Study Commentary on Ezra-Nehemiah*, 62; Davies, *Ezra and Nehemiah*, 10–12.

Offerings (1:6–11)

The third movement in the text also follows the decree of Cyrus but with more detail. The gifts are presented in three major stages: encouragement from the people (1:6), gifts from Cyrus (1:7–10), and receipt by Sheshbazzar (1:11). The major changes are marked by the subjects of the main verbs. First, the people surrounding are the subject of חזק ("encourage"), then King Cyrus brought out (יצא) articles, and finally Sheshbazzar brought the articles up (עלה). It should be noted that Mithredath is most likely the subject of ספר in verse 8, but this should be understood as a dependent clause. Cyrus brought the vessels out by the hand of Mithredath, and so the counting of the vessels by Mithredath is a description of Cyrus bringing out the vessels by his hand. This is then further detailed by a noun phrase listing the vessels and their quantities.[6]

Goswell sees the response of the people and the list of returnees as a chiasm: the people rise (1:5), goods are given (1:6), movement of goods (1:7–11), and movement of people (2:1–70).[7] However, this division is unconvincing. First, verses 9–10 do not mention the movement of goods but their quantity. In the chiastic structure, there should be a parallel to this in verse 6 but no quantities are mentioned in that verse. Second, the alternation between people and goods then goods and people relies upon a somewhat artificial division between verses 6 and 7. The text transitions from gifts by the people in the communities to gifts by Cyrus, but this does not appear to be a break in the text on the same level as verses 5 and 6. Verse 5 is about leaders rising up to leave, whereas verse 6 describes gifts given by other people (change in characters and action). However, verses 6 and 7 describe gifts and donations but the person giving them changes from the people to Cyrus (same action but different characters). So, the four-part chiastic structure does not seem as clear as Goswell's division might indicate.

---

6. Whether this list was copied from an original inventory or created by the author/editor of Ezra does not affect the function of it in the text. This list also contains some numerical issues. For a discussion of these see Segal, "Numerical Discrepancies in the List of Vessels in Ezra I 9–11," 122–29.

7. Goswell, *Study Commentary on Ezra-Nehemiah*, 62.

List of Returnees (2:1–67)

The fourth section of the return migration is the list of returnees.[8] This passage begins with "and these (are) sons of the province who came up." This introduction ties Ezra 2:1 with Ezra 1:11. Sheshbazzar brings the offerings "with the exiles who came up from Babylon to Jerusalem." Read in this way, the list of returnees is an expansion of the people who Sheshbazzar brought back to Jerusalem on his return.

This is against Williamson, who claims that "apart from its position, the list has no connection with chap. 1." One of his proofs is that Sheshbazzar is not mentioned, but his name would not be expected in the list if it is a list of people who "went up with Sheshbazzar" from Ezra 1:11.[9] Halpern claims it originally listed the return for Zerubbabel not Sheshbazzar, which was a different return, because Sheshbazzar is not mentioned in Ezra 2 or Neh 7. Zerubbabel's later migration is conflated with Sheshbazzar's return here so that the first (failed) migration by Sheshbazzar does not seem abortive.[10] Goswell claims that the list of returnees parallels Ezra 1:7–11 based upon parallels like Nebuchadnezzar (1:7 and 2:1), the word "number" (1:9 and 2:2), vessels and people being broken down into groups, "other vessels" and people without genealogy (1:10 and 2:59–63), and the final total number (1:11 and 2:64–67). He also claims that Sheshbazzar should be added to the list to make twelve leaders.[11]

My interpretation is between Halpern and Goswell. Regardless of whether the list originally referred to Sheshbazzar's migration, Zerubbabel's migration, or both because the leaders returned in the same migration, the intention of the author in this passage is clear. The ending of chapters one and two with vessels given for temple service and the omission of the twelfth leader, indicates that this is intended to be the migration ordered by Cyrus and fulfilled by Sheshbazzar. Whether they were originally separate migrations is less relevant for the discussion of the function of the list

---

8. Williamson analyzes the structure of Ezra 2 as: "heading (1–2), lists of lay people (3–35), of priests (36–39), Levites (40), singers (41), gatekeepers (42), and other temple servants (43–58), and of those whose genealogies could not be proved (59–63); totals (64–67); summary of gifts for the temple building (68–69), and conclusion (70)." Williamson, *Ezra, Nehemiah*, 28; Becking, *Ezra-Nehemiah*, 40.

9. Williamson, *Ezra, Nehemiah*, 30. See also Clines, *Ezra, Nehemiah, Esther*, 44–46; Myers, *Ezra-Nehemiah*, 15.

10. Halpern, "Historiographic Commentary on Ezra 1–6," 89, 96, 125.

11. Goswell, *Study Commentary on Ezra-Nehemiah*, 64–65, 69.

The Literary Structure of the Return Migrations

within its current setting, which makes it entirely dependent upon Ezra 1 (contra Williamson).

This list, then, could have been placed as a subsection of "given to Sheshbazzar and taken to Jerusalem" in the chapter diagram. However, the length of the list, organization, and detail of the individuals (including the questionable ancestry) indicates that this is functioning as more than a simple inventory list (unlike Ezra 1:9–10). The discussion of ancestry and consequences for not providing enough genealogical detail is one of the primary indicators that this has a more significant function and should be treated as a major section rather than solely as an expansion of Sheshbazzar's return in Ezra 1:11. This section is intimately tied with Sheshbazzar's action in 1:11, but it is more than a list of details explaining that verse.

Within this section are three subsections. The first section is the list of names which can be divided into leaders (2:1–2a), people of Israel (2:2b–35),[12] priests (2:36–39), Levites and temple personnel (2:40–58), people without genealogy (2:59–60), and priests without genealogy (2:61). The final two groups (people and priests without genealogy) are separated from the rest of the list by an introductory verse (2:59). The extended introduction lists their place of origin and inability to show their ancestry, and this extended identifier sets these people apart from the rest of the community. They are part of the name list, but special attention is paid to their place of origin and lack of records.

This list of returnees and special focus on the people with unknown ancestry leads to the next subsection which is the exclusion of the priests without genealogy (2:62–63). The shift in the text is marked by an absence of names. The people being excluded are simply "these" (אלה). The last time that this pronoun was used, it was to introduce the list of names "and these are the ones who came up from . . . but they were not able to give evidence of their father's house" (2:59). This is an introductory formula that precedes the list of names. However, in Ezra 2:62, the antecedent to the pronoun is the list of people in the preceding verses, and they are not only searching but also being considered unclean by others. So, the primarily nominal clauses have changed to verbal clauses with active verbs and no individuals named. The lack of names includes the subsequent verse (v. 63) because

---

12. Williamson argues that this could be further subdivided into people identified by family (vv. 2–20) and two sets of people identified by location (vv. 21–28, 29–35). Williamson, *Ezra, Nehemiah*, 33. Becking only divides this in two parts. Becking, *Ezra-Nehemiah*, 40. So also Shepherd and Wright, *Ezra and Nehemiah*, 24–25; Steinmann, *Ezra and Nehemiah*, 170.

the governor is only referred to by the title not by name.[13] So, this second subsection describes the treatment of the people bracketed off in the name list as different from the rest of the community.

The final subsection is the conclusion (2:64–67). The change is indicated by phrase "the whole assembly" (v. 64). Though the total number of people mentioned in the name list does not add up to the number given here (42,360), the verse is clearly intended to provide the total number of people and animals in the return.[14] This summary also ties together this entire section. Ezra 2:1 began with a list of names and locations, and Ezra 2:64–67 concludes this section by giving the total number of people in the list and additional people and animals not counted in the earlier list.

Amount of Gold, Silver, and Clothing for the Temple (2:68–69)

After the list of returnees, the text shifts to Jerusalem. The phrase "when they arrived at the house of Yahweh which is in Jerusalem" orients this text around the location (2:64). The previous section was focused upon the list of people. Even the section about the people without records does not state where the governor's decision took place or even what city or province the governor oversaw, but focuses on their genealogy and the number of people (2:63). By contrast, this section only mentions "some heads of the fathers" (with a partitive מן), but the name or number of leaders is not provided. However, the text does provide the quantity and type of offering that they made (2:69). This section, then, orients the activity at the temple in Jerusalem and focuses upon the quantity of gold, silver, and clothing provided.

---

13. Goswell thinks the governor is Sheshbazzar but with little proof. Goswell, *Study Commentary on Ezra-Nehemiah*, 69.

14. Williamson argues for the inclusion of women in the total to harmonize the numbers. Williamson, *Ezra, Nehemiah*, 38. Becking claims no satisfactory explanation can be found without a totally different tradition or redefining "returnees." Becking, *Ezra-Nehemiah*, 44; Clines, *Ezra, Nehemiah, Esther*, 60; Steinmann, *Ezra and Nehemiah*, 176. Redditt argues that the redactor is indicating that not all who returned are considered "true Israel." Redditt, "Census List in Ezra 2 and Nehemiah 7," 223–40. For additional discussion of the numbers of people who returned in comparison with the list in Neh 7, see Allrik, "Lists of Zerubbabel (Nehemiah 7 and Ezra 2) and the Hebrew Numeral Notation," 21–27.

The Literary Structure of the Return Migrations

Israel Lives in the Cities (2:70)

The concluding verse summarizes the passage. The focus returns to the people groups mentioned in the list at the beginning of chapter two (though in a different order) but also in their location. Though the gifts to the temple are no longer mentioned, the listing of the people groups and setting of the location within their cities brings together the two major sections of chapter two through the two emphases (people and location).

EZRA

1. Introduction of Ezra (7:1–6)
2. Movement from Babylon to Jerusalem (7:7–10)
    A. Some sons of Israel migrated also (7:7)
    B. Desire to teach the Law (7:10)
3. The decree of Artaxerxes (7:11–26)
    A. Transcription of the decree (7:12–26)
        i. Any of the people may leave (7:13)
        ii. Offerings (7:15–24)
            a. From Artaxerxes (7:15)
            b. From the people (7:16)
            c. Given to Ezra for the temple (7:17–20)
            d. From other treasurers (7:21–23)
        iii. No taxes on religious personnel (7:24)
        iv. Authority given to Ezra (7:25–26)
4. Blessing to God for decree (7:27–28a)
5. Leaders rise up to go (7:28b)
6. List of returnees (8:1–14)
7. Gathering of specialized temple personnel (8:15–20)
8. Fasting for the journey (8:21–23)
9. Weighing gold and silver offerings for the temple (8:24–30)

10. Move to Jerusalem and remaining there three days (8:31–32)

11. Weighing of offerings for the temple (8:33–34)

12. Returnees sacrifice, deliver edicts, and support the temple (8:35–36)

Introduction of Ezra (7:1–6)

The beginning of this section is a series of nominal clauses. This separates the passage from the previous chapter ("and after these things") and identifies the time period ("in the reign of Artaxerxes"), as well as the lineage and occupation of Ezra (priest and scribe). This is the largest narrative break in Ezra. The primary Israelite character changes, the king changes, and the location changes. Dumbrell also notes that the emphasis on the temple seems to disappear here or at least be changed into an emphasis on temple provisions by the Persian king.[15]

Once Ezra is identified by genealogy, he is further identified as the one who went up from Babylon, a scribe skilled in the Mosaic Law and the one God blessed with favor before the king (7:6). Kellerman notes the awkwardness of the lengthy genealogy here and claims that vv. 1a, 6, and 8–10 are Chronistic but verses 1b–5, and 7 are from a "list-happy interpolator."[16] Wilhelm In der Smitten claims that a long genealogy interrupts the narrative flow, regardless of whether it is original or secondary.[17] The length of this genealogy is unique in Ezra-Nehemiah, and the lack of a verb until verse 6 creates a need for the subject ("this Ezra") to be repeated. The discussion of redaction history is beyond the scope of this work, but noting the uniqueness of the genealogy and redaction hypothesis confirms the narrative shifts presented here.

The continued focus upon Ezra in verse 6 is signaled by the fronting of the third-person pronoun and the name Ezra in the first clause and the third-person pronoun and scribe in the second clause. The other clauses follow the verb-subject word order because Ezra is not the subject.[18] This verse, then, continues to identify Ezra but instead of his genealogy, he is described by his actions and his skills. Christopher Hays notes that the

15. Dumbrell, "Theological Intention of Ezra-Nehemiah," 68.
16. Kellermann, *Nehemia*, 57–59.
17. In der Smitten, *Esra*, 8. See also Gunneweg, *Esra*, 120.
18. The verb-subject clauses are "which Yahweh the God of Israel gave" and "the king gave to him."

description of Ezra in verse 6 functions as a *merismus*, giving Ezra earthly (the king granted his requests) and heavenly (the hand of God was upon him) authority.[19]

Movement from Babylon to Jerusalem (7:7–10)

This section changes focus from the person of Ezra to the people migrating to Jerusalem. This is shown by the addition of other people groups, defined dates, and repeated references to location. Verse 7 does not mention Ezra at all. Unlike later verses (7:13, 28), in verse 7, people groups went up to Jerusalem but not "with Ezra." The lack of reference to Ezra is a sharp change from the previous verses. Even the singular verbs lack explicit reference to Ezra until verse 10. It must be inferred from verse 6 that Ezra is the person making the migration even though he is not explicitly named.

Daniels even claims that this lack of Ezra reference implies this is a secondary addition to verses 1–6 and verses 8–10.[20] Martin Noth considered verses 8–10 to be a secondary addition but added prior to verse 7. He asserted this because verse 6 is separated from the causal sentence in verse 10 and verse 9bβ is a shortened repetition of verse 6b.[21] However, Daniels does not find this division convincing because verse 9bβ ties "the good hand of his God" to the events of both verse 6 (favor with the king) and verses 8–9 (successful travel).[22] These redactional arguments aside, the shift in perspective from verse 6 to verse 7 is important for identifying the new narrative movement.

In addition to the other people mentioned, these verses also solidify the date of the migration. Ezra 7:1 stated that these events took place in the reign of Artaxerxes, but these verses state the exact month. The importance of the date is shown by the repetitive way in which the dates are provided. Verse 7 claims it was the seventh year, verse 8 claims they arrived in Jerusalem in the fifth month of the seventh year, and verse 9 explains that they left Babylon in the first month and arrived in Jerusalem on the first of the fifth month. This emphasis on dates is a departure from the general dating of the

---

19. Hays, "Silence of the Wives," 63.

20. Daniels, "Composition of the Ezra-Nehemiah Narrative," 313, 315; Goswell, *Study Commentary on Ezra-Nehemiah*, 138–39; Hoglund, *Achaemenid Imperial Administration in Syria-Palestine and the Missions of Ezra and Nehemiah*, 226.

21. Noth, *Überlieferungsgeschichtliche Studien*, 125.

22. Daniels, "Composition of the Ezra-Nehemiah Narrative," 312.

reign of Artaxerxes earlier, and it focuses the narrative on the migrations rather than the individual.

The emphasis on migration is also shown through the repeated locations and movements. The people went up to Jerusalem (7:7), he came to Jerusalem (7:8), he began to go up from Babylon and came to Jerusalem (7:9), and Ezra desired to teach in Israel (7:10). So, the focus in this section is no longer solely on the person of Ezra but on the migration itself.

Pakkala claims that verse 7 is a late addition that interrupts the flow of the narrative because it includes the Levites, which indicates the editor was apparently unaware of Ezra 8:15b–20.[23] A challenge to this claim is that the point of Ezra 8:15b–20 is to show how the Levites did in fact go to Jerusalem with Ezra. If the summary statement in Ezra 7:7 *did not* mention Levites, that would indicate ignorance of 8:15b–20 because the passage shows the special care Ezra took to include Levites. Ezra 7:7, then, should be seen as cohesive in the narrative with the passage about Ezra retrieving Levites from Iddo, regardless of whether one views it as original or a late addition.

The description of the migration is in summary form and the wording of Ezra 7:9–10 echoes verse 6 (going up from Babylon, the hand of God upon Ezra, and his study of the Law). The similarity of the final verses at the end of each section draws them together. Read together, these first two sections create a prologue for the rest of the narrative. They identify Ezra, who writes in the first person starting in 7:27, the people migrating, and date of the migration. These sections identify in quick summary the new characters and events that will be detailed over the next two chapters but do not mention Artaxerxes issuing a decree. Ezra 7:11 starts, "And this is a copy of the letter," but there is no mention of a letter in the previous verses. For this reason, these first two sections should be seen as a prologue defining the characters and the overall migration. The next section begins to detail the decree and events that have been given in summary form here.

The Decree of Artaxerxes (7:11–26)

The transcription of the letter of Artaxerxes dictates the events that will happen in the rest of this chapter and chapter eight. The transcription of the letter is in Aramaic, so lexical parallels between the decree in chapter seven

---

23. Pakkala, "Disunity of Ezra-Nehemiah," 215.

The Literary Structure of the Return Migrations

and the actions of Ezra in chapter eight are difficult to make, but the basic movements are the same.[24]

This section begins with an introduction stating that this is a letter given by Artaxerxes to Ezra. Steinmann considers Ezra 7:12 to be the beginning of the Ezra Memoir with 7:11 being a description of the letter made by the author/compiler of the book of Ezra who wrote Ezra 7:1–10 and reworked the Ezra Memoir to fit the rest of the chapter.[25] However, I am following the narrative break rather than changes in sources, so the narrative shift occurs clearly at the end of Ezra 7:10 regardless of whether the author/editor changes in that verse.

The statement in 7:11 mirrors the introductory first line of the letter itself (v. 12). However, their titles are different in each statement. In Ezra 7:11, it is "king Artaxerxes," but 7:12 calls him "Artaxerxes, king of kings." Also, Ezra 7:11 states, "Ezra the priest, the scribe, learned of the words of the laws of Yahweh and his statutes to Israel," whereas Ezra 7:12 states, "Ezra the priest, the scribe of the law of the God of heaven." Both introductory phrases indicate that the letter is a personal correspondence. Though the letter gives certain privileges to Ezra, it is written to Ezra specifically, not just a general broad command to all people.

After Artaxerxes introduces himself and Ezra, the letter then transitions to the main body of the text.[26] The text begins with Artaxerxes allowing the people to return to Jerusalem (7:13). However, Artaxerxes does not just allow the people to leave but allows them to leave "with you (Ezra)." The importance of this is borne out in the next verse, which starts, "Since you are being sent by the king." So, even though the people are the ones allowed to return, Artaxerxes is centering this upon his command to Ezra. They can return with Ezra because Ezra is the one being sent back to inquire of God on behalf of Persia. The offerings detailed by Artaxerxes also relate to the command for Ezra to inquire of God as they are all tied to providing for the temple and performing the sacrifices in accordance with the law of God (7:15–20).

---

24. For the function of the embedded document and discussion of its origin, see Jones, "Embedded Written Documents as Colonial Mimicry in Ezra-Nehemiah," 158–81; Hogue, "Return from Exile," 66; Grabbe, *Judaism from Cyrus to Hadrian*, 1:33–34. Hays claims that the Aramaic is intended to draw the readers' attention and provides "at least a patina of verisimilitude." Hays, "Silence of the Wives," 64; Burns, *Ezra, Nehemiah*, 38.

25. Steinmann, *Ezra and Nehemiah*, 285, 296.

26. וכענת is a common transition marker in letters. See Ezra 4:10–11, 17 and the related כען in Ezra 4:13–14, 21; 5:16–17; 6:6. Steinmann, *Ezra and Nehemiah*, 239, 292.

Separation of the People, Separation of the Land

Ezra 7:21–24 begins a second decree, or at least a second section of the decree. Artaxerxes begins by identifying himself as Artaxerxes the king and repeating that he is issuing a decree (just like Ezra 7:12–13). Artaxerxes is still the antecedent of the first-person pronouns but now the treasurers beyond the River are the antecedent to the second-person pronouns. The main concern of this passage is still the functioning of the temple and concern for divine favor for the Persian king. However, Artaxerxes is no longer commanding Ezra to return and resume cultic functions; he is now commanding the treasurers to assist in cultic function and provide supplies to Ezra.

The second-person pronouns change to Ezra in verses 25–26. This third section of the decree provides Ezra additional powers to teach the law and judge people. Though the temple and cultic functions are not mentioned in these verses, they relate to the command in verse 14: "Inquire according to the law of your God which is in your hand." So, the decree of Artaxerxes begins with the law (even verse 12 calls Ezra "the scribe of the law of the God of heaven") and ends with Ezra's ability to enforce the law.[27]

Blessing to God for Decree (7:27–28a)

The response of Ezra to the decree is the beginning of his first-person account. Ezra's benediction is entirely dependent upon the decree of Artaxerxes so even though this is the first time that first-person pronouns have been used (outside of royal decrees), it must be considered part of this narrative section.

The blessing is divided into two actions. First, Yahweh put it in the king's heart to adorn the temple. Second, Yahweh provided favor for Ezra before the king and his officials.[28] So, the first part of the blessing draws directly from the decree. Ezra is thankful for the decree to return to Jerusalem and restart the cult. The second part of the blessing points forward to Ezra's gathering of leaders because he obtained favor with the king. Hays notes that the phrasing in this section mirrors Ezra 7:6 where Ezra was described as having favor before God and the king.[29] However, here Ezra's approval extends beyond the king to include his fellow Israelites as well.

---

27. For a similar three-part division of the decree, see Hamilton, *Exalting Jesus in Ezra and Nehemiah*, 61–67; Steinmann, *Ezra and Nehemiah*, 297–98.

28. Becking, *Ezra-Nehemiah*, 117.

29. Hays, "Silence of the Wives," 65.

The Literary Structure of the Return Migrations

Leaders Rise up to Go (7:28b)

Though many commentators treat Ezra 7:27–28 as a single movement in the text, the subject change indicates that they are separate activities.[30] In Ezra 7:27–28a, Yahweh is the subject as the one who put desires in the king's heart and who gave Ezra favor before the royals. However, in Ezra 7:28b, Ezra is the subject who is encouraged and gathers the leaders. This builds upon the latter part of the blessing because it is from the king's favor that Ezra is encouraged and able to gather leaders.

List of Returnees (8:1–14)

The introductory line of the list reflects the ending of Ezra 7:28b. In Ezra 7:28, it is "from the heads of Israel to go up with me," and Ezra 8:1 begins with, "And these are the heads of the fathers and the genealogies of those who went up with me." This makes the name list an expansion of the summary statement in Ezra 7:28b. So, Ezra gathers heads of Israel to go up with him, and now these heads are listed in detail.

The genealogical list does not have any major structural divisions after verse 2. It can be divided by the two priests (8:2), a son of David (8:2), and laity divided into twelve families (8:3–14).[31] However, these are all introduced by "of the sons of" and so the narrative structure does not differentiate between the three groups.[32]

Gathering of Specialized Temple Personnel (8:15–20)

Ezra 8:15 resumes the first-person narrative, with Ezra again gathering the people. This is the first point in this chapter where the location of the events is given. Previously, the movements were described (going from Babylon to Jerusalem) but not where the specific events took place. Now the gathering

---

30. Steinmann considers them one movement. Steinmann, *Ezra and Nehemiah*, 281–82; Redditt, *Ezra-Nehemiah*, 173.

31. Redditt understands verses 13–14 to reference two houses that "came later," that is not with Ezra. However, אחרון could mean "last" or "after" indicating that these are the final names in the list (which is how most translations understand it). Redditt, *Ezra-Nehemiah*, 180.

32. The laity are divided into twelve families which shows their significance as the true Israel. Steinmann, *Ezra and Nehemiah*, 281, 304–5; Becking, *Ezra-Nehemiah*, 120; Hamilton, *Exalting Jesus in Ezra and Nehemiah*, 73.

is happening at the river which runs to Ahava, where they camped for three days (v. 15).

The significant number twelve is present in the eleven leaders (nine leading men and two teachers) plus Ezra.[33] Ezra is the subject of verses 15–17, with him gathering, sending, and explaining the mission that the leaders are to accomplish. The subject changes, though, in verse 18. In this verse, the leaders are the subject, bringing the Levites back, and this introduces another short list of names (8:18–20).

Pakkala claims that verses 15b–20 are a late addition because three days is not enough time to accomplish these tasks and the duplication of "the river Ahava" in verse 21.[34] Goswell understands the three days as the time that Ezra inspects the camp to discover the missing Levites but not the time that it took to bring the Levites to the camp.[35] However, nothing in the text forces all or part of the activities to take place within the three-day encampment. Instead of viewing all the activities as taking place within three days, it is equally possible that they took place after three days. In this way, Ezra observed the lack of Levites after they had assembled for three days at the river. Though I am not directly addressing redactional issues in Ezra-Nehemiah, the coherence of the narrative and the logical progression of time within this unit is important to maintain the coherence of the narrative.

Fasting for the Journey (8:21–23)

After the Levitical genealogy, Ezra is again the subject of the main verbs. He proclaims a fast and claims he was ashamed to ask for help. The location of the narrative at the river of Ahava is restated, and the speech of Ezra and the leaders to the king is presented as reported speech.

The change from singular to plural in Ezra 8:22 is continued in verse 23. So, Ezra proclaims a fast and explains how he was ashamed (vv. 21–22a). However, the community spoke about God's protection, and they also fast and pray together (vv. 22b–23). The resumption of first-person pronouns in 8:21 begins a new narrative section after the short name list. Internal cohesion within the section is created by the mirroring of the actions, Ezra

33. Steinmann, *Ezra and Nehemiah*, 281.
34. Pakkala, "Disunity of Ezra-Nehemiah," 211.
35. Goswell, *Study Commentary on Ezra-Nehemiah*, 156. Becking rejects multiple sources here but without much discussion. Becking, *Ezra-Nehemiah*, 123.

proclaiming a fast, and the people responding by fasting, as well as Ezra being ashamed to ask for help and the people proclaiming God's favor to the king. Each action of Ezra has a corresponding action or response by the people (with Ezra).

The section closes with God listening to their prayers which validates the direct speech and the actions taken by Ezra and the people (fasting and praying). The resolution "and he listened to our entreaty" provides closure by changing to the third-person singular (from first-person subjects) and resolving the concern of the first verse in the section (8:21).

Weighing Gold and Silver Offerings for the Temple (8:24–30)

This section begins with the first-person singular "I set apart" (8:24). The switch to singular from plural, as well as a new type of action (not fasting and praying), indicates that this is a new section within the narrative.

This section is entirely focused upon the actions of Ezra. He selects the priests and Levites, he measures out the items for them to carry, and he speaks in recorded speech. The only action that the leaders perform in this section is accepting the items from Ezra (8:30). The section ends with the acceptance of the gifts by the leaders that Ezra presented in 8:25.

Move to Jerusalem and Remaining Three Days (8:31–32)

The group of returnees departs from the river Ahava. The change in location and date formula (twelfth of the first month) indicates that this is a new segment of the narrative. The pronouns change from first-person singular and third-person plural in the last section to first-person plural. Now Ezra is not acting upon the leaders in his group, but they are all travelling together (Ezra and the group) in three movements: departing from Ahava, arriving in Jerusalem, and remaining in Jerusalem.

Weighing Offerings for the Temple (8:33–34)

The emphasis shifts in Ezra 8:33 to the articles for the temple. This is signaled by the *niphal* form of שׁקל without an active subject ("the silver, gold, and articles were weighed").

Steinmann believes that Ezra presented and counted the offerings to the officials, but nothing explicitly mentions this.[36] In fact, the change from first-person active verbs to a passive third-person verb removes Ezra from the scene. Ezra may have been the one presenting the items, but the text appears to intentionally omit him or any other character as the active giver. This is followed by a list of people who received the gifts, specifically the priests and the Levites. Verse 34 reiterates the point of verse 33, only adding that the weight was recorded when they were weighed and presented.

Returnees Sacrifice, Deliver Edicts, and Support the Temple (8:35–36)

The focus returns to the exiles in this section. This serves as a conclusion to the narrative as the exiles fulfill the remaining points of the decree in quick succession. Goswell notes that Ezra is not named in 8:36, and the terminology of aiding the people and the temple is drawn from the Cyrus decree as well as Artaxerxes's decree.[37] The exiles offer burnt offerings, as commanded by Artaxerxes in Ezra 7:17, and deliver letters to the governors to obtain support for the temple, as commanded by Artaxerxes in Ezra 7:21–23.[38] The clause states that the governors supported the people and temple, which ends the narrative with the exiles living in Jerusalem with assistance from the local governors.[39]

---

36. Steinmann, *Ezra and Nehemiah*, 280.

37. Goswell, *Study Commentary on Ezra-Nehemiah*, 162.

38. Contra Steinmann who claims that Ezra was the one sacrificing and presenting letters. Steinmann, *Ezra and Nehemiah*, 280. The verbs are all third-person plural and refer to the plural subject "sons of the captivity" in verse 35.

39. Many scholars believe these two verses switch from first-person narrative to third-person. However, this is not conclusive since Ezra is not mentioned in these verses (by pronoun or name). See Steinmann, 317; Blenkinsopp, *Ezra-Nehemiah*, 171–73; Breneman, *Ezra, Nehemiah, Esther*, 146; Fensham, *Books of Ezra and Nehemiah*, 121–22; Williamson, *Ezra, Nehemiah*, 116, 122; Allen and Laniak, *Ezra, Nehemiah, Esther*, 67; Redditt, *Ezra-Nehemiah*, 186.

The Literary Structure of the Return Migrations
SHESHBAZZAR AND EZRA
Table 1. Sheshbazzar and Ezra

Sheshbazzar	Ezra
1. Cyrus issues a decree (1:1–4)	3. The decree of Artaxerxes (7:11–26)
A. God stirs and Cyrus writes (1:1)	
B. Transcription of the decree (1:2–4)	A. Transcription of the decree (7:12–26)
i. Any of the people may leave (1:3)	i. Any of the people may leave (7:13)
ii. People support the returnees (1:4)	
2. Leaders rise up to go (1:5)	
3. Offerings (1:6–11)	ii. Offerings (7:15–24)
A. From the people (1:6)	a. From Artaxerxes (7:15)
B. From Cyrus (1:7–10)	b. From the people (7:16)
C. Given to Sheshbazzar and taken to Jerusalem (1:11)	c. Given to Ezra for the temple (7:17–20)
	d. From other treasurers (7:21–23)
	iii. No taxes on religious personnel (7:24)
	iv. Authority given to Ezra (7:25–26)
	4. Blessing to God for decree (7:27–28a)
	5. Leaders rise up to go (7:28b)
4. List of returnees (2:1–67)	6. List of returnees (8:1–14)
A. Name list (2:1–61)	
i. Leaders (2:1–2a)	
ii. People (2:2b–35)	
iii. Priests (2:36–39)	
iv. Levites (2:40–58)	
v. Unclear ancestry people (2:59–60)	
vi. Unclear ancestry priests (2:61)	7. Gathering of specialized temple personnel (8:15–20)
B. Exclusion (2:62–63)	

73

C. Total numbers (2:64–67)	
	8. Fasting for the journey (8:21–23)
5. Amount of gold, silver, clothing given for the temple (2:68–69)	9. Weighing gold and silver offerings for the temple (8:24–30)
	10. Move to Jerusalem and remaining there three days (8:31–32)
	11. Weighing of offerings for the temple (8:33–34)
6. Israel lives in the cities (2:70)	12. Returnees sacrifice, deliver edicts, and support the temple (8:35–36)

The literary structure of the return narratives for Sheshbazzar and Ezra have many similarities, as shown in table 1. Starting with the decree, both narratives state the name of the king and then transcribe the words of the decree in first person. The transcription in Ezra 7 switches to Aramaic while Ezra 1 is in Hebrew, but the contents of the decrees are quite similar. Both narratives grant the people permission to leave before describing gifts that are donated by the Persian king as well as the general population. In both cases the gifts are for the temple, though one is for building the temple while the other is supporting the cultic practices.

After the initial decree to return, both narratives contain a list of personnel who are returning with a special emphasis on cultic officials and ancestry.[40] Though the list in Ezra 8 is solely by father's household and Ezra 2 has some toponym entries, the importance of ancestry especially for the cultic officials is shown in the exclusion of priests with unknown ancestry (2:61–63) and the search for Levites (8:15–20). Once the returnees arrive in Jerusalem, gold and silver donations to the temple are counted and a summary of Israel living and worshiping in the land concludes both narratives.

Though the details and prominent characters are different, the return narratives have a similar pattern. Each of them has a transcribed royal decree, donations for the temple from the king and surrounding people, a list of returnees with an emphasis on the cultic personnel, a list of donations for the temple once they arrive in Jerusalem, and finally a statement of settlement within the land. Bedford has a similar list of parallels between Sheshbazzar's return and Ezra's return. However, he does not mention that the parallel narrative elements are, for the most part, in the same order in both narratives.[41] Though only two migrations might not be enough examples to

40. Burns, *Ezra, Nehemiah*, 40.
41. Bedford, "Diaspora," 154.

argue for a Robert Alter style "type scene," they clearly show an underlying pattern.[42] The major movements in the narrative overlap surprisingly often and in many places are in the same order.[43]

NEHEMIAH

1. Introductory formula (1:1)

2. Judeans return to Susa (1:2–3)

    A. Nehemiah questions Judean returnees (1:2)

    B. Bad news in reported speech (1:3)

3. Nehemiah mourns (1:4–11)

    A. Fasted and prayed (1:4)

    B. Penitential prayer in reported speech (1:5–11a)

    C. Nehemiah's position (1:11c)

4. Nehemiah before the king in reported speech (2:1–8)

    A. Nehemiah describes the state of Jerusalem (2:1–3)

    B. Nehemiah requests to rebuild (2:4–5)

    C. Artaxerxes grants the request (2:6–8)

5. Move to the provinces beyond the River (2:9–10)

    A. Letters sent to officials (2:9)

    B. Displeased outsiders (2:10)

6. Arrival and assessment (2:11–16)

    A. Arrival and stay (2:11)

    B. Small group of leaders convened by Nehemiah (2:12)

    C. Nehemiah's survey (2:13–15)

    D. Officials excluded (2:16)

7. Plan of action (2:17–20)

    A. Assessment and plan in reported speech (2:17)

---

42. Alter, *Art of Biblical Narrative*, 60.

43. Hamilton lists these return migrations as parallel structures as well. Hamilton, *Exalting Jesus in Ezra and Nehemiah*, 72.

B. Reported response of agreement (2:18)

   C. Strife and response in reported speech (2:19–20)

8. List of people resolving the problem (3:1–32)

Introductory Formula (1:1)

The introductory formula is a unique mixture of third-person and first-person narrative. Nehemiah, or an editor, introduces the book as the words of Nehemiah, but then the next sentence dates the activities from the point of view of Nehemiah (in the first-person). So, clearly the first line is intended to stand outside of the actual narrative, which is dictated through Nehemiah's experience.

The date formula is also interesting because it does not contain the royal reference until the next chapter. This makes the date meaningless at this point in the text because "the month Kislev, in the twentieth year" does not state to what event the twentieth year refers. The debates about whether it was the twentieth year of Nehemiah's royal service, a textual corruption (omission), or an indication of the reliance upon Ezra thereby indicating that these should be a unified text are outside of the scope of this literary structure analysis.[44]

As the text stands, the date formula is missing the referent for the year. In Neh 2:1, Nehemiah goes before Artaxerxes in the twentieth year of his reign in the month Nisan. Since the Persian regnal year typically began in Nisan, it is unlikely that Neh 1:1 refers to the twentieth year of Artaxerxes's reign.[45] Since the dates would not line up properly and the text omits the reference to the king, it is likely that this is the twentieth year of some other important event. The event itself might never be known for certain, but it is important to note that the initial date formula does not highlight the Persian king but Nehemiah's words and his residing in Susa.

---

   44. Campbell claims that the partial date formula indicates these books should be read as a unity. Campbell, "Structure, Themes, and Theology in Ezra-Nehemiah," 402.

   45. Steinmann, *Ezra and Nehemiah*, 386.

The Literary Structure of the Return Migrations

Judeans Return to Susa (1:2–3)

This section begins with Hanani and others meeting Nehemiah in Susa. The primary actors are the Judeans, but it is all related to Nehemiah. So, Hanani is described as the brother of Nehemiah while the rest are unnamed others, their direct speech is in response to Nehemiah's inquiry about the state of Jerusalem, and even the introduction to the speech keeps Nehemiah in view as "they said to me," rather than simply "they said."

Nehemiah Mourns (1:4–11)

The subject of the verbs shifts in this section. Though Nehemiah asked about the state of the people and city of Jerusalem, the primary actors were the Judeans returning to Susa in the previous section. They returned and also provided the recorded speech. However, this section has a short introduction followed by a recorded prayer. The Judeans are not mentioned in this section, and, in fact, their speech is only referred to as "these words," but the speakers are not identified (Neh 1:4).

The reported prayer has a concentric structure:

A. God is great and full of lovingkindness (1:5)

  B. Petition for God to hear his servant (1:6)

    C. Confession of sins against God (1:7)

      D. Petition to remember the promise to Moses (1:8–9)

    C'. Return from sins and redemption (1:10)

  B'. Petition for God to be attentive to his servant (1:11a)

A'. Petition for success and compassion from God (1:11b)[46]

---

46. This structure is the thematic movement of the prayer, rather than lexical or phrase repetition. Goswell has a similar breakdown but there are some differences in the sections. Goswell, *Study Commentary on Ezra-Nehemiah*, 204. Becking and Williamson divide the prayer into almost identical thematic sections but do not discuss whether the structure is concentric. Becking, *Ezra-Nehemiah*, 173; Williamson, *Ezra, Nehemiah*, 167. Though I think Goswell's interpretation as concentric rather than linear makes the repeated themes clearer, the primary point of this partitioning of the text is to show the seven points that Nehemiah is making in this prayer. Steinmann only has a three-part structure to the prayer: a plea and confession (vv. 5–7), a plea for God to remember his promises to restore Israel and the land (vv. 8–10), and another plea for God to hear and grant favor before the king (v. 11a). Steinmann, *Ezra and Nehemiah*, 390. However, this misses the parallel lines, especially between verses 6 and 11a.

Baltzer argues that the penitential prayer draws upon language from Deut 7, 9, 30, and 1 Kgs 8. His comparisons lead to his conclusion that Nehemiah uses "servant of God" on three levels (Moses, Nehemiah, and the Israelites) with the intention of placing the authority of Moses upon Nehemiah to enforce the Law of Moses.[47] Therefore, the primary focus of the prayer is the Law of Moses and specifically the need for the people to adhere to it. This is shown not only by the use of "servant of God" but also by the center of the chiastic structure and the thematic development throughout the prayer. Nehemiah starts with a confession of the people's disobedience to the law, then states the promises and curses for following or disobeying the law, and finally states that the people have been redeemed by God and delight in his name. This last section suggests that the people are now following the law because they have been redeemed and delight in God. In this way the prayer centers upon the Law of Moses and the relationship of the Israelite people to it.

The final statement in this section links the prayer to the dialogue in the next section. The prayer ends with the cryptic statement "grant him mercy before this man."[48] In the next clause Nehemiah identifies himself as the cupbearer to the king, which explains which man from whom he requests mercy. This statement also introduces the next scene where Nehemiah is before the king. So, it defines the unnamed man in the prayer (the king) and explains why Nehemiah is serving the king in the next chapter.

---

47. Baltzer, "Moses Servant of God and the Servants," 121–30. See also Polaski, "Nehemiah," 40–41; Smith, "Influence of Deuteronomy on Intercessory Prayers in Ezra and Nehemiah," 345–65; Goswell, *Study Commentary on Ezra-Nehemiah*, 205–7; Becking, *Ezra-Nehemiah*, 174.

48. Blenkinsopp argues that this prayer "has probably been spliced into the memoir by an editor" because it mentions prayer day and night but does not mention the bad news the Nehemiah received nor his upcoming request to the king. Blenkinsopp, "Nehemiah Autobiographical Memoir," 135. See also Talstra, "Discourse of Praying: Reading Nehemiah 1," 219–36; Wright, *Rebuilding Identity*, 9–10. Clines claims that Nehemiah likely used traditional religious language when praying. Clines, *Ezra, Nehemiah, Esther*, 138. For a discussion of the connections between the prayer and the actions of Nehemiah see Klingbeil and Klingbeil, "'Eyes to Hear,'" 91–102; Becking, *Ezra-Nehemiah*, 173.

However, the origin of the prayer is an argument from silence and formulaic prayer does not necessarily indicate that it is not original to the memoir. The theological function is clear. It is most likely not a detailed transcription of Nehemiah's daily prayer but that does not indicate late editing, in the same way that the interaction between Nehemiah and Artaxerxes is not a word for word transcription of their conversation but it is integral to the memoir. See Allen and Laniak, *Ezra, Nehemiah, Esther*, 88–90.

The Literary Structure of the Return Migrations

Nehemiah before the King in Reported Speech (2:1–8)

Besides the new chapter, the date formula in this text indicates a new movement in the narrative. The date is the month of Nisan in the twentieth year of Artaxerxes and, as argued above, indicates that the date in Neh 1:1 is most likely not meant to be read as referring to the twentieth year of Artaxerxes's reign. The beginning of this segment with ויהי also indicates that the narrative has jumped forward in time.⁴⁹

The first verse provides the background to the dialogue. Not only does it provide the date, but also the location, presenting wine before the king, and the circumstance, Nehemiah's sad expression. The king's first speech addresses this circumstance.

The dialogue begins with the question of the king, and this sets the dialogue pattern that repeats three times, with some significant changes in the third interaction. The pattern is: first, the king asks a question in recorded speech, then Nehemiah narrates his reaction, and finally he responds in a recorded speech.⁵⁰ In the first interaction, the king asks why Nehemiah is sad but not ill. Nehemiah narrates that he is afraid and then responds with a recorded speech about the ruined state of Jerusalem (2:2–3). In the second interaction, the king asks what Nehemiah would request. Nehemiah narrates that he prayed to God and then responds in a recorded speech that he would like to return to rebuild the city (2:4–5). The king asks how long Nehemiah will be gone in the final dialogue. Nehemiah narrates that he gave the king a definite time and then requests letters for passage and building materials in reported speech (2:6–8).

The third interaction is unique because the narrated section answers the king's question, but the direct speech of Nehemiah addresses a secondary issue (the need for letters from the king). In the other two interactions, the narrated section gives Nehemiah's response to the king's speech, but it is Nehemiah's speech that answers the king's question. This last section is also unique because it concludes with a narrated response by Artaxerxes. After Nehemiah's request for letters, the king does not have another recorded speech. Nehemiah only narrates that the king granted his request (2:8).

---

49. Harmelink, "Exploring the Syntactic, Semantic, and Pragmatic Uses of וַיְהִי in Biblical Hebrew," 445.

50. Goswell claims this question-and-answer pattern is similar to King Ahasuerus and Esther (Esth 5:3–8; 7:1–6) and so could be a type scene of a courtier making a request to his royal master. Goswell, *Study Commentary on Ezra-Nehemiah*, 211.

This third interaction breaks the pattern of the first two dialogue cycles and completes the dialogue section. Nehemiah records that he received his requests because of God's hand upon him, which could refer to the entire interaction since he received permission to go as well as the letters he requested. The insertion of this narrative sentence also indicates that the dialogue section is complete because it is placed where a recorded speech from the king would be expected based upon the previous two interactions.

Move to the Provinces beyond the River (2:9–10)

This section is separated from the previous one in three ways. First, there is no recorded speech, while the last section was primarily recorded speech. Second, the geographic location has changed to the provinces beyond the River. Third, the king is no longer a prominent character and the only mention of him is as the one who sent the officers with Nehemiah (2:9).

Two major movements in the narrative occur within this section. First, Nehemiah narrates his arrival in the provinces beyond the River. He indicates that he arrived, gave letters to the governors, and was sent by the king with officers and horsemen. Though the subject of the verb changes in the final clause from first-person (Nehemiah) to third-person (king), the focus is still upon the journey to the provinces and specifically the company that was travelling. This complements the first two clauses which define the place that they arrived and the items that they delivered.

The second movement is the reaction of two named individuals: Sanballat the Horonite and Tobiah the Ammonite (2:10). This is the first introduction of these characters, and they are the subjects of the main clauses while Nehemiah is referred to only as "a man" (אדם). The change from Nehemiah being referred to in the first-person to Nehemiah as a man indicates that this is a separate event in the text even though it is predicated on Nehemiah's arrival and distribution of letters in 2:9.

Becking believes that Neh 2:1–9 is a literary unit and verses 10–18 are a second unit. He points to the *petucha* after verse 9 as an indication that the break should be there.[51] However, Hamilton divides the text between Neh 2:1–8 and 2:9–20 based upon geographic movement.[52] Many other scholars claim that Neh 2:1–10 is a literary unit and 2:11–20 is a second

---

51. Becking, *Ezra-Nehemiah*, 178.

52. Hamilton, *Exalting Jesus in Ezra and Nehemiah*, 105; Thomas, *Ezra & Nehemiah*, 214, 226; McConville, *Ezra, Nehemiah, and Esther*, 77–81.

literary unit.⁵³ However, I view the pericope as verses 9–10 because of the geographical movement of Nehemiah. In verse 9, Nehemiah goes to the governors, and in verse 11, Nehemiah arrives in Jerusalem. From a literary point of view, the change in geographic location indicates a different point in the narrative and so a different literary segment.⁵⁴

Arrival and Assessment (2:11–16)

The next movement in the text resumes the first-person narrative after the actions of Sanballat and Tobiah in verse 10. Nehemiah describes the conclusion of his travel to Jerusalem and his subsequent stay for three days. He then arises at night and assembles a small group of leaders in secret (2:12). The next section is an itinerary of his inspections (2:13–15). Verses 13 and 15 reiterate the fact that the events are happening at night, most likely to emphasize the secrecy of Nehemiah's activities. After Nehemiah's itinerary, the exclusion of the officials is reiterated, though the description of the excluded people as "those who did the work" foreshadows the conversation of the next section.

This section is tied together by the repetition of לילה ("night") and the emphasis on Nehemiah's secrecy at the beginning and end. Though the section begins with Nehemiah's recruitment of a few men, all the primary verbs in the itinerary are first-person and singular, which emphasizes Nehemiah's actions.

Plan of Action (2:17–20)

Nehemiah 2:17 begins new section because it changes from narrative to reported speech, and it changes thematically from Nehemiah's secret activities to his recruitment of the officials for his cause. In the previous section, only Nehemiah was the subject of the verbs (in the first person), but here the officials speak and work. Also, the adversaries mock Nehemiah and have a recorded speech. In addition, the speech by Nehemiah does not reference his investigation but appeals to their knowledge of the ruined state of the city.

---

53. Williamson, *Ezra, Nehemiah*, 177–85; Fensham, *Books of Ezra and Nehemiah*, 158–64; Blenkinsopp, *Ezra-Nehemiah*, 210–19; Becker, *Esra/Nehemia*, 63–66; Schunck, *Nehemia*; Allen and Laniak, *Ezra, Nehemiah, Esther*, 96.

54. Redditt, *Ezra-Nehemiah*, 237–38.

The antecedent of the plural pronoun (להם) in the introduction to Nehemiah's first speech is the same groups that were excluded from Nehemiah's exploration in the previous verse. The speech itself does not appeal to Nehemiah's inspection, and even the description of the city gates follows the phrasing of the Judeans in Neh 1:3 more closely than Nehemiah's assessment in 2:13 (וּשְׁעָרֶיהָ נִצְּתוּ בָאֵשׁ in 1:3 and 2:17 versus וּשְׁעָרֶיהָ אֻכְּלוּ בָאֵשׁ in 2:13).[55]

Verse 18 continues the speech but in summary form. Nehemiah's recorded speech followed by a summary of his speech highlights the recorded section. Nehemiah is highlighting the state of the walls and the need for rebuilding while passing over the details of his interaction with Artaxerxes and journey to Jerusalem. This summary of Nehemiah's speech is immediately followed by the response of the people in recorded speech. The recorded speech is "let us rise and build," which echoes the call for the people to build in the recorded speech in verse 17. This again highlights the city of Jerusalem and glosses over Nehemiah's recounting of his journey to the city and interactions with the king. Even the summary statement at the end of this verse states that the people began to do the good work but does not indicate their response to the rest of Nehemiah's speech.

The final two verses of this section are quite different from the preceding verses. This segment is a conversation between Nehemiah and his adversaries. The change in verses 19–20 is indicated by the change in subject of the main verb in verse 19. In the previous verses Nehemiah and unnamed Judean leaders are the primary speakers, but in verse 19, Sanballat, Tobiah, and Geshem hear, mock, despise, and finally speak to the Judeans. The verb שמע in verse 19 lacks an object. So, the actions of the adversaries are dependent upon the actions of Nehemiah and the Judeans. Though verse 18 has a summary statement ("they strengthened their hands to the good work"), verse 19 must be part of the same pericope. The text does not define what the adversaries heard, so it must be inferred from the actions immediately preceding, in verse 18.

The speech by the adversaries addresses both the building work by the Judeans (though only opaquely: "what is this thing which you are doing?") and the consent of the king. However, Nehemiah's response does not address the consent of the king.[56] Instead, his speech uses the same phrase

---

55. Esler, "Ezra-Nehemiah as a Narrative of (Re-Invented) Israelite Identity," 423.

56. Van Wijk-Bos, *Ezra, Nehemiah, and Esther*, 57; Becking, *Ezra-Nehemiah*, 191; Steinmann, *Ezra and Nehemiah*, 411.

as the Judeans in verse 18, "we will arise and build."[57] This continued emphasis on building in the recorded speech of Nehemiah and the repetition of the exact phrase from the Judeans' recorded speech, ties verse 20 to the preceding verses. For this reason, though the prominent characters that Nehemiah is interacting with have changed, verses 19–20 must be read as part of the same section as verses 17–18.

List of People Resolving the Problem (3:1–32)

This section begins with verbs echoing the statements by Nehemiah and the Judeans. Eliashib and his brothers rise up and build just like Nehemiah proposed and the people promised (2:18, 20). However, instead of a *yiqtol* followed by a *weqatal*, both verbs are in the *wayyiqtol* form in Neh 3:1. So in the previous chapter, the people and Nehemiah were going to rise and build in the future, but in Neh 3:1 both actions are in the past.[58]

The repetition of the actions from the recorded speeches of the last chapter indicates that this is the fulfillment of their plans. The itinerary starts in the north then moves to the west side of the wall and completes the circuit around the south and east sides.[59] The people are described in various ways throughout the list. There are priests, Levites, Nethinim, people from nearby towns, people identified by their ancestry, and people identified by their occupation. The location of people groups does not seem to be divided by these attributions. In other words, the priests and all the cultic personnel do not repair a section to themselves while all the goldsmiths repair another section and all the people from other towns repair a third section. Instead, the people of Mizpah repair a section next to Uzziel the goldsmith, who is next to Hananiah the perfumer, who is then followed by a city official, Rephaiah (3:7–9). This mixture of people also applies to cultic

---

57. For the cohortative use of the yiqtol נָקוּם in verse 18 versus the future meaning of the same verb and conjugation in verse 20 see Steinmann, *Ezra and Nehemiah*, 406; Joüon and Muraoka, *Grammar of Biblical Hebrew: Part Three: Syntax*, 2:374, §114b; Van der Merwe, Naudé, and Kroeze, *Biblical Hebrew Reference Grammar*, §19.3, 148.

58. Van der Merwe et al., *Biblical Hebrew Reference Grammar*, §21.2, 165–66.

59. For a detailed discussion of the locations of the gates and area enclosed by the wall see Avi-Yonah, "Walls of Nehemiah," 239–48; Williamson, "Nehemiah's Walls Revisited," 81–88; Burns, *Ezra, Nehemiah*, 58; Ussishkin, "On Nehemiah's City Wall and the Size of Jerusalem during the Persian Period: An Archaeologist's View," 101–30; Finkelstein, "Jerusalem in the Persian (and Early Hellenistic) Period and the Wall of Nehemiah," 501–20.

personnel as the Nethinim repair a section of the wall next to the people from Tekoa followed by sections repaired by priests (3:26–28). The Levites repair a section of the wall on the southeast, quite far from the repairs by the Jerusalem priests on northern and eastern sides (3:17). In addition, the section of the wall near the houses of the Nethinim was not repaired by the Nethinim but by the goldsmiths (3:31–32).

Some of the people identified as priests elsewhere are only identified by their genealogy (3:29). Zadok son of Immer and Shemaiah son of Shecaniah are most likely priests. Immer was a priest who returned with Sheshbazzar (Ezra 2:37, 10:20; Neh 7:40, 11:13). Shecaniah was also mentioned as a priest who returned with Zerubbabel in Neh 12:6. However, in Neh 3:29 these individuals are mentioned as making repairs after the priests. This could identify them as one of the priests making repairs, but it could also indicate that they are simply beside the priests because this same formula ("after them/him") is used for Hananiah, Hanun, Meshullam, and Malchijah (3:30–31), but none of these individuals are described as priests in Ezra-Nehemiah, and Malchijah is identified as a goldsmith, not a priest.[60] So, the separation between cultic and non-cultic personnel in the building summary is blurred, and the purpose for identifying some individuals by occupation, others by location, and others by genealogy is unclear.

This section concludes with repairs at the sheep gate, which is where the chapter began (3:32). This conclusion of the circuit around the city and the beginning of the next verse with a focus on Sanballat with his brothers in Samaria indicates that the name list concludes this section.

NEHEMIAH WITH SHESHBAZZAR AND EZRA

Table 2. Sheshbazzar/Ezra and Nehemiah

Sheshbazzar/Ezra	Nehemiah
1. Persian king issues decree	1. Introductory formula (1:1)
A. Transcription of the decree	2. Judeans return to Susa (1:2–3)
2. Offerings	A. Nehemiah questions Judean returnees (1:2)
A. From the king	B. Bad news reported speech (1:3)
B. From others	3. Nehemiah mourns (1:4–11)

60. See further discussion in Steinmann, *Ezra and Nehemiah*, 433.

The Literary Structure of the Return Migrations

Sheshbazzar/Ezra	Nehemiah
C. To the Judean leader	A. Fasted and prayed (1:4)
3. Leaders rise up to go	B. Penitential prayer in reported speech (1:5–11a)
4. List of returnees	C. Nehemiah's position (1:11c)
5. Weighing of gold and silver for the temple	4. Nehemiah before the king in reported speech (2:1–8)
6. Concluding statement: settlement	A. Nehemiah describes the state of Jerusalem (2:1–3)
	B. Nehemiah requests to rebuild (2:4–5)
	C. Artaxerxes grants the request (2:6–8)
	5. Move to the provinces beyond the River (2:9–10)
	A. Letters sent to officials (2:9)
	B. Displeased outsiders (2:10)
	6. Arrival and assessment (2:11–16)
	A. Arrival and stay (2:11)
	B. Small group of leaders convened by Nehemiah (2:12)
	C. Nehemiah's survey (2:13–15)
	D. Officials excluded (2:16)
	7. Plan of action (2:17–20)
	A. Assessment and plan in reported speech (2:17)
	B. Reported response of agreement (2:18)
	C. Strife and response in reported speech (2:19–20)
	8. List of people resolving the problem (3:1–32)

The left column of table 2 shows the major elements shared in the first two migrations. These literary movements are not only shared between Sheshbazzar's and Ezra's returns, but they are also in the same order. Nehemiah's return is remarkably different. The lack of overlap makes comparison difficult. None of the major literary features are shared.

The prayer of Nehemiah at the beginning of the narrative does not have a parallel in the Ezra or Sheshbazzar narratives. Ezra proclaims a fast by the river, but this does not begin the narrative, nor does the text contain a transcribed prayer (Ezra 8:21–23).

Artaxerxes has a dialogue with Nehemiah but does not make any official pronouncement or provisions for the return. Bedford tries to draw a parallel between Ezra's return and Nehemiah's return by noting, "Like Ezra, Nehemiah is recognized by the Persian king Artaxerxes as not only having a legitimate interest in Judean affairs, but also as being a legitimate leader from the diaspora for the community in Judah."[61] However, this masks the difference between Artaxerxes's decree given to Ezra and his permission given to Nehemiah. Though they are both recognized as legitimate leaders, one is commanded to return through a recorded decree while the other is given permission within a recorded dialogue. Nehemiah requests letters from the king for building materials and safe travel but these are not transcribed in the text (Neh 2:7–8). The interchange between Nehemiah and Artaxerxes is a recorded conversation rather than a transcribed decree like the other two migrations.

The recorded dialogue with Nehemiah and Artaxerxes does not mention offerings for the temple or the city of Jerusalem. Both Sheshbazzar and Ezra were given precious gifts from the king for the rebuilding of the temple and reinstitution of the cult, and these provisions were mentioned in the recorded decrees. However, Nehemiah received letters for provisions from the governors but only by request, and Artaxerxes does not detail the provisions nor weigh out any gold or silver items.

The leaders that rise to leave with Sheshbazzar and Ezra are not in Nehemiah. He was given officers and horsemen, but these are not described as leaders of the people of Israel (or even Israelites at all) nor do they play a significant role in the conversation with Artaxerxes. This is unlike the specifically Judean leaders and the emphasis on them in the decrees in Ezra 1 and 7.

Nehemiah delivers letters to the governors from the king but does not deliver any materials to the temple or any officials in Jerusalem. Both Ezra and Sheshbazzar conclude with a record of valuable items being delivered to the temple and a record that they were weighed out to the officials there.

Finally, Nehemiah does not contain a list of returnees. The list of names in Ezra 2 and 8 are specifically those who went up to Jerusalem.

---

61. Bedford, "Diaspora," 156.

The Literary Structure of the Return Migrations

However, the list of people in Neh 3 are rebuilders of the wall. As noted above, Nehemiah's return mentions officers and horsemen returning but no leaders and no other individuals. This migration is centered almost solely upon Nehemiah, whereas the migrations of Sheshbazzar and Ezra focus upon the community, cultic personnel, and genealogical records to prove their inclusion in the new community.

This comparison of the return migrations contrasts a few scholars' interpretation of the parallel structures in Ezra-Nehemiah, most recently put forth by George Van Pelt Campbell.[62] Campbell draws parallels between Ezra 1–10 and Neh 1–10.[63] However, this chapter by chapter paralleling ignores major narrative points. Broadly, the return migration in Ezra 1 is matched by a return migration in Neh 2, but this breaks down in the details. Also, the parallel of Ezra 2 and Neh 3 is placed under the heading "List," most likely because they are clearly different types of lists (unlike Ezra 2 and Ezra 8, which are both lists of returnees).

Campbell's alignment of Ezra 7 with Neh 8 is challenging as well. Not only does Campbell invert the order of Nehemiah (Ezra 7 is paired with Neh 8, but Ezra 8 is paired with Neh 7), the title of Ezra 7 and Neh 8 is "Emphasis on the law."[64] However, this heading misses the entire focus of Ezra 7: the return migration. The emphasis on the law in Ezra 7 is subsumed under the instructions to return and reinstate the cult found in the transcribed decree of Artaxerxes which comprises most of the chapter.

A similar structural argument has been presented by Raeyong Kim as a repeated cycle in Ezra 1–6, 7–10, and Neh 1–13, consisting of five elements: decree/permission, list/people, enemy, work, result.[65] The challenge with this view, as much as Campbell's article, is that the details do not align. For example, Kim claims that "like Zerubbabel, Ezra and Nehemiah each return to Jerusalem with many people (Ezra 8:1–14; Neh 2:8–11)," but this is not substantiated by the text.[66] Soldiers and horsemen returned with Nehemiah, but the number of people is not mentioned, and they are not identified as Judeans, unlike the other migrations. This organization also

---

62. Campbell, "Structure, Themes, and Theology in Ezra-Nehemiah." A similar, though more abbreviated form of this argument is presented in Williamson, *Ezra, Nehemiah*, xlix; Grabbe, *Ezra-Nehemiah*, 64–66.

63. Campbell, "Structure, Themes, and Theology in Ezra-Nehemiah," 397.

64. Campbell, "Structure, Themes, and Theology in Ezra-Nehemiah," 397.

65. Kim, "Historiographic Characteristics of Ezra-Nehemiah," 112.

66. Kim, "Historiographic Characteristics of Ezra-Nehemiah," 112.

forces Ezra 7 to be concerned with dissolving marriages. Since Ezra 7–10 is paralleled with Ezra 1–6, the decree of Cyrus to rebuild the temple (Ezra 1) and its accomplishment in Ezra 6 must find its parallel in the decree of Artaxerxes (Ezra 7) and its accomplishment in Ezra 10.[67] However, Ezra 9–10 details the separation from foreign wives, but the decree of Artaxerxes does not mention marriage at all. The details of the narratives undermine the parallel structures posited by Kim. It is closer than Campbell's comparison but still glosses over details like the thematic shift between Ezra 7–8 and 9–10 as well as the difference between Artaxerxes's permission in Neh 2 and the Persian decrees in Ezra 1 and 7.

CONCLUSION

As shown in the previous chapter, the migration accounts of Ezra and Sheshbazzar overlap significantly while Nehemiah contrasts sharply. In addition to the thematic differences shown in chapter two, the narrative structures are remarkably different. The Ezra and Sheshbazzar accounts contain many of the same major movements, and the overlapping literary movements are in the same order. However, Nehemiah does not contain any of these literary movements. Nehemiah's migration does not focus on bringing a community out of exile and reestablishing the cult; instead it focuses upon the rebuilding of the wall by a community that appears to be already established. The major literary movements in Neh 1–3 will be revisited in chapter six in comparison with Ezra 9–10 to show that this is a much closer parallel to Neh 1–3 than the other two return migrations.

---

67. Kim, "Historiographic Characteristics of Ezra-Nehemiah," 112–13.

Chapter 4

Dissolving Marriage

Ezra 9–10, Nehemiah 9–10, and 13:23–29

IN THIS CHAPTER I will apply the same thematic analyses from chapter two to passages about intermarriage in Ezra-Nehemiah: Ezra 9–10, Neh 9–10, and Neh 13:23–29. This will set up the discussion of the literary structure of these passages in the next chapter. In this chapter, I will first explain where each literary unit begins and ends. The goal is to show that these are complete literary units within the broader narrative of Ezra-Nehemiah. Then each passage will be examined for the prominent characters and primary concerns. After examining each passage for these primary themes, I will compare them together within this same framework in the final section of this chapter. I will show that Ezra 9–10 and Neh 13:23–29 have a single prominent character who narrates largely in the first person (Ezra and Nehemiah respectively), but the narrative of Neh 9–10 is distinct because it is principally driven by the Levites, and specifically the Levites named in Neh 9:4–5. In the same way, the primary concern in Neh 9–10 is God's favor through separation and temple contributions by the Israelite community, but Ezra 9–10 and Neh 13:23–29 are concerned with intermarriage, though with different emphases.

EZRA 9–10

The narrative movement of the marriage conflict in Ezra 9–10 can be diagrammed as follows:

Separation of the People, Separation of the Land

1. Leaders approach Ezra, bad news reported speech (9:1–2)
2. Ezra mourns (9:3–15)
   A. Ezra appalled (9:3)
   B. People gather (9:4)
   C. Penitential prayer in reported speech (9:5–15)
3. Ezra and Shecaniah in reported speech (10:1–5)
   A. Crowd gathers before the temple (10:1)
   B. Shecaniah describes the state of the people (10:2)
   C. Shecaniah proposes a covenant (10:3–4)
   D. Ezra rises to initiate the covenant (10:5)
4. Move to the chamber of Jehohanan (10:6–8)
   A. Proclamation to assemble (10:7)
   B. If unheeded, lose possessions and excluded (10:8)
5. Arrival in Jerusalem within three days (10:9)
6. Plan of action (10:10–15)
   A. Assessment and plan in reported speech (10:10–11)
   B. Reported response of agreement (10:12)
   C. Request for delay in reported speech (10:13–15)
7. Investigating the problem (10:16–17)
8. List of people resolving the problem (10:18–24)

The separation of Ezra 9–10 from Ezra 8 is shown by the change in time and the change in voice. The final verses of Ezra 8 are in the third person while Ezra 9:1 begins with "the princes approached me." In addition, a move forward in time is indicated by the phrase, "now when these things were completed" (9:1).[1] Based upon the date given in Ezra 10:9, the intermarriage events of Ezra 9–10 took place about four and a half months after the events of chapter eight, which Steinmann claims is 4 Ab to 17 Kislev.[2]

---

1. Clines, *Ezra, Nehemiah, Esther*, 119; Van Wijk-Bos, *Ezra, Nehemiah, and Esther*, 40.
2. Steinmann, *Ezra and Nehemiah*, 325; Mangan, *1–2 Chronicles, Ezra, Nehemiah*, 172; Myers, *Ezra-Nehemiah*, 76.

Dissolving Marriage

Finally, the actors in Ezra 8:35–36 are the exiles while Ezra 9:1 begins with the princes.[3]

Steinmann divides the text at Ezra 8:33, claiming that this is the second unit of Ezra's ministry.[4] However, this division is unlikely because the thematic emphasis is different. The temple donations delivered in Ezra 8:33–34 are addressed repeatedly throughout Ezra 7–8, but they are not mentioned in Ezra 9–10 at all. Similarly, the main crisis of Ezra 9–10 is intermarriage, but this is not mentioned in Ezra 7–8.[5] So, it is more likely that the narrative break takes place at the chapter division where the focus turns to mixed marriages rather than Ezra 8:33, where the emphasis is on provisions for the temple.[6]

Prominent Character: Ezra

Chapter nine switches to the first person after the third-person narrative in Ezra 8:35–36. The rest of the chapter is written from Ezra's point of view, and the longest reported speech, which is actually a prayer, is put in the mouth of Ezra (9:6). According to Fried, Ezra's prayer and his actions portray him as a second Moses.[7] Even when the passage changes to third person in chapter ten, Ezra is still the primary speaker, and his speech drives the narrative and the actions of the other characters.[8] Hays notes the Moses imagery can even be seen in the response of the people to Ezra's commands in Ezra 10.[9]

Chapter nine begins with a statement of the issue by a group of leaders. However, the introduction to their speech indicates that the focus is upon Ezra, first because they are unnamed (just called "princes") and, second,

---

3. Schoville claims scholars generally agree chapters 9–10 are all part of a single event. Schoville, *Ezra-Nehemiah*, 117; Williamson, *Ezra, Nehemiah*, 127; Daniels, "Composition of the Ezra-Nehemiah Narrative," 321.

4. Steinmann, *Ezra and Nehemiah*, 70.

5. Allen and Laniak, *Ezra, Nehemiah, Esther*, 71.

6. For discussions of the original location of Neh 8 between Ezra 8 and 9 see Allen and Laniak, *Ezra, Nehemiah, Esther*, 71; Schoville, *Ezra-Nehemiah*, 118. However, Goswell rejects this insertion on literary grounds. Goswell, *Study Commentary on Ezra-Nehemiah*, 168–69.

7. Fried, "Who Wrote Ezra-Nehemiah—and Why Did They?," 486–90.

8. See Janzen's argument that Ezra is portrayed as the administrative head of the community in this passage. Janzen, *Witch-Hunts, Purity and Social Boundaries*, 37–53.

9. Hays, "Silence of the Wives," 68.

because the narrative specifically describes them as approaching Ezra ("they approached me"). The focus remains on Ezra rather than the leaders, even in the verses following the speech as the leaders and their speech are not mentioned. In verse 3, Ezra tore his robe "when he heard this matter." This clearly refers to the speech of the leaders but does not mention them directly, nor does it explicitly state that it is their speech. Allen and Laniak even claim that the princes' speech did not bring new information to Ezra but simply the opportunity to enforce his teaching.[10] In the same way, verse 4 states that people gathered to Ezra. These people are only defined as "all who trembled at the words of God on account of the unfaithfulness of the exiles." So, the references to the community no longer identify their social status. The leaders and their speech become "this matter" and then "all who trembled at the words of God on account of the unfaithfulness of the exiles" gather. None of these references identify the social standing of the people, or even that they heard or were reacting to a recorded speech. The gathering of the people is instead tied to the actions of Ezra in the preceding verse (v. 3), and they gather to Ezra, not the princes.

Ezra 9:5 introduces Ezra's prayer. This introduction is first-person singular, with Ezra as the speaker, but the prayer is first-person plural after the introductory line in Ezra 9:6. In the prayer, the concern of intermarriage is stated as a prohibition by the prophets without any naming of the individuals or social groups presently involved, even though verse 2 identified them as the princes and rulers, nor any explicit mention of the reported speech in verse 1 nor the princes who reported it to Ezra. In reference to the prayer, Goswell claims, "By allowing Ezra as a key participant to make the theological evaluations, the narrator makes Ezra a powerful spokesman for the message of the narrative."[11] Hays claims that the prayer "serves to refract the voice of God" and drives the theological message with the support of the prophets and God himself.[12]

Chapter ten switches to the third person but again focuses upon Ezra's actions. The covenant is proposed by Shecaniah (vv. 2–4) but is predicated on the mourning and prayer of Ezra in chapter nine and fulfilled by Ezra in the remaining part of chapter ten. Hays describes him as an agent confirming Ezra's view in chapter nine.[13] So, Shecaniah acts as a linkage between

---

10. Allen and Laniak, *Ezra, Nehemiah, Esther*, 74; Schoville, *Ezra-Nehemiah*, 118.
11. Goswell, *Study Commentary on Ezra-Nehemiah*, 171.
12. Hays, "Silence of the Wives," 66–67.
13. Hays, "Silence of the Wives," 67.

Dissolving Marriage

two acts of Ezra: mourning and assembling the people. He does not begin the action but reacts to the crisis in Ezra 9–10:1. The focus here is still on Ezra as he speaks specifically "to Ezra" and recounts Ezra's assessment of the people's sinfulness (10:2). He also concludes his speech with "arise, for the matter is yours, and we will be with you, be courageous and act" (10:4). This is an open-ended call for Ezra to be the primary actor in the process of establishing the covenant.

The speech by Shecaniah drives Ezra's actions in the next verse, but then Ezra appears to go beyond Shecaniah's call in verse 6. The two primary requests in Shecaniah's speech are mirrored in verse 5, though in reverse order ("Ezra rose" and made the people "take the oath" in verse 5 versus "let us make a covenant" in verse 3 and "arise" in verse 4). The wording of Shecaniah's speech includes "those who tremble at the commandment of our God" (v. 3). However, "all who trembled at the words of the God of Israel" were already gathered to Ezra in 9:4 (repeated vaguely as "a very large assembly" in 10:1) and the oath in verse 5 includes "priests, Levites, and all Israel."[14] So, if the people who Shecaniah is concerned about were already gathered to Ezra and the oath in verse 5 included an even broader group of people ("all Israel"), the call to assemble and the investigation of the matter in the rest of chapter ten go beyond Shecaniah's request. In addition, the oath that the people swear is to "do according to this word," which clearly points to the speech of Shecaniah. Ezra appears to have been unsatisfied with the simple covenant agreement and so investigated and imposed penalties of his own.[15] For this reason, Shecaniah can be seen as moving Ezra from mourning into action, but his speech does not present or command the actions throughout the narrative.[16]

The next series of events again begins with Ezra fasting and mourning (10:6; cf. 9:3, 4b–5; 10:1). This section is the gathering of the people to Ezra. Though the proclamation was made by an unnamed group (10:7), Ezra

---

14. Contra Clines, who translates 10:5 as "leaders . . . of the lay Israelites" but without discussing how וְכָל־יִשְׂרָאֵל can be translated this way (rather than "and all Israel"). Clines, *Ezra, Nehemiah, Esther*, 127.

15. For a discussion of the confiscation of property for those who did not arrive in Jerusalem and the development of the practice of extirpation in the second temple period, see Horbury, "Extirpation and Excommunication," 13–38.

16. Blenkinsopp claims that the covenant swearing should have been settled at 10:5, so the continuing narrative in 10:6–44 is an alternate version that has been added to the original story. Blenkinsopp, *Judaism, the First Phase*, 65–66.

is the first person named and the one who addresses the crowd (10:10).¹⁷ He commands the people to make a confession, in recorded speech, and the unnamed assembly responds in agreement (10:10–11). Ezra's speech reflects his prayer from chapter nine in assessing the people as unfaithful and guilty. However, Ezra commands them to make a confession (תודה) not swear an oath (שׁבע) like verse 5 nor cut a covenant (ברית) like verse 3. Though swearing an oath and cutting a covenant are similar, making a confession is quite different. Mayer notes that the confession is part of sacral law in the Old Testament along with the identification of the parties (10:7–9) and restitution (10:18–44). However, the invitation to doxology is missing in this text, though it is present in a similar text in Josh 7.¹⁸ Leslie C. Allen also calls this a "doxology of judgment, a praising acknowledgment that God is in the right," citing Ezra 10:11 and Josh 7:19.¹⁹ With this interpretation, the confession is an acknowledgment of guilt, which is an activity distinct from the command for making a covenant or swearing an oath. This again confirms that Ezra is pushing the narrative forward through his speech and actions rather than simply fulfilling the speech of Shecaniah.

After the people respond to Ezra and raise concerns about fulfilling his command, it is Ezra who again leads the narrative. The people responded to Ezra with a request to be mediated by their leaders (10:14) and so Ezra selected the leaders himself (10:16).²⁰

To summarize, Ezra 9–10 is focused upon Ezra's actions and leadership.²¹ He has the longest recorded speeches, these speeches are referenced within the speeches of the other characters, and he is named as the lead character who organizes the people of Israel within the narrated sections.

---

17. Davies claims that Ezra's mourning causes other people to act by calling the gathering. He interprets this as Ezra's rhetorical presence shrinking as the number of Israelites in attendance grows. However, this minimizing of Ezra's involvement could only be argued for 10:7–8 and even in this no other individuals are named. Davies, *Ezra and Nehemiah*, 68.

18. Mayer, "ידה Ydh: III. Usage.," 442.

19. Allen, "3344 ידה," 408.

20. Schoville, *Ezra-Nehemiah*, 131; Davies, *Ezra and Nehemiah*, 69; Myers, *Ezra-Nehemiah*, 86; Clines, *Ezra, Nehemiah, Esther*, 130; Larson and Dahlen, *Ezra, Nehemiah, Esther*, 120. Contra Goswell who claims that the exiles chose for themselves. He claims that 1 Esd 9:16 has Ezra selecting leaders, but this is contrary to the Masoretic text. Goswell, *Study Commentary on Ezra-Nehemiah*, 190.

Steinmann notes it is a *niphal* ("be selected") but does not indicate who is doing the selecting. Steinmann, *Ezra and Nehemiah*, 358.

21. Thomas, *Ezra & Nehemiah*, 179–82.

Dissolving Marriage

Primary Concern: Foreign Wives

The primary concern of Ezra 9–10 is introduced in the first two verses: the men have married foreign wives and so have their sons. Steinmann claims this is the dominant issue through which God conveys the problem of mixing with pagan elements and the need for repentance.[22] Hamilton claims that the internal challenge of intermarriage with the people of the land in Ezra 9–10 is parallel with the external challenge from the people of the land in Ezra 3–6.[23] These might be broadly similar, but they are quite different in literary presentation. Multiple kings, decrees, and letters are mentioned in Ezra 3–6, while the Persian government is completely ignored in 9–10. Also, multiple Judean leaders are acting in the narrative in 3–6 while Ezra is the dominating figure in 9–10. Regardless of the relationship with other narratives in book of Ezra, the focus on wives as Israel's transgression is reiterated throughout Ezra 9–10.[24]

Ezra's prayer claims the command of the prophets is to not give Israelite daughters to the nations or to take their daughters for Israelite sons (9:12). However, he does not state the exact way that the people are breaking this commandment except that they are "intermarrying with the people who commit these abominations" (9:14).

The precise marriage situation that was mentioned in Ezra 9:2 is reiterated by Shecaniah as marrying foreign wives (10:2). Shecaniah's proposed oath involves putting away wives and children, but the unfaithfulness is tied only to the foreign wives.

Ezra echoes this emphasis on foreign wives in his speech before the assembly (10:10). He includes separating from the people of the land as well as foreign wives as the solution for the problem, but the unfaithfulness again is tied specifically to foreign women. In the same way, the people's speech states, "Let all those in our cities who have married foreign wives come at appointed times" (10:14). Both speeches emphasize that foreign wives are the primary concern in the narrative.

---

22. Steinmann, *Ezra and Nehemiah*, 319–20. For a discussion of foreign women and ideology in Ezra 9–10 and Jeremiah, see Leuchter, "Exegesis of Jeremiah in and beyond Ezra 9–10," 62–80.

23. Hamilton, *Exalting Jesus in Ezra and Nehemiah*, 82.

24. Becking notes that it is foreign women not men or children in this passage, unlike Deut 7, which includes foreign men and women. Becking, *Ezra, Nehemiah, and the Construction of Early Jewish Identity*, 60; Blenkinsopp, *Ezra-Nehemiah*, 59.

Separation of the People, Separation of the Land

Beyond the reported speech, the narrative emphasizes foreign women specifically in Ezra 10:18 and 19. The final verse of the passage mentions that all the people listed married foreign wives, but only some of them had children (v. 44). So, the narrator is not denying the existence of children but focusing primarily on the wives. The children from these mixed marriages or foreign husbands with Israelite wives are never linked to Israel's unfaithfulness. Beyond the missing connection to unfaithfulness, Israelite women marrying foreign men is not even mentioned as an action occurring in Yehud at the time, children are only mentioned twice (10:3, 44), and only once as part of the solution to Israel's sin (v. 3).

The primary concern of the passage is presented not only as a problem but also with a solution. So, the people of Israel marrying foreign wives is the crisis that begins the passage, but the narrative resolves the issue by removing the foreign women from the community. Ezra 10 resolves the crisis presented in Ezra 9 twice. First, the people swear an oath to perform the proposal of Shecaniah's speech (10:5). Then the people agree to follow Ezra's command for confession and a list of the people resolving the issue is transcribed (10:12–44). Both Ezra and Shecaniah call for the removal of foreign wives. Their speeches do not address future intermarriage but those that have already taken place. So, the resolution of the foreign wives crisis is to confess the sin and dissolve the current marriages rather than to discontinue the practice of intermarriage in the future.

NEH 9–10

The narrative movement of the marriage conflict in Neh 9–10 can be diagrammed as follows:

1. Sons of Israel gather in fasting, sackcloth, and dirt (9:1)

2. Israel separated from foreigners and stood (9:2–3)

    A. Confessed their sins (9:2)

    B. Confessed iniquities of fathers (9:2)

    C. Read the Law (9:3)

    D. Confessed and worshiped (9:3)

3. Levites stood on their platform and cried out (9:4)

4. Levites recorded prayer (9:5–38)

Dissolving Marriage

5. List of people on the sealed document (10:1–29)

   A. Officials (10:1)

   B. Priests (10:2–8)

   C. Levites (10:9–13)

   D. Leaders (10:14–27)

   E. Others (10:28–29)

6. Contents of the document (10:30–39)

   A. No intermarriage (10:30)

   B. Sabbath observance (10:31)

   C. Temple tithes (10:32–39)

This passage follows from the feasting in the previous chapter. Some scholars have claimed that Neh 9 is out of place because the people were feasting in Neh 8, but they are mourning in Neh 9.[25] In addition, Neh 8 is often seen as displaced Ezra material because it focuses upon Ezra and reading the Law, which follows from Artaxerxes's decree in Ezra 7.[26] Some scholars have also claimed that Neh 9–10 originally followed Ezra 10 because the service beginning with separation in Neh 9 would fit nicely after the investigation of the intermarriage in Ezra 10.[27] However, Clines claims that this lays too much weight on Neh 9:2a because nothing in the Levites' prayer references mixed marriage.[28]

Regardless of the source theory, the time reference, change of tone (rejoicing to mourning), and the switch from Ezra to the Levites as the

---

25. Myers, *Ezra-Nehemiah*, 165–66; Williamson, *Ezra, Nehemiah*, 308–10; Schoville, *Ezra-Nehemiah*, 221. Wright claims Neh 9–10 is a younger stratum of text than 8:13–18. Wright, *Rebuilding Identity*, 318. Fried claims a similar view to Wright. Fried, "Torah of God as God," 295. For an argument that the mourning is out of place in the narrative, see Fried, "Who Wrote Ezra-Nehemiah—and Why Did They?," 5; Welch, "Source of Nehemiah IX," 130–37.

26. Koch, "Ezra and the Origins of Judaism," 192; Pakkala, "Original Independence of the Ezra Story in Ezra 7–10 and Neh 8," 17–24; Pakkala, "Disunity of Ezra-Nehemiah"; Laird, "Political Strategy in the Narrative of Ezra-Nehemiah," 1, 3.

27. Burns, *Ezra, Nehemiah*, 75–76; Myers, *Ezra-Nehemiah*, 165; Rudolph, *Esra und Nehemia Samt 3. Esra*, 154; Grabbe, "Law of Moses in the Ezra Tradition," 95–96. Larson and Dahlen present the option but do not commit to this reordering of the text. Larson and Dahlen, *Ezra, Nehemiah, Esther*, 228.

28. Clines, *Ezra, Nehemiah, Esther*, 189.

prominent character indicates that Neh 9 is a separate convocation.[29] The chapter begins by stating that it was the twenty-fourth day of the month, which is two days after the previous festival.[30] As Becking notes, there is no festival in the Israelite calendar on this date, so it is unclear why the people are gathering, and it is unrelated to the gathering of the previous chapter.[31]

Nehemiah 10 and 11 are clearly separate sections of text. Not only is chapter ten an embedded document, but chapter eleven begins with the leaders living in Jerusalem and the rest of the people living in their cities. Chapter eleven does not mention the solemn assembly nor the document that was signed.[32]

Prominent Character: Levites

Nehemiah 9 begins with an assembly of Israelites. The people are described as a collective in mourning, reading the Law, and confessing their sins. The first mention of specific groups and individuals is in verse 4. Not only are the Levites mentioned, but eight specific individuals are named twice (though the names are slightly different between verses 4 and 5).[33] These individuals then have a recorded speech that spans the rest of chapter nine. The end of the Levites' prayer mentions the significant people who signed the document that will be presented in chapter ten: the leaders, Levites, and

---

29. Steinmann, *Ezra and Nehemiah*, 531; Redditt, *Ezra-Nehemiah*, 294; Pakkala, "Disunity of Ezra-Nehemiah," 208; Pakkala, *Ezra the Scribe*, 180–84. Daniels believes that Neh 8–10 derives from a single source but part of it was lost in the redaction process which caused a disrupted transition between Neh 8 and 9–10. Daniels, "Composition of the Ezra-Nehemiah Narrative," 326.

Davies claims there are three phases in Neh 8–9 (8:1–12, 8:13–18, 9:1–37) followed by the result in Neh 10. In this scheme, Neh 9–10 is the final phase and conclusion. Davies, *Ezra and Nehemiah*, 119–20; Eskenazi, *In an Age of Prose*, 96; Duggan, *Covenant Renewal in Ezra-Nehemiah (Neh 7:72b–10:40)*, 139.

30. Steinmann, *Ezra and Nehemiah*, 531.

31. Becking, *Ezra-Nehemiah*, 255. See also the discussion in Duggan, *Covenant Renewal in Ezra-Nehemiah (Neh 7:72b–10:40)*, 141. Contra Goswell who claims the chronological note forges a close connection. Goswell, *Study Commentary on Ezra-Nehemiah*, 295.

32. Many scholars connect Neh 11 with Neh 7 because of the focus on the population of Jerusalem that is interrupted by chapters 8–10. Goswell, *Study Commentary on Ezra-Nehemiah*, 323; Redditt, *Ezra-Nehemiah*, 214, 313; Burns, *Ezra, Nehemiah*, 81.

33. Steinmann discusses the leaders and two different groups of Levites. Steinmann, *Ezra and Nehemiah*, 532.

priests (9:38). This again reflects the focus on Levites and leadership within this passage.[34]

The sealed document recorded in chapter ten lists the names divided by the governor, priests, Levites, and leaders of the people (10:1–27). Even the summary of the rest of the people divides between "people, priests, Levites, gatekeepers, singers, temple servants, and all who had separated from the foreign people" (10:28). So, the prominent characters leading the prayer in Neh 9 are one of the primary groups signing the document in Neh 10. This document also mentions the necessity for contributions to the temple function and concludes with the promise of the Levites and priests ministering in the temple (10:37–39).

This passage contains a small narrative with an embedded prayer and an embedded oath document. Both the prayer and the document are presented by the Levites, and the document emphasizes the contributions for the Levites even more than the priests (10:34, 37–39).[35] The introductory narrative (9:1–4) only names Levites, and the rest of the people are simply called "the sons of Israel." So, this passage does not emphasize an individual but a group. The leaders generally are important, priests and other leaders are named, but the Levites are emphasized specifically in the narrative, by the recording of their prayer, and through their activities in the embedded document.

Primary Concern: God's Favor

The primary concerns of the passage are addressed in the prayer in chapter nine and the embedded document in chapter ten.[36] The prayer of the Levites ends with "we are slaves today . . . we are in great distress, now because of all this we are making a written agreement" (Neh 9:36–38). The prayer

---

34. Goswell claims this focus on the Levites was prepared for by the gradual disappearance of Ezra in Neh 7–8. Goswell, *Study Commentary on Ezra-Nehemiah*, 296–97.

35. The list of document signers also lists family names for most people but individual names for the Levites. See Steinmann, *Ezra and Nehemiah*, 558; Schoville, *Ezra-Nehemiah*, 234; Burns, *Ezra, Nehemiah*, 80; Boice, *Nehemiah*, 107–08; Myers, *Ezra-Nehemiah*, 176.

36. Häusl argues that Neh 9–10 belong close together because chapter nine serves as the preparation for the conclusion for the contract fulfilled in chapter ten. Häusl, "Searching for Forces of Group Cohesion in the Books of Nehemiah and Isaiah," 61.

Separation of the People, Separation of the Land

presents the problem, the people are in distress, and the solution presented in the passage, a sealed document.[37]

The solution to the distress is proper worship and obedience to the Law. The people separate themselves from foreigners to read the Law, confess, and worship on the twenty-fourth day of the month (9:1–3). The precise purpose behind their gathering and confession is not stated until the end of the Levites' prayer. The history of Israel is recounted with an emphasis on God's continued patience and restoration despite the sin of the people.[38] This cycle leads into the main point of the prayer: the current sons of Israel have sinned and now are suffering and enslaved (9:37). Because of this situation they are making an agreement before God (9:38). So, the narrative in chapter nine introduces the Levites' prayer which provides the primary concern for the passage: find favor with God by following the Law.[39]

The document shows the specific laws and ordinances that the people deemed necessary to entreat God's favor.[40] The first two ordinances are about mixing with the people of the land: no intermarrying and no commerce on holy days or the sabbath (10:30–31).[41] All the remaining ordinances are about contributions to the temple and the roles of the priests and Levites in the functioning of the temple (10:32–39).[42] This emphasis on the support of the temple is confirmed by the final line of the document: "thus we will not neglect the house of our God" (10:39). So, most of the document is about the continued attention to the temple, which fits with the goal of entreating God's favor which was stated at the end of the Levites' prayer.

The issue of intermarriage is only explicitly mentioned in one verse (10:30). The other references about "separating from the foreign people" are likely about participation in the solemn assembly (9:2; 10:28).[43] How-

---

37. For a discussion of anti-Achaemenid language in the prayer see Janzen, "Yahwistic Appropriation of Achaemenid Ideology and the Function of Nehemiah 9 in Ezra-Nehemiah," 839–56. He argues that the prayer looks for a divine plan beyond the Achaemenid rule.

38. Steinmann, *Ezra and Nehemiah*, 548.

39. Steinmann, *Ezra and Nehemiah*, 550.

40. Each of the ordinances are found in the Pentateuch. See the list in Steinmann, *Ezra and Nehemiah*, 562.

41. Thiessen claims that Neh 10 emphasizes separation of the exiles from the impure nations. Thiessen, "Function of a Conjunction," 63–79.

42. Steinmann, *Ezra and Nehemiah*, 562.

43. See Steinmann's argument that 9:2 is about participating in the assembly. Blenkinsopp, *Ezra-Nehemiah*; Becking, *Ezra-Nehemiah*; Steinmann, *Ezra and Nehemiah*, 531.

Dissolving Marriage

ever, many scholars compare these chapters to Ezra 9–10 because of the recorded prayer and oath against intermarriage.[44] The challenge is that the primacy of intermarriage shown in Ezra 9–10 is not found in this passage. Ezra's prayer explicitly states intermarriage as a concern, but the prayer of the Levites does not (Ezra 9:12, 14). Also, the passing reference to mixed marriage in Neh 10:30 is outweighed by the lengthy treatment of temple contributions, whereas the entire list of names in Ezra 10 is people who have separated from foreign wives. Therefore, the oath to refrain from marrying foreign people is not the primary concern of the passage but only one part of the promises intended to bring God's favor and deliverance.

NEH 13:23–29

The narrative movement of the marriage conflict in Neh 13:23–29 can be diagrammed as follows:

1. Nehemiah noticed Jews married foreign women, had foreign children (13:23–24)

2. Nehemiah contended with them (13:25–27)

   A. Cursed them, struck them, pulled out their hair (13:25a)

   B. Made them swear an oath (13:25b)

   　i. Reported speech/content of oath (13:25c)

   　ii. Reported speech/Solomon's sin (13:26)

   　iii. Reported speech/present sinfulness of the people (13:27)

3. Nehemiah drove away a son of Joiada (13:28)

4. Appeal to God for recognition (13:29)

The segmentation of the text in Neh 13 is fairly easy to define. The narrative events are separated by Nehemiah's pleas to God for recognition.[45] So, Neh 13:22 ends with, "About this remember me, my God, and have pity on me according to your great lovingkindness." Besides the versification, the initial pronoun, זאת, connects verse 22 with the events of the preceding

---

44. Steinmann, *Ezra and Nehemiah*, 335; Myers, *Ezra-Nehemiah*, 178; Philip Esler, "Ezra-Nehemiah as a Narrative of (Re-Invented) Israelite Identity," 425; Campbell, "Structure, Themes, and Theology in Ezra-Nehemiah," 397.

45. Blenkinsopp, *Essays on Judaism in the Pre-Hellenistic Period*, 136–37.

passage. This section, 13:15–22, is concerned with commerce on the sabbath and so is thematically distinct from the intermarriage crisis of verses 23–29 as well.

The final verse of the passage being examined here states, "Remember them, my God, because they have defiled the priesthood, and the covenant of the priesthood, and the Levites." This again reflects the actions from the preceding verses and specifically the interaction with the son of Joiada in the preceding verse.[46]

The two following verses are about the appointment of priests and Levites to their tasks and also ends with the plea, "Remember me, my God, for good" (13:31). So, verses 30–31 are a short unit that is separate thematically from the passage concerning intermarriage and textually by Nehemiah's plea in 13:29.[47]

Therefore, Neh 13:23–29 can be treated as its own pericope. The textual signal of Nehemiah's plea to God separates the section on both sides. The theme of the section, intermarriage, is also distinct from the preceding and following passages.

Prominent Character: Nehemiah

This section, and all of chapter thirteen, is written in the first-person. Not only is this narrated by Nehemiah in the first-person, he is also the character performing the primary actions in the text. Nehemiah saw the people intermarrying (v. 23) and then contended, cursed, struck, pulled out the hair, and made the people swear (v. 25). He also drives away one of the sons of the high priest and then calls upon God to remember them for defiling the priesthood (vv. 28–29).

In addition to being the subject of nearly all the primary verbs in the narrative section, Nehemiah is the speaker for the only recorded speech in this section (vv. 25–27). The only person mentioned as an individual, rather than a people group (v. 23), is the son of Joiada (v. 28). However, he is

---

46. Schoville, *Ezra-Nehemiah*, 266; Goswell, *Study Commentary on Ezra-Nehemiah*, 359–60; Myers, *Ezra-Nehemiah*, 216.

47. Redditt treats Neh 13:28–31 as a single unit about purifying the priesthood and temple. However, he does not address the appeal to God in verse 29 or the issue of intermarriage being the same in 13:23–27 and 28–29. Redditt, *Ezra-Nehemiah*, 334; Burns, *Ezra, Nehemiah*, 91.

Dissolving Marriage

not mentioned by name but only relationship, son of Joiada and son-in-law of Sanballat.

In this way, Nehemiah is the prominent character in the passage. The characters he is contending with are only named as Jews and women from Ashdod, Ammon, and Moab (v. 23) and the son of Joiada and Sanballat (v. 28). None of the other characters are named, and none of them have any primary actions within the narrative events.

Primary Concern: Mixed Families

Nehemiah condemns the people for marrying foreign women and having children who have lost their Jewish identity (vv. 23–24). However, he also removes one of the sons of Joiada, son-in-law of Sanballat the Horonite (v. 28). So, the narrative condemns the marriage with foreign women, the children of these marriages who do not speak Judean, and priests who are in mixed marriages.

Nehemiah's speech emphasizes the marriage of Judeans with foreign wives through a description of Solomon's sin and the current actions of marrying foreign wives (vv. 26–27). The wording of the oath indicates that the people are prohibited from marrying in either direction, Judean husband and foreign wife or Judean wife and foreign husband (v. 25). The main concern in Neh 13:23–29 is mixed families within the Judean community. Though foreign wives are emphasized, mixed children and foreign husbands are also condemned.

The crisis is presented as mixed families and the solution is swearing an oath not to intermarry (13:25). The only indication of a resolution for those who have already intermarried is the removal of the son of Joiada from the priesthood (v. 28). However, this is not presented as a normative practice. Nehemiah's standard practice might have been to remove the people who intermarried from the community and allow the mixed families to remain intact, but it is unclear. His actions with the people in verse 25 describes his violent reaction and how he made them swear an oath. If the people swearing the oath not to intermarry were those who were already intermarried, then it seems likely that they remained in the community. However, if the people who swore the oath were the members of the community who had not intermarried, then the outcome of those who intermarried is unknown (also his violent actions against people who have not intermarried would be confusing). In any event, Nehemiah appears to favor, or at least provide the option of, removal from the community rather than divorce based upon the interaction with the son of Joiada.

COMPARISON OF EZRA 9–10, NEH 9–10, AND NEH 13:23–29

Unlike the return migrations in Ezra-Nehemiah, there are few overlapping themes in these passages. Ezra 9–10 and Neh 13:23–29 are more similar to each other than Neh 9–10 is to either of them but there are still some distinct differences. All three passages will be compared within the same framework of prominent character and primary concern that was used for each individually.

Prominent Character

Ezra 9–10 and Neh 13:23–29 focus upon a single character, Ezra and Nehemiah, respectively. However, Neh 9–10 focuses upon the community as a whole and the Levites specifically. This initial overlap between the actions of Ezra and Nehemiah is less clear when the details are examined. Kraemer notes the difference between the Ezra passage and the two Nehemiah passages in terms of priestly emphasis. He notes that Ezra is portrayed as a priest, but in the other two passages the actions are performed by Levites and Nehemiah.[48]

Ezra is the primary agent in the narrative but receives information from other characters, specifically leaders (9:1), Shecaniah (10:2–4), and the people (10:12–13). In Neh 13, though, the other characters are mute and unnamed. Even as Nehemiah contends with them, makes them swear an oath, and removes a particularly egregious offender, the characters have no responses nor names (outside of family lineage in Neh 13:28).

The characters in Neh 9–10 are represented somewhere between Ezra 9–10 and Neh 13:23–29. The only ones with a recorded speech are the Levites (Neh 9:4–38). However, the people who signed the document are listed at least by ancestry if not by name (Neh 10:1–29). So, the other characters are almost mute because they do not make substantial contributions to the narrative events, unlike in Ezra 9–10, but they are named and listed in the

---

48. Kraemer, "On the Relationship of the Books of Ezra and Nehemiah," 85.

embedded document, which is a major focus of the narrative, unlike Neh 13:23–29.

A similar challenge in the narratives is the use of recorded speeches by the prominent characters. Ezra and the Levites both have lengthy recorded prayers (Ezra 9:6–15; Neh 9:5–38) and, even more significantly, the prayers recount the history of Israel with a focus on the people's unfaithfulness juxtaposed with God's restorative actions. McConville also notes that both prayers indicate Persian rule was a burden, which breaks from some of the more positive views of Persia expressed in Ezra-Nehemiah.[49] Nehemiah 13:29 has a call for God's remembrance, but this short prayer is a call for God to remember the current defilement, not a recounting of Israel's history nor a plea for God's restoration. However, Ezra and Nehemiah both have recorded speeches where they address the people directly about their sin of intermarriage (Ezra 10:10–11; Neh 13:25–26), but the Levites do not address the people directly and, in fact, they do not have any recorded speech besides the prayer.

The single focus on an individual joins Ezra 9–10 and Neh 13:23–29 together. However, the relationship of the prominent character to the background characters and the narrative movement overall is dramatically different. The narrative in Ezra centers around Ezra's actions, but it is not solely Ezra, whereas the narrative in Neh 13:23–29 is solely accomplished by Nehemiah to the point that no other characters are even explicitly named. Both prominent characters address the sin of the people directly to the people in a recorded speech.

The third text, Neh 9–10, shares elements with both passages and illuminates the significant differences between them. Though the focus on a group of Levites rather than an individual separates it from the other two, Ezra and the Levites both present a lengthy prayer.[50] On the other side, Nehemiah and the Levites are the only ones performing actions, while Ezra contains speeches from other individuals and groups.

In this way, the narratives are each distinct. The presentations of the prominent character or characters are slightly different in each text. The way in which they interact with other characters and move the plot forward

---

49. McConville, "Ezra-Nehemiah and the Fulfilment of Prophecy," 208–10.

50. For a comparison of how this prayer is used in connection with purity and the cult see Janzen, "Sacrifice as Cultic Expression of the Law," 206–07. Kim claims that the prayers share similar Deuteronomic quotations. Kim, "Historiographic Characteristics of Ezra-Nehemiah," 117–19.

are also different, specifically whether it is the prominent character acting alone or in conversation with secondary characters.

Primary Concern

The primary concern of each text is also unique, though Ezra 9–10 and Neh 13:23–29 have the most overlap. However, Smith-Christopher claims that the social concern of Ezra 9–10 and Neh 13:23–31 is different because Ezra might be about an internal religious struggle while Nehemiah is about external marriage for political and social gains.[51] Eskenazi and Judd also suggest that Ezra 9–10 is an internal struggle based upon a more literal translation of Ezra 9:1 as "not separated themselves from the people of the land whose abhorrent practices are like those of the Canaanites." So, the *kaph* is a simile that leaves the actual ethnic background of the women obscure, unlike Neh 13 where they clearly speak foreign dialects.[52]

All three passages share a similar phrase: "Do not give your daughters to their sons, nor take their daughters for your sons" (Ezra 9:12; Neh 10:30; 13:25).[53] However, the Nehemiah passages are within the oath context whereas Ezra claims to be quoting the Law in his prayer. This is the most significant overlap between Neh 9–10 and the other two passages. Outside of this phrase, the emphasis on God's favor through obedience in Neh 9–10 is much broader than the passages specifically focused upon marriage.[54]

Nehemiah 13:23–29 and Ezra 9–10 both emphasize marrying foreign women as the sinful act that the people were engaged in (Ezra 9:2; 10:10–11, 14, 17–19; Neh 13:23, 26).[55] However, the issue of children is highlighted

---

51. Smith-Christopher, "Mixed Marriage Crisis in Ezra 9–10 and Nehemiah 13," 243–65.

52. Eskenazi and Judd, "Marriage to a Stranger in Ezra 9–10," 268; Williamson, *Ezra, Nehemiah*, 125; Amzallag, "Authorship of Ezra and Nehemiah in Light of Differences in Their Ideological Background," 277–78.

53. The mixed marriage events point to a desire by Ezra and the Levites for a greater salvation that is still yet to come for the Judean community. McConville, "Ezra-Nehemiah and the Fulfilment of Prophecy," 211–13.

54. For a discussion of the different roles of the common people in Ezra 9–10 and Neh 9–10 see Korada, "Seeing Discontinuity in Chronicles-Ezra-Nehemiah through Reforms," 287–306.

55. Olyan explains that both passages describe intermarriage as polluting the community. Olyan, "Purity Ideology in Ezra-Nehemiah as a Tool to Reconstitute the Community," 1–16. For the relationship of Ezra and Nehemiah to the Persian empire and possibility that ethnic boundaries are part of the Persian policy, see Maier, "'Foreign'

Dissolving Marriage

by Nehemiah but almost absent in Ezra. Children are only mentioned twice in Ezra and only in connection with the foreign wives (in 10:3, Shecaniah proposes to put both wives and children away and in 10:44, some of those married to foreign wives also had children with them). However, Nehemiah makes a special point that these children do not retain the Judean language and do not belong to the people of Yehud (13:24).[56] This focus upon the relationship of the children to the community and their language shows that Nehemiah considers the children to be a concern apart from, and perhaps even greater than, the wives. Therefore, the primary concern in Ezra 9–10 can be summarized as foreign wives, but Neh 13:23–29 is mixed families (including both foreign wives and mixed children). Blenkinsopp also believes that Judean women marrying foreign men is alluded to in Neh 13:25, though it is absent in Ezra 9–10. He also claims that the exclusion of foreigners in Neh 9–10 includes men and women and so is closer to Neh 13 than Ezra 9–10.[57]

A second point of disagreement between the two passages is the solution for those who have already married foreign wives or had mixed children. Ezra commands the people to separate from the foreign wives and even compiles a list of people who divorced their wives. Yonina Dor understands this to be a purifying ritual whereby outsiders could be accepted into the community rather than a literal command for divorce from foreign women, but this interpretation is unconvincing.[58] However, Neh 13:23–29 does not instruct the people to leave their foreign wives and children.[59] He

---

Women in Ezra-Nehemiah," 79–98. For a discussion of Ezra's emphasis on pollution of the land and Nehemiah's emphasis on the obstruction of the restoration of the community, see Rainey, "'Their Peace or Prosperity,'" 158–81.

56. For a deeper discussion of language and ethnicity in Neh 13, see Southwood, "'And They Could Not Understand Jewish Speech,'" 1–19; Thon, "Sprache und Identitätskonstruktion," 557–76.

57. Blenkinsopp, *Judaism, the First Phase*, 66–67, 70.

58. Dor, "Rite of Separation of the Foreign Wives in Ezra-Nehemiah," 173–88.

59. Steinmann, *Ezra and Nehemiah*, 97; Rothenbusch, "Question of Mixed Marriages between the Poles of Diaspora and Homeland," 65; Thomas, *Ezra & Nehemiah*, 184; Burns, *Ezra, Nehemiah*, 91; Ben Zvi, *Social Memory among the Literati of Yehud*, 532. Gabizon claims Ezra's focus on the foreign wives imputing impurity to the children might be one source for the matrilineal descent in modern Judaism but also notes that Neh 13 does not assume any pollution in the lineage by the foreign women (it is a political and economic issue). Gabizon, "Development of the Matrilineal Principle in Ezra, Jubilees, and Acts," 148–52.

fights with the people and makes them swear an oath not to intermarry but does not provide a solution for those who have already married (13:25).⁶⁰

The incident with the son of Joiada also shows a very different response to the problem than Ezra's solution (13:28). Instead of requiring him to divorce his foreign wife, Nehemiah removes him from office. It appears that he remained married to the daughter of Sanballat, the text does not indicate otherwise, but he is no longer considered part of the priesthood.⁶¹ The priests who married foreign wives in Ezra's narrative put away their wives and offered a sacrifice but appear to still be considered priests (Ezra 10:18–19).

CONCLUSION

Unlike the Sheshbazzar and Ezra return migrations, the passages about intermarriage do not appear to share prominent characters or concerns. The passages focused upon Nehemiah and Ezra share the focus on a single character rather than a group like the Levites in Neh 9–10. In the same way, Nehemiah and Ezra are concerned broadly with intermarriage but their narrower focus (children and families versus foreign wives) and their resolutions are very different (divorce versus removal from office). The oath by the Levites is dramatically different and concerns community purity and temple support more broadly than just intermarriage. In the next chapter I will discuss the literary structure of each passage and explore the similarities and differences in the presentation of the events of the three narratives.

---

60. Clines opens the possibility that Neh 13:25 and 27 might hint at Nehemiah dissolving marriages but concludes that it is unclear and remains an open question. Clines, *Ezra, Nehemiah, Esther*, 246.

61. Schoville posits that the son of Joiada found refuge in his father-in-law's house. Schoville, *Ezra-Nehemiah*, 266. Myers considers the possibility that the son of Joiada refused to divorce his wife and that is why he was expelled. However, nothing in the text indicates this interaction. Myers, *Ezra-Nehemiah*, 218.

Chapter 5

The Literary Structure of Ezra 9–10, Nehemiah 9–10, and Nehemiah 13:23–29

THE PREVIOUS CHAPTER FOCUSED upon thematic elements of the mixed marriage passages. This chapter will explore their literary structures. First, the structural patterns in the Ezra, Levites, and Nehemiah passages will be discussed individually. These structures will then be compared for similar elements and ordering.

EZRA 9–10

1. Leaders approach Ezra, bad news reported speech (9:1–2)
2. Ezra mourns (9:3–15)
    A. Ezra appalled (9:3)
    B. People gather (9:4)
    C. Penitential prayer in reported speech (9:5–15)
3. Ezra and Shecaniah in reported speech (10:1–5)
    A. Crowd gathers before the temple (10:1)
    B. Shecaniah describes the state of the people (10:2)
    C. Shecaniah proposes a covenant (10:3–4)
    D. Ezra rises to initiate the covenant (10:5)
4. Move to the chamber of Jehohanan (10:6–8)

Separation of the People, Separation of the Land

    A. Proclamation to assemble (10:7)

    B. If unheeded, lose possessions and excluded (10:8)

5. Arrival in Jerusalem within three days (10:9)

6. Plan of action (10:10–15)

    A. Assessment and plan in reported speech (10:10–11)

    B. Reported response of agreement (10:12)

    C. Request for delay in reported speech (10:13–15)

7. Investigating the problem (10:16–17)

8. List of people resolving the problem (10:18–24)

Leaders Approach Ezra (9:1–2)

This section begins the narrative with a recorded speech and a narration in the first person. The events are situated in relation to the previous chapter with the line "when these things were completed" (9:1). However, the narration changes from the third-person "they delivered" to the first-person "approached me" in this section. The location of the interaction is not provided but it might have been in front of the temple based upon the reference to the house of God in Ezra 10:1.[1]

Though the narrative is told from Ezra's point of view, the prominent characters in this section are the princes. They are the ones approaching Ezra and the ones who have the recorded speech. In the first two verses, Ezra is only the object of the verb ("they approached me"), and even this occurs only once (9:1).

The speech contains three parts. First, the problem is identified: the people of Israel have not separated and acted according to the abominations of the other people groups (9:1b).[2] Second, the precise way in which they have mixed with the other nations, and the cause of the abominations, is presented in a כי clause: they have taken wives for themselves and their

---

    1. Clines, *Ezra, Nehemiah, Esther*, 119.

    2. Interestingly these people groups are not current to Ezra's time. Allen and Laniak, *Ezra, Nehemiah, Esther*, 72–74. For a discussion of the theological and historical significance of these names, see Goswell, *Study Commentary on Ezra-Nehemiah*, 119. Graham proposes a connection between these foreign peoples and the genealogy of the assassins of Joash in 2 Chronicles 24:26 (son of a Moabite woman and son of an Ammonite woman). Graham, "Connection Proposed between II Chr 24,26 and Ezra 9–10," 256–58.

The Literary Structure of Ezra 9–10, Nehemiah 9–10, and Nehemiah 13:23–29

sons (9:2a). Finally, the people most responsible are named: princes and officials (9:2b). This structure creates a full description of the problem. They start with a broad claim of mixing to the narrower issue of foreign wives and from the broad claim of Israel, priests, and Levites being involved to the princes and officials being the primary people responsible. So, both halves of Ezra 9:2 are necessary to clarify the two-part general claim of Ezra 9:1b (who acted and what they did).

The term שׂר is used for the princes who were leaders in the unfaithfulness, 9:2b, and this is the same term for those who approached Ezra in 9:1a. For this reason, it has been argued that the final clause ("the hands of the princes and rulers have been foremost in this unfaithfulness") is not part of the recorded speech. Instead, it has been argued to be part of Ezra's commentary on the situation.[3] However, the princes implicating themselves or their colleagues is not necessarily a problem and requires certain assumptions about the princes that are beyond what is stated in the text (i.e., that they would not implicate themselves). The princes approached Ezra with the issue of intermarriage and if they or their close colleagues were involved, then they would have an even better knowledge of the problem.

Textually, this clause fits more closely with the speech because the next verse begins with "and when I heard." If this phrase does not follow the speech directly, the sequence becomes confusing. In Becking's reading, the princes speak, Ezra comments that they are the ones committing the sins, and then Ezra says, "and when I heard." Instead, it is more likely that the princes speak, and Ezra's response begins with "and when I heard."

Ezra Mourns (9:3–15)

After the speech by the princes, the narrative focus shifts to Ezra. This is still presented in the first-person, but Ezra now takes the primary actions and has the recorded speech. The first verse references the previous section but obliquely. Ezra does not mention the princes, their speech, or even the precise problem. The only reference Ezra makes is to "this matter" (הַדָּבָר הַזֶּה). This vague reference is not clarified until well into Ezra's prayer in verse 12.

The narrative contains three movements and two of them are performed by Ezra. First, Ezra mourns by tearing his garment and robe, pulling his hair, and sitting down appalled (9:3). The next movement is the

---

3. Becking, *Ezra-Nehemiah*, 143.

gathering of people to Ezra (9:4).⁴ Interestingly, the people are gathering because of the unfaithfulness of the exiles. However, the speech by the princes did not mention the exiles at all, it named sons of Israel, priests, Levites, princes, and officials. Undoubtedly, the sons of Israel and exiles are often used interchangeably in Ezra-Nehemiah, but it is notable that their identification does not match the speech from Ezra 9:1–2. Just like Ezra's reference to "this matter" in verse 3, the narrative again does not address the speech of the princes directly. This verse ends with a reiteration of Ezra's posture and the duration of it ("until evening"). The final action introduces Ezra's speech (10:5). This reiterates Ezra's mourning posture from verse 3 and his move to a posture of prayer (kneeling with arms raised).

Each of Ezra's movements begin with a temporal reference: "when I heard" (וּכְשָׁמְעִי) in verse 3 and "at the evening offering" (וּבְמִנְחַת הָעֶרֶב) in verse 5. However, the second movement is performed by those who tremble at the words of God but without a specific time indication (simple *waw*). The response of the people is also followed by a reiteration of Ezra's seated astonishment with a simple *waw* conjunction. So, Ezra appears to move the narrative forward not only by performing two of the three primary movements but also by his connection with the temporal references within the text.

Ezra's prayer in recorded speech spans the rest of the chapter (9:6–15). It begins in the first-person singular but transitions to the first-person plural in the first verse (9:6). Williamson divides the prayer into five sections.⁵ First, Ezra confesses that he and the people are standing in their guilt (vv. 6–7).⁶ Then, he reflects upon God's grace to the remnant (vv. 8–9) and makes a more specific confession of their sin of intermarriage (vv. 10–12).⁷

---

4. For a discussion of the group "the people who tremble at the word of the Lord" in post-exilic writings, see Blenkinsopp, "Trito-Isaiah (Isaiah 56–66) and the Gôlāh Group of Ezra, Shecaniah, and Nehemiah (Ezra 7–Nehemiah 13)," 661–77.

5. Williamson, *Ezra, Nehemiah*, 128; Becking, *Ezra-Nehemiah*, 147. Duggan divides the prayer into three major parts: confession of people's guilt in the past (vv. 6–7), God's mercy and the people's decision in the present (vv. 8–14), and summary confession of God's righteousness and the people's guilt (v. 15). Duggan, "Ezra 9:6–15," 169.

6. For the constructive role of Ezra's shame and guilt in spurring the people to action, see Kang, "Positive Role of Shame for Post-Exilic Returnees in Ezra/Nehemiah," 257–59. Smith discusses verbal connections with Deuteronomy and the pessimistic view of Israel's past and the community's present situation in Ezra's prayer. Smith, "Influence of Deuteronomy on Intercessory Prayers in Ezra and Nehemiah." Emmanuel Usue claims that the negative view of foreigners comes from a partial and narrow reading of the Abrahamic and Mosaic covenants by Ezra. Usue, "Is the Expulsion of Women as Foreigners in Ezra 9–10 Justifiably Covenantal?," 158–69.

7. For a discussion of the stake metaphor in Ezra 9:8 and its thematic connection with

Williamson calls the next two sections, "statement of future intent" (vv. 13–14) and "concluding general confession" (v. 15).[8] However, his descriptions of these sections obscure the primary purpose. Verses 13–14 are not expressing a positive intention but rather the potential result if they continue in their current sins (God will destroy them). The language in this section does not reflect a new intention but mirrors the sin described in verses 11–12. A more apt description is "concern for future punishment." Similarly, the final verse is a general confession but contains elements from the statement of God's grace ("left to us an escaped remnant" לְהַשְׁאִיר לָנוּ פְּלֵיטָה v. 8 and "we are left an escaped remnant" נִשְׁאַרְנוּ פְלֵיטָה v. 15) and the introductory confession ("guilt" אשמה vv. 6, 7, 15).[9] This, then, is not just another general confession but a recapitulation of God's grace and the people's guilt from the first two sections of the prayer. Steinmann divides between verse 15a and 15b as confession and grace but does not discuss the clear recapitulation of the opening section of the prayer. He also claims that the prayer alternates between three confessions (9:6–7, 10–12, 15b) and three statements of God's grace (9:8–9, 13, 15a). This alternation is partially true, but the outline is missing verse 14 entirely and misses the movement from general confession to intermarriage confession to recapitulation of guilt.[10]

Ezra and Shecaniah in Reported Speech (10:1–5)

This section continues the narrative from Ezra 9:5, when he was praying at the evening offering.[11] Though this section is linked temporally with chapter nine ("and while Ezra was praying and confessing, weeping and bowing"), it is no longer written in the first person. The narrative has shifted to speaking about Ezra in the third person. Many scholars have debated about

---

the rest of the prayer, see Moffat, "Metaphor at Stake in Ezra 9:8," 290–98.

8. Williamson, *Ezra, Nehemiah*, 128; Schoville, *Ezra-Nehemiah*, 120–21. Goswell has a similar structure but considers verses 13–15 as a single unit. Goswell, *Study Commentary on Ezra-Nehemiah*, 171, 177–78.

9. For a discussion of the challenging grammatical construction in Ezra 9:15, see Byun, "Paradoxical Situation and God's Righteousness in Ezra 9:15," 467–73.

10. Steinmann, *Ezra and Nehemiah*, 334.

11. Dor claims that the prayer is a separate document with the narrative composed around it. Dor, "Composition of the Episode of the Foreign Women in Ezra IX-X," 34. Pakkala claims that the prayer was an expansion to the Ezra material. Pakkala, *Ezra the Scribe*, 258.

Separation of the People, Separation of the Land

the relationship between the two chapters primarily because of this shift in person.[12] Daniels claims that this is a narrative connection technique and is a direct continuation of the reform begun in Ezra 9, so they should be part of a single narrative.[13] Dor, however, claims that the prayer is a separate source from the narrative of chapter ten but that the wording of the narrative at the beginning of chapter nine obscures any clear distinction between the two chapters. So, it is a single narrative with the prayer inserted within it.[14] While the origin of these passages may remain unknown, they are clearly intended to be read together in their current form. Besides the connection of Ezra praying in 9:5 and 10:1, the narrative crisis of Ezra 9 remains unresolved without this section. In chapter nine, the leaders present a crisis and Ezra mourns and prays but no solution or final punishment is provided. Ezra's prayer anticipates punishment if they continue sinning but does not indicate whether this occurs (Ezra 9:14). In the same way, the beginning of Ezra 10 is confusing without the prior statement of Israel's sin. The first verse refers to his confession and weeping as well as the crowd weeping. However, this tearful response comes before Shecaniah's identification of the problem and so creates an introductory verse that is difficult to understand without chapter nine. These two chapters are being treated as one text because they are both necessary to create a coherent and resolved narrative.

This section, Ezra 10:1–5, contains three movements: the people gather (v. 1), Shecaniah's direct speech (vv. 2–4), and Ezra's resolution to the proposal (v. 5). This section contains strong connections to Ezra 9, even beyond Ezra 9:4–5 and 10:1. Shecaniah's speech refers to the foreign wives as "from the people of the land" like Ezra's prayer (9:11, 10:3). Also, Shecaniah refers to the people as "those who tremble at the commandment of our God," which is similar to the description in Ezra 9:4, "all who tremble at the words of the God of Israel."

The final verse of this section resolves the issue according to the method presented by Shecaniah. Ezra responded to the call to arise and act by rising up and making the people swear an oath. The full resolution to Shecaniah's speech is shown by the actions and the people involved. Shecaniah proposes to "make a covenant with our God to put away the wives and their children" and Ezra makes the people "swear an oath to do according

---

12. Williamson, *Ezra, Nehemiah*, 127, 148.
13. Daniels, "Composition of the Ezra-Nehemiah Narrative," 321–22.
14. Dor, "Composition of the Episode of the Foreign Women in Ezra IX–X," 27.

The Literary Structure of Ezra 9–10, Nehemiah 9–10, and Nehemiah 13:23–29

to this word" (vv. 3, 5). The final clause is "and they swore an oath" (v. 5). So, the actions complete the request. They should make a covenant, so the people swear an oath.

The people involved in the oath also indicates the complete fulfillment of Shecaniah's proposal. Ezra makes the leaders of the priests, the Levites, and all Israel swear the oath (10:5). Whether the very large assembly that gathered to Ezra in verse 1 constituted all Israel, by the time of this oath, Ezra had brought all Israel to him. So, this passage contains a proposal by Shecaniah and a fulfillment of the proposal by Ezra which involved all the people of Israel.[15]

Move to the Chamber of Jehohanan (10:6–8)

The connection between this section and the previous section is weak.[16] Ezra rose up and moved from the temple to the chamber of Jehohanan, but his continuation at the temple is unclear in the previous passage. Ezra began kneeling before the temple in Ezra 10:1, but then he rose up and made the people swear in verse 5. Now he is arising again and moving away from the temple. Whether he was still at the temple during the oath swearing, the repetition of rising up in verse 6 highlights the disjointedness of these sections.

In addition to the repetition, Shecaniah is no longer mentioned, and Ezra is still mourning. Though Shecaniah had the only recorded speech in the previous section, here Ezra is performing the main actions and the only other named character is Jehohanan, and even then, it is just identifying the owner of the room.[17] Ezra's fasting and mourning in the section fits awk-

---

15. Contra the view that it was only the leaders swearing the oath. Schoville, *Ezra-Nehemiah*, 127; Allen and Laniak, *Ezra, Nehemiah, Esther*, 79–80; Larson and Dahlen, *Ezra, Nehemiah, Esther*, 117. Moffat claims that שׂרי refers to all three nouns in succession and acknowledges that this is an unusual construction (normally it would occur before each noun) but cites three other times where "leaders" refers to a series of nouns (1 Chron 13:1; Ezra 8:29; Jer 29:2). Moffat, *Ezra's Social Drama*, 115–16.

16. Schoville places this verse with 10:1–5 under the heading "Effect of Ezra's Prayer" but does not explain how it is related to the preceding verses. He only addresses the questions of Jehonanan's genealogy. Schoville, *Ezra-Nehemiah*, 127–28. Dor divides Ezra 10 between the short narrative (vv. 2–6) and the long narrative (vv. 7–44) and claims that these are two separate textual traditions that have been placed next to each other. Dor, "Composition of the Episode of the Foreign Women in Ezra IX–X," 35.

17. The identification of Jehohanan as the son or grandson of Eliashib has created many questions about the date of these events. Burns, *Ezra, Nehemiah*, 46; Myers,

wardly with the resolution proposed and fulfilled in the previous section. If making a covenant with God brought hope for Israel (10:2), then Ezra should be celebrating the covenant, not continuing to mourn.[18] However, verse 6 continues with Ezra performing the same actions as Ezra 9.

One potential explanation for the continued mourning, and Shecaniah's disappearance from the narrative, is that Shecaniah's proposed solution was unsatisfactory to Ezra. Ezra completed the covenant proposal but did not believe that it fully absolved the community of their sin. For him, more work needed to be done, and the people needed to assemble for a full investigation (or reassemble since all Israel was swearing with Ezra in verse 5).

The resolution to Ezra's continued mourning is to call for an assembly of all the exiles in Jerusalem (10:7–8). The proclamation is issued by an unnamed plural subject in verse 7. Steinmann claims that the leaders and the elders are the ones who issued the proclamation.[19] Though he does not state it explicitly, this interpretation most likely comes from verse 8 where the forfeiture of property is "according to the counsel of the princes and elders." However, the princes and the elders were not the most recent subjects of the narrative. The most recent action was Ezra going to the chamber of Jehohanan, so it is likely that these are the ones who issued the proclamation. Ezra, and potentially Jehohanan, could be issuing a proclamation that contains the guidance of the princes and elders. Nothing about the counsel of the leadership within the proclamation requires that the proclamation be sent by them.

Arrival in Jerusalem within Three Days (10:9)

After the proclamation was sent out, the people gathered. Interestingly, the proclamation was sent through Judah and Jerusalem (10:7), but the men of Judah and Benjamin gathered (10:9). The movement in the previous section was from the chamber of Jehohanan to all of Jerusalem and Judah, in this section the people from Judah and Benjamin gather before the house of God in Jerusalem.

The narrative emphasizes time in a way that it has not in the previous sections of this passage. The events have been dated relative to other events: "when they things had been completed" (9:1), "when I heard about

Ezra-Nehemiah, 85–86; Clines, *Ezra, Nehemiah, Esther*, 127.

18. Dor, "Composition of the Episode of the Foreign Women in Ezra IX–X," 37.
19. Steinmann, *Ezra and Nehemiah*, 351.

the matter" (9:3), "while Ezra was praying" (10:1). However, this verse dates the gathering to "the ninth month, on the twentieth day of the month." This date allows scholars to date the entire episode, assuming the events of chapter nine occurred roughly three days before this.[20]

So, the new date formula and the change in movement shows that this is a new section from the previous one. The verse is also set apart from the following section because it focuses just on the migration of the people. Though it does anticipate further actions, otherwise the people are left sitting and trembling in the rain, it does not indicate why they are waiting there. The proclamation in the previous section was for the men to assemble or forfeit their possessions. So, assembling in the rain fulfills that proclamation on its own.

Plan of Action (10:10–15)

Ezra's recorded speech drives the narrative forward. The proclamation and assembly are unclear without his speech. The people could have been gathering to register their property with the officials in Jerusalem, since forfeiture was the punishment, or record the genealogy of their wives, since Ezra was mourning the unfaithfulness by intermarriage. However, Ezra's speech identifies the precise purpose for the gathering that was not explicit in the previous two sections: separating from the people of the land and the foreign wives.

The speech of Ezra is reminiscent of Shecaniah, though with quite different word choices. Both speeches begin with a confession of unfaithfulness by marrying foreign wives (though Shecaniah uses first-person plural and Ezra second-person plural) (Ezra 10:2, 10). They also propose a solution: Shecaniah desires to make a covenant to put away the wives and Ezra desires to make a confession to separate from foreign wives and the people of the land (Ezra 10:3, 11). However, Ezra's speech does not contain the positive statement of Shecaniah, "and yet there is hope for Israel in spite of this" (Ezra 10:2).[21]

Another important difference between Shecaniah's speech and Ezra's speech is the focus on action in Ezra's speech. Shecaniah requests a covenant to be made according to counsel and according to the law. Shecaniah ends

---

20. See Becking, *Ezra-Nehemiah*, 139; Steinmann, *Ezra and Nehemiah*, 325.

21. Goswell also notes the similarity but with less detail. Goswell, *Study Commentary on Ezra-Nehemiah*, 180.

his speech commanding Ezra to rise and act. Ezra's actions in the narrative then confirm that making the covenant was what Shecaniah had proposed and called Ezra to do (10:4–5).

However, confession is only the first part of the solution in Ezra's speech.[22] He proposes to make a confession, do God's will, and separate from the foreign people and wives. Unlike Ezra's narrated response to Shecaniah's recorded speech, the community has a recorded speech in this section (10:12–14). The people respond with confession but then address the challenge of Ezra's call for separation. They state that the number of people involved and the rainy season will make the process lengthy so there should be leaders appointed to investigate and resolve the issue. This shows that they understood Ezra's call to be more than just communal confession; it required separation. So, Shecaniah proposed a covenant to put away foreign wives, which Ezra fulfilled, but Ezra proposed a community-wide action to separate from the people of the land and the foreign wives. His emphasis on communal action is indicated by the assembly's speech and the details of the investigation process.

The final verse in this section is a narrative conclusion to the proposal. Four individuals are named as standing against the rest. It is does not clarify whether the individuals are against the slower counterproposal by the assembly or if they are against Ezra's requirement to put away foreign wives.[23] Whichever proposal they are standing against, this text summarizes the final response to the conversation started by Ezra. The people still appear to be gathered at the temple and responding to Ezra's speech.

Investigating the Problem (10:16–17)

This section begins with a statement that resumes from the speech of the assembly rather than the dissenters of verse 15. The shift to a new section is

---

22. Gitay notes that the narrative surrounding Ezra's speech portrays him as hesitant to issue the order to separate from foreign wives and the people's hesitancy to carry out the separation order, even though they believe that they are defiling the holy seed. For this discussion see Gitay, "Designed Anti-Rhetorical Speech," 57–68.

23. Goswell, *Study Commentary on Ezra-Nehemiah*, 189. Myers claims that they wanted immediate action. Myers, *Ezra-Nehemiah*, 86; Clines, *Ezra, Nehemiah, Esther*, 130. Larson and Dahlen claim they wanted immediate action because they identify Meshullam as the leader in Ezra 8:16 and Neh 8:4 and Shabbethai in Neh 8:7–8. So, they were strong leaders who wanted strong action. Larson and Dahlen, *Ezra, Nehemiah, Esther*, 120.

The Literary Structure of Ezra 9–10, Nehemiah 9–10, and Nehemiah 13:23–29

shown by the change in name for the people, the actions of the people, and the date formula.

The first line, "and the sons of the exile did it," uses a term for the assembly that was not present in the previous section. They were called "the assembly" (הַקָּהָל) in verses 12 and 14, but "the exiles" (הַגּוֹלָה) was only used in verses 7–8. In these verses, "the exiles" did not refer to the assembly gathered at the temple but all the people in the land of Judah that were called to assemble. The use of this term in Ezra 10:16 most likely implies that the assembly before the temple has ended, and the actions are taking place after the exiles have returned to their homes, perhaps even including some exiles who were not present in the assembly.

The second indication of a new section is the action by Ezra and the exiles. The section begins with a summary statement, "the exiles did it," followed by an explanation of what they did, Ezra selecting leaders and their convening to investigate. The introductory summary statement introduces the series of actions that were based upon the speech. These actions are in narrative, rather than recorded speech, and are clearly happening after the assembly, recorded speeches, and dissenting opinions.

The final indication of a separate section is the date formula. The assembly was dated to "the ninth month on the twentieth day of the month" (10:9). The reconvening of the leaders is dated to the "first day of the tenth month" (10:16). This move forward in time along with the change in characters indicates that a shift in the narrative is happening here. The counter-proposal provided by the assembly is being narrated.

This section concludes with another date formula, the completion of the investigation on the first day of the first month (10:17). So, this narrative block spans the selection of leaders, start of the investigation, and completion of the investigation.

List of People Resolving the Problem (10:18–24)

This section is typically interpreted as an embedded document.[24] Whereas the previous sections were either narrative or recorded speech, this is a list within only two verses of narration (10:19 and 44). The list is divided into priests (vv. 18–22), Levites (vv. 23–24), and the sons of Israel (vv. 25–43). In the section on priests, the sons of Jeshua are separated from the sons of Immer, Harim, and Pashhur by the note that the sons of Jeshua pledged to

---

24. See discussion in Steinmann, *Ezra and Nehemiah*, 364.

put away their wives and offered a ram as a sacrifice (v. 19). The Levites are also divided further into singers and gatekeepers (v. 24).[25]

The concluding statement of the name list is also the conclusion of the book. The statement reiterates that all the people in the list married foreign wives, and some had children with them (10:44). This conclusion fits the name list document but does not clearly address the concerns of the narrative. The author identifies the people on the list as marrying foreign wives but does not explicitly state that all these separated from their foreign wives (which would be the logical conclusion to the narrative). Only by the placement of this name list after the investigation section (10:16–17) is it clear that these are the guilty people who are solving the issue presented by the princes in Ezra 9:1 through the command to separate by Ezra (10:11).

NEH 9–10

1. Sons of Israel gather in fasting, sackcloth, and dirt (9:1)

2. Israel separated from foreigners and stood (9:2–3)

    A. Confessed their sins (9:2)

    B. Confessed iniquities of fathers (9:2)

    C. Read the Law (9:3)

    D. Confessed and worshiped (9:3)

3. Levites stood on their platform and cried out (9:4)

4. Levites recorded prayer (9:5–38)

5. List of people on the sealed document (10:1–29)

    A. Officials (10:1)

    B. Priests (10:2–8)

    C. Levites (10:9–13)

    D. Leaders (10:14–27)

    E. Others (10:28–29)

6. Contents of the document (10:30–39)

    A. No intermarriage (10:30)

---

25. For a comparison of the names and numbers with Ezra 2, see Steinmann, *Ezra and Nehemiah*, 364–67; Schoville, *Ezra-Nehemiah*, 131–35.

B. Sabbath observance (10:31)

   C. Temple tithes (10:32–39)

Sons of Israel Gather (9:1)

Nehemiah 9 begins with a date formula and the gathering of the sons of Israel. The date is based upon the festival in Neh 8. The events of Neh 9 took place two days after the festival and assembly in the previous chapter.[26] Though a date is given, the location is not provided in this verse.

The date formula ("the twenty-fourth of this month") indicates chapter nine is a new movement in the narrative and so does the summary statement in this verse. Nehemiah 9:1 states the way that the people assembled, and the next two verses detail the actions of the people after they gathered. "The people assembled with fasting, sackcloth and dirt." This summarizes the way that the people assembled (in mourning) and who assembled (the sons of Israel). The actions that take place during this assembly will be described in the subsequent verses.

Israel Separated from Foreigners and Stood (9:2–3)

This section of the narrative details the actions of the sons of Israel after they gathered. When the Israelites gathered in their mourning attire, they separated themselves from foreigners, stood, and confessed their sins (9:2). Verse 1 stated that the Israelites gathered, and this verse explains who precisely gathered, that they were standing, and their action of confession.

Verse 3 then goes into deeper detail about their actions while standing and confessing. They read the Law for a fourth of the day and then confessed and worshiped for another fourth of the day. So, the first three verses of Neh 9 focus upon the actions of the Israelites in increasing detail. The sons of Israel gather in mourning, and they separate from foreigners, stand, and confess sins. Their time of standing confession was specifically divided between reading the Law and confessing sins.

---

26. Steinmann, *Ezra and Nehemiah*, 531.

Levites Stood on their Platform (9:4)

This section changes from the people of Israel to the Levites. This section also provides the location of the events. The Levites stood on their platform and cried out to God. The location and actions of the sons of Israel are not mentioned in the rest of this chapter. Presumably, they are standing before the Levites' platform, but they are no longer the focus of the passage. The remainder of this chapter is focused upon the speech of the Levites.

Levites Recorded Prayer (9:5–38)

The Levitical prayer is introduced by a new set of Levitical leaders. The names mostly overlap but not entirely. Some scholars have posited that this is a duplication in the text with a scribal error or a remnant from the combination of two originally independent pieces of narrative.[27] Steinmann argues that these different names are different leaders. The group crying out on the platform is a different set of Levites from the Levites offering the prayer recorded in the rest of the chapter, and the five overlapping names are people who were leaders in both groups.[28] Whether these names originated from two separate documents, or the lists were originally the same but became corrupted through transmission, the way they are presented currently seems to support Steinmann's view. The Levites listed in Neh 9:4 cried with a loud voice and then another group of Levites is listed, and they begin the prayer (9:5). The second list of Levites interrupting the two actions (crying out and the recorded speech) indicates that the people in this list are performing a separate action from the preceding list and action.

Nehemiah 9:5 introduces the speakers and begins the recorded prayer that comprises the rest of chapter nine.[29] The prayer can be divided into

---

27. Clines claims this is a scribal error. Clines, *Ezra, Nehemiah, Esther*, 191.

28. Steinmann, *Ezra and Nehemiah*, 532; Becking, *Ezra-Nehemiah*, 264; Kidner, *Ezra and Nehemiah*, 111; Larson and Dahlen, *Ezra, Nehemiah, Esther*, 229; Duggan, *Covenant Renewal in Ezra-Nehemiah (Neh 7:72b–10:40)*, 145–46. Schoville lists both options but is undecided. Schoville, *Ezra-Nehemiah*, 223.

29. Boda claims this is prayer is part of a covenant ceremony and argues that it has connections to the Persian period along with Ezra 9 and Neh 5. Boda, *Praying the Tradition*, 32–38; Becking, *Ezra, Nehemiah, and the Construction of Early Jewish Identity*, 89–93. For the use of the prayer in constructing a social identity in the postexilic community tied to the collective memory of Israel's history, see Mtshiselwa, "Remembering and Constructing Israelite Identity in Postexilic Yehud," 1–6. Myers lists each clause of the prayer and its linguistic relationship to other Old Testament texts.

three major parts: praise, history, and pledge, along with further subdivisions in the history section.[30] The first part of the prayer is a blessing directed to God and is described as a doxology by Becking (9:5b).[31]

The second part of the prayer comprises the majority of the text, verses 6–31, and recounts the history of the world and Israel.[32] This can then be further subdivided into the history of the world, verse 6, and the history of Abraham's descendants, verses 7–31, through the repetition of "You are Yahweh" in verses 6 and 7.[33] The history of Abraham's descendants can then be further broken down into cycles of God's compassion and the people's rebellion: Abraham (vv. 7–8), exodus (vv. 9–12), Sinai (vv. 13–15), rebellion and compassion (vv. 16–17), desert wandering (vv. 18–22),

---

Myers, *Ezra-Nehemiah*, 167–70. For the use of the Abrahamic covenant in the prayer, see Bautch, "Appraisal of Abraham's Role in Postexilic Covenants," 42–63; Holmgren, "Faithful Abraham and the 'amānâ Covenant Nehemiah 9,6–10,1," 249–54; Mermelstein, "When History Repeats Itself," 113–42. For a discussion of the scriptural reflection and unique literary relationship of Neh 9 to earlier parts of the Hebrew Bible, see Newman, "Nehemiah 9 and the Scripturalization of Prayer in the Second Temple Period," 112–23; Rendtorff, "Nehemiah 9," 111–17.

Clines claims that there is a rhythmic and metrical character to the prayer but current knowledge about Hebrew poetry makes deeper analysis difficult. Clines, *Ezra, Nehemiah, Esther*, 193.

30. The three-part division is asserted by Boice, *Nehemiah*, 101–04; Eskenazi, "Nehemiah 9–10," 1–19. Redditt divides the prayer into four parts: verses 6–8, 9–15, 16–31, and 32–37. However, the two middle sections should be seen as a single major section because they both deal with the history of God's relationship to Abraham and his descendants. Redditt, *Ezra-Nehemiah*, 297.

Thomas divides the prayer into seven sections: verses 6, 7–16, 17–25, 26–31, 32–35, 36–37, 38. However, he is does not clearly address all the verses in each section but only a single verse in most of them. Thomas, *Ezra & Nehemiah*, 355–56.

For a discussion of chiastic structure in the prayer and specifically a critique of Bliese, see Boda, "Chiasmus in Ubiquity," 55–70; Bliese, "Chiastic Structures, Peaks and Cohesion in Neh 9.6–37," 208–15. For an examination of the literary sections of the prayer and implications for its composition, see Chrostowski, "Examination of Conscience by God's People as Exemplified in Neh 9,6–37," 253–61.

31. Becking, *Ezra-Nehemiah*, 264.

32. Gili Kugler analyzes the themes of the Levites' prayer and argues that it is distinct from the other prayers in Ezra-Nehemiah and Daniel. He believes it is a pre-exilic prayer inserted into the text. Kugler, "Present Affliction Affects the Representation of the Past," 605–26. Rendsburg claims that the prayer originated in northern Israel based upon linguistic evidence. Rendsburg, "Northern Origin of Nehemiah 9," 348–66. Leuchter identifies inter-Levitical disputes within the prayer and its setting showing that it is a response to elitist and exclusivist views. Leuchter, "Inter-Levitical Polemics in the Late 6th Century BCE," 269–79.

33. Steinmann, *Ezra and Nehemiah*, 532.

conquest of the promised land (vv. 23–25), rebellion (v. 26), pre-monarchy (vv. 27–29), monarchy (vv. 30–31), late monarchy to exile (vv. 32–35), current state (vv. 36–37).[34]

The final part of the prayer is the pledge (9:38).[35] This bridges the themes of the history of Israel in the recorded speech with the document embedded in the next chapter. In the Hebrew text this verse is the first verse of chapter ten and so not part of the prayer but an introduction to the sealed document. However, this reading is less likely. It is true that the verse is no longer petitioning God directly, nor is it recounting the history of Israel like the rest of the prayer, but it is still speaking in the first-person plural, and the introductory clause refers directly to the bad state of the people ("now because of all this").[36] Perhaps this is a separate speech from the prayer, but it is still presented as recorded speech by the Levites and not part of the document.[37] For this reason, regardless of the versification, this

---

34. Becking contains a similar breakdown but with some significant differences in verses 27–35. Becking, *Ezra-Nehemiah*, 262–63. Goswell contains a similar division but less detailed. Goswell, *Study Commentary on Ezra-Nehemiah*, 289–310. Boda divides the prayer as hymnic introduction (9:5), creation (9:6), Abraham (9:7–8), exodus (9:9–11), wilderness–Sinai (9:12–23), conquest–life in the land (9:24–31), request (9:32–37). This is similar to my interpretation but paired slightly differently. Boda, "Torah and Spirit Traditions of Nehemiah 9 in Their Literary Setting," 479.

Van Wijk-Bos divides the prayer into three sections: covenant with Abraham (vv. 7–8), exodus and wilderness wandering (vv. 9–22), and possession and loss of land (vv. 23–31). Van Wijk-Bos, *Ezra, Nehemiah, and Esther*, 80.

Allen and Laniak claim that the shift happens in verse 32 because of the pronoun change. However, they do not explain why the passage is in the past tense and refers to Assyria and Israelite kings (vv. 32, 34). Allen and Laniak, *Ezra, Nehemiah, Esther*, 134; Schoville, *Ezra-Nehemiah*, 230–32.

35. Glatt-Gilad claims that the "pledge" is the only connecting element between Neh 9 and 10. This highlights the need for Torah and temple faithfulness. Glatt-Gilad, "Reflections on the Structure and Significance of the 'amānāh (Neh 10,29–40)," 386–95.

36. Becking claims the pronoun binds the verse to the preceding text. Becking, *Ezra-Nehemiah*, 282; Waltke and O'Connor, *Introduction to Biblical Hebrew Syntax*, §17.4; Wright, *Rebuilding Identity*, 214. Contra Clines who claims the connection in verse 38 to the prayer is not clear at all and should be seen as a heading for the signed document. Clines, *Ezra, Nehemiah, Esther*, 200. Larson and Dahlen assert that Neh 9:38–10:39 originally stood after Neh 13 and so it is part of the pledge referring to the sinful actions of chapter thirteen. Larson and Dahlen, *Ezra, Nehemiah, Esther*, 242.

37. Becking advocates for this being part of the prayer and lists scholars who believe it is not part of the prayer. Becking, *Ezra-Nehemiah*, 282. Some scholars believe it is closely linked to the prayer. Goswell, *Study Commentary on Ezra-Nehemiah*, 312; Hamilton, *Exalting Jesus in Ezra and Nehemiah*, 182.

should be included as part of the prayer, or at least a recorded speech, by the Levites.

List of People on the Sealed Document (10:1–29)

The document begins with a list of names and an introduction identifying them as the names on the sealed document (10:1).[38] Nehemiah the governor is the first name on the list followed by the priests (vv. 1–8), the Levites (vv. 9–13), and the leaders of the people (vv. 14–27). After the list of individuals, the rest of the people, priests, Levites (divided into gatekeepers and singers as well), temple servants, and all who separated themselves from the people of the land with their families are included (10:28).[39]

Contents of the Document (10:30–39)

The document switches from third-person plural in the last section to first-person plural in this section.[40] This section of the document details what the people are agreeing to and so naturally is presented in the first person from the point of view of the signers: "we agree/pledge." The stipulations can be divided into three groups, which can then be further subdivided: intermarriage (10:30), sabbath observance (v. 31), and temple support (vv. 32–39).[41] The first two are only one verse each, but it should be noted that

---

38. For a discussion of the document as an independent source and a discussion about how the style of the agreement is different from the rest of Nehemiah, see Becking, *Ezra-Nehemiah*, 284–87; Clines, "Nehemiah 10 as an Example of Early Jewish Biblical Exegesis," 111–17. Many scholars claim that it is either an embedded document or based upon an independent document. Grabbe, *Judaism from Cyrus to Hadrian*, 1:39–40; Rudolph, *Esra und Nehemía Samt 3. Esra*, 173; Clines, *Ezra, Nehemiah, Esther*, 200; Williamson, *Ezra, Nehemiah*, 328; Jones, "Embedded Written Documents as Colonial Mimicry in Ezra-Nehemiah," 174.

39. For a deeper discussion and identification of the names included in the list, see Jepsen, "Nehemia 10," 87–106. Lau argues that Neh 10:28 is a rare inclusivist viewpoint in Ezra-Nehemiah because anyone who participates in the Passover can be joined to the community of true Israel. Lau, "Gentile Incorporation into Israel in Ezra-Nehemiah?," 356–73.

Sivertsev argues the opposite of Lau, claiming that the signing of the covenant began a movement towards sectarianism that continued into the Dead Sea sects. Sivertsev, "Sects and Households," 59–78.

40. Becking, *Ezra-Nehemiah*, 287.

41. See Steinmann, *Ezra and Nehemiah*, 562; Goswell, *Study Commentary on*

the sabbath regulations include commerce on holy days and the sabbatical year.[42]

The final section of this document concerns the functioning of the temple (10:32–39). First, the people agree to pay an annual tax for the service of the temple (vv. 32–33). Then the people agree to do what is commanded in the law. First, to cast lots for supplying wood for the temple (v. 34),[43] then to bring the first fruits (vv. 35–37).[44]

The final two verses of the temple provisions section explain the actions of the priests and Levites when they receive these tithes (vv. 38–39). This details that the priests are with the Levites when they receive them, and the Levites bring them to the temple. The final statement of the document is "thus we will not neglect the house of our God." Though this concludes the entire agreement, it more directly addresses the final temple provisions section. The emphasis on temple provisions and specifically upon temple provisions according to the law addresses the concerns of the Levites' prayer in chapter nine, in which forgetting God and disobeying the law are repeated concerns (cf. 9:16–17, 26, 29, 34). So, even though this final verse relates explicitly only to Neh 10:32–39, it also covers the broader concern of neglecting God and the law.[45]

NEH 13:23-29

1. Nehemiah noticed Jews married foreign women, had foreign children (13:23–24)

Ezra-Nehemiah, 315; Thomas, *Ezra & Nehemiah*, 366; Van Wijk-Bos, *Ezra, Nehemiah, and Esther*, 83–86. Myers makes a comparison between the provisions in the document and the description of issues in Neh 8. Myers, *Ezra-Nehemiah*, 175.

42. Levering separates the sabbath day law from the sabbath year law. Levering, *Ezra & Nehemiah*, 192.

43. For a discussion of the wood festival in Qumran documents and the connection to wood donations in Neh 10, see Crawford and Hoffmann, "Note on 4Q365, Frg. 23 and Neh 10:33–36," 429–30.

44. Steinmann only divides between the tax (vv. 32–33) and keeping the law (34–39). Steinmann, *Ezra and Nehemiah*, 563–64. Becking divides between tax (32–33), casting lots for wood (34), and providing agricultural surplus (35–39). Becking, *Ezra-Nehemiah*, 289–91; Allen and Laniak, *Ezra, Nehemiah, Esther*, 140–41. Schoville contains a similar one to mine except he has vv. 35–36 as first fruits and 37–39 as tithes. Schoville, *Ezra-Nehemiah*, 238.

45. Clines, *Ezra, Nehemiah, Esther*, 210.

The Literary Structure of Ezra 9–10, Nehemiah 9–10, and Nehemiah 13:23–29

    2. Nehemiah contended with them (13:25–27)

        A. Cursed them, struck them, pulled out their hair (13:25a)

        B. Made them swear an oath (13:25b)

            i. Reported speech/content of oath (13:25c)

            ii. Reported speech/Solomon's sin (13:26)

            iii. Reported speech/present sinfulness of the people (13:27)

    3. Nehemiah drove away a son of Joiada (13:28)

    4. Appeal to God for recognition (13:29)

Nehemiah Noticed Jews Married Foreign Women (13:23–24)

The section begins with a time reference: "also in those days" (13:23). This indicates that the events of this section took place roughly contemporaneously to the preceding events. However, by introducing this section as happening contemporaneous to the previous section, the author indicates that they interpret it as a separate action. Two separate events happened in those days (the sabbath conflict and the intermarriage conflict).[46]

Two issues are seen by Nehemiah in this section. He saw Jews had married foreign women and their children not being able to speak the Judean language. Though Nehemiah focuses on foreign wives in his speech and expulsion of the son of Joiada, he also condemns the children that result from these marriages.

Nehemiah Contended with Them (13:25–27)

This section describes Nehemiah's reactions to his discovery in Nehemiah 13:23–24. His reactions are first physical and then verbal. He physically contends, curses, strikes, and pulls the hair out of the people who have intermarried. Nehemiah also makes them swear an oath, and this recorded speech takes up the majority of this section.

First, Nehemiah states the oath in the second person, likely indicating the words that the people are to swear.[47] After this, Nehemiah provides a warning from Israelite history: Solomon was a great king loved by God but

---

46. Schoville, *Ezra-Nehemiah*, 263.
47. Steinmann, *Ezra and Nehemiah*, 611.

still fell into sin because of intermarriage (13:26). The final part of Nehemiah's speech is a question that ties the initial oath formula with Solomon's sin. Nehemiah moves the conversation from Solomon's intermarriage to the present sin of intermarriage that he has witnessed.

Nehemiah Drove Away a Son of Joiada (13:28)

This section changes from recorded speech to action. Unlike the first section (Neh 13:23), this section does not indicate Nehemiah's observation. In this verse, Nehemiah simply states that a son of Joiada was also the son-in-law of Sanballat. The emphasis is placed upon Nehemiah's solution, driving him away, rather than his learning of the situation.

Appeal to God for Recognition (13:29)

This first-person appeal to God directly relates only to Neh 13:28.[48] Nehemiah asks God to remember those defiling the priesthood, covenant of the priesthood, and the Levites. However, verses 23–24 state that Jews were intermarrying, not just cultic personnel. Nehemiah's oath also appears to address the community as a whole and uses the example of Solomon's sin, who was neither a priest nor a Levite. So, the son of Joiada is the only mention of a priest in this passage.

Becking solves this puzzle by combining verses 28–29 so that the appeal to God only relates to the preceding verse.[49] However, this does not consider the function of these appeals throughout Neh 13. These appeals reflect God's observation of the entire preceding pericope (13:14, 22). This, then, should be an appeal for all the actions against intermarriage, not just the final action.[50] In addition, the pronoun is plural (להם) in verse 29, so it does not fit as a conclusion for an interaction with a single son of Joiada.

---

48. Contra Van Wijk-Bos who divides the text as 13:23–28 and 13:29–31 commenting that "remember them" can stand as the leading line of the passage and not a direct response to the preceding verse. Van Wijk-Bos, *Ezra, Nehemiah, and Esther*, 97–98.

49. Becking, *Ezra-Nehemiah*, 329; Allen and Laniak, *Ezra, Nehemiah, Esther*, 166; Goswell, *Study Commentary on Ezra-Nehemiah*, 360. Williamson claims this is a secondary addition, but the redaction layers are outside the scope of this work. Williamson, *Ezra, Nehemiah*, 394.

50. See Schoville's comparison with Neh 6:14, Schoville, *Ezra-Nehemiah*, 266.

The Literary Structure of Ezra 9-10, Nehemiah 9-10, and Nehemiah 13:23-29

"Remember them" should refer to multiple people defiling the priesthood, not just a single son intermarrying.

This conclusion clearly relates to the incident with the son of Joiada, but it should also be understood as a summary of the entire pericope. As Steinmann notes, this is an intensification of the issue. Intermarriage occurred among the Jews, and it even extended to the cultic personnel.[51] So, this is not strictly focused upon the cultic personnel to the exclusion of the other people in the pericope but addressing the most egregious sin, which is the defilement of the cult. In this way, the appeal to God completes the entire passage but with a specific emphasis on the most problematic situation, intermarriage by the cultic personnel.

COMPARISON

Table 3. Return migrations

Ezra	Levites	Nehemiah
1. Leaders approach Ezra, bad news in reported speech (9:1-2)	1. Sons of Israel gather in fasting, sackcloth, and dirt (9:1)	1. Nehemiah noticed Jews married foreign women, had foreign children (13:23-24)
2. Ezra mourns (9:3-15)	2. Israel separated from foreigners and stood (9:2-3)	2. Nehemiah contended with them (13:25-27)
A. Ezra appalled (9:3)	A. Confessed their sins (9:2)	A. Cursed them, struck them, pulled out their hair (13:25a)
B. People gather (9:4)	B. Confessed iniquities of fathers (9:2)	
	C. Read the Law (9:3)	
C. Penitential prayer in reported speech (9:5-15)	D. Confessed and worshiped (9:3)	
3. Ezra and Shecaniah in reported speech (10:1-5)	3. Levites stood on their platform and cried out (9:4)	

---

51. Steinmann, *Ezra and Nehemiah*, 612; Allen and Laniak, *Ezra, Nehemiah, Esther*, 164; Larson and Dahlen, *Ezra, Nehemiah, Esther*, 275.

Separation of the People, Separation of the Land

A. Crowd gathers before the temple (10:1)		
B. Shecaniah describes the state of the people (10:2)	4. Levites recorded prayer (9:5–38)	
C. Shecaniah proposes a covenant (10:3–4)		
D. Ezra rises to initiate the covenant (10:5)	5. List of people on the sealed document (10:1–29)	
4. Move to the chamber of Jehohanan (10:6–8)	A. Officials (10:1)	
A. Proclamation to assemble (10:7)	B. Priests (10:2–8)	
B. If unheeded, lose possessions and excluded (10:8)	C. Levites (10:9–13)	
5. Arrival in Jerusalem within three days (10:9)	D. Leaders (10:14–27)	
6. Plan of action (10:10–15)	E. Others (10:28–29)	
A. Assessment and plan in reported speech (10:10–11)	6. Contents of the document (10:30–39)	B. Made them swear an oath (13:25b)
B. Reported response of agreement (10:12)	A. No intermarriage (10:30)	i. Reported speech/content of oath (13:25c)
C. Request for delay in reported speech (10:13–15)	B. Sabbath observance (10:31)	ii. Reported speech/Solomon's sin (13:26)
7. Investigating the problem (10:16–17)	C. Temple tithes (10:32–39)	iii. Reported speech/present sinfulness of the people (13:27)
		3. Nehemiah drove away a son of Joiada (13:28)
8. List of people resolving the problem (10:18–24)		4. Appeal to God for recognition (13:29)

Unlike the Sheshbazzar and Ezra return migrations, none of the intermarriage passages are similar enough to demonstrate a pattern of narrative movements in the same order. Similar themes appear in all three of them though. Ezra and the Levites have recorded prayers of confession that include a history of Israel's unfaithfulness.[52] These two passages also contain a name list, though Ezra's is a list of people who put away foreign wives, while Nehemiah 10 is a list of people who signed the document. So, Ezra's intermarriage crisis and the Levites' document-signing passage have two points of contact, but even within these similar points, there are significant differences (Ezra versus the Levites praying and the name lists being people leaving their foreign wives versus signing the document).

Ezra's intermarriage crisis is also similar to Nehemiah's crisis in Neh 13. Each of these are dominated by a single character rather than a group (as it is in Neh 9–10). Nehemiah and Ezra both make the people swear an oath in recorded speech rather than a signed document. Nehemiah drove away the son of Joiada, and the people listed at the end of Ezra put away their foreign wives. Even within these points of similarity, there are significant differences. Nehemiah drove away a priest who intermarried, while Ezra recommended the people separate from the foreign wives. In addition, the oath-swearing by Ezra is followed by a response from the people agreeing to fulfill it, while Nehemiah is the only recorded speech in the passage and the response of the people is not provided even in the narration. Even the prominent character being an individual is different because Nehemiah is the only character performing any action in Neh 13:23–29, but the princes, Shecaniah, and people all interact with Ezra and have recorded speeches in Ezra 9–10. Becking notes some differences in the details of the portrayal as well: Ezra pulls out his hair, but Nehemiah pulls out other people's hair; Ezra prays while Nehemiah preaches; and Ezra includes himself in the sin, but Nehemiah rebukes others.[53]

Finally, Neh 9–10 and 13:23–29 have only one point of commonality: swearing an oath. Even this is different because Nehemiah does not mention the people who agreed to his oath, and it appears to be given verbally rather than embedded in a written document like Neh 10. David Glatt-Gilad notes that the written and signed covenant in Neh 10 is unique in the Hebrew Bible and, even if it is a fabrication and not an original document,

---

52. Japhet notes these two prayers are the strongest emphases on God's justice in Ezra-Nehemiah. Japhet, "Theodicy in Ezra-Nehemiah and Chronicles," 432–35. For a lexical comparison, see Duggan, "Ezra 9:6–15." Harm Van Grol discusses the concepts of servitude in Ezra 9 and Neh 9. Van Grol, "'Indeed, Servants We Are,'" 209–27. Van Grol also tries to demonstrate links between Ezra 9 and Ezekiel 36 as well as Isaiah. Van Grol, "Exegesis of the Exile-Exegesis of Scripture?," 31–61.

53. Becking, *Ezra, Nehemiah, and the Construction of Early Jewish Identity*, 104.

it is unlike the verbal commitments recorded in Ezra 10 and Neh 13.[54] More broadly, the issues addressed in Neh 10 appear in Neh 13, sabbath observance and tithes to the temple, but this is beyond the mixed marriages section.[55]

CONCLUSION

All three passages share a similar phrase: you shall not give your daughters to their sons, nor take their daughters for your sons (Ezra 9:12; Neh 10:30; 13:25). However, a single overlapping phrase is not enough to indicate shared narrative structure. The elements that overlap are still portrayed quite differently and they are not in the same order. This makes an identification of a type-scene for this passage difficult. The first two migration passages shared numerous structural elements in the same order and so appeared to follow a pattern. However, none of these passages have a significant overlap, so no pattern can be discerned between them.

Some scholars have posited that Ezra 9–10 is a retelling of the same historical event as Neh 13:23–28.[56] If this view is combined with the view that Neh 9–10 was originally placed between Ezra 8 and 9, then all three passages are about the same event. This argument relies upon rearranging the text to fit a historical reconstruction or viewing the Ezra 9–10 and Neh 13:23–28 as deriving from separate literary traditions before being combined.[57] However, the text portrays the events very differently. Nehemiah tears out the hair of the transgressors while Ezra tears out his own hair, and Ezra commands removing foreign wives while Nehemiah only removes the priest from his position. In addition, the narrative structures differ

---

54. Glatt-Gilad, "Voluntary Nature of the Nehemiah Covenant in Rabbinic Literature," 6–7.

55. See discussion in Becking, *Ezra-Nehemiah*, 287; Goswell, *Study Commentary on Ezra-Nehemiah*, 315; Becking, *Ezra, Nehemiah, and the Construction of Early Jewish Identity*, 100–02; Davies, *Ezra and Nehemiah*, 123–24; Boda, "Torah and Spirit Traditions of Nehemiah 9 in Their Literary Setting," 488–90; Blenkinsopp, "Nehemiah Autobiographical Memoir."

56. Becking disagrees with scholars who claim that the events are about the same crisis but then claims, "Ezra 9–10 is a fictional message that applies the theme of Neh. 13 to the crisis recalled in Josephus." So, in some sense, Ezra 9–10 is recasting Neh 13, even if they are not the same historical event. Becking, *Ezra-Nehemiah*, 138.

57. See Becking's earlier position in Becking, *Ezra, Nehemiah, and the Construction of Early Jewish Identity*, 106.

The Literary Structure of Ezra 9–10, Nehemiah 9–10, and Nehemiah 13:23–29

considerably, as noted in this chapter. So, whether the historical events behind the text are the same, the way that the text portrays them are entirely different. For this reason, they should be treated as unique narratives and, based upon their themes and structure, they are describing different narrative events.

In the following chapters, I will propose a different structural pattern for the outlier in the migrations, Neh 1–3:32, and the intermarriage crisis of Ezra 9–10. Neither of these fit a discernible pattern with the passages that share the same themes (intermarriage or migration), but they are similar to each other. After analyzing the texts, I will also discuss the thematic and theological significance of this comparison.

Chapter 6

The Literary Structure of Ezra 9–10 and Nehemiah 1–3

IN THE PREVIOUS CHAPTERS, I have shown that Ezra 9–10 and Neh 1–3 do not follow the literary structure of the passages that are most similar to them thematically. In this chapter, I will compare the literary structures of these two passages to show that they contain a significant number of parallels. Since I analyzed them individually in previous chapters, I will only compare them here. The similarities in literary structure discussed in this chapter will provide a framework for comparing the shared literary themes of the passages in the next chapter.

COMPARISON OF EZRA 9–10 AND NEH 1–3

Table 4. Ezra 9–10 and Neh 1–3

Ezra 9–10	Neh 1–3
	1. Introductory formula (1:1)
1. Leaders approach Ezra, bad news in reported speech (9:1–2)	2. Judeans return to Susa (1:2–3)
	A. Nehemiah questions Judean returnees (1:2)
	B. Bad news reported speech (1:3)
2. Ezra mourns (9:3–15)	3. Nehemiah mourns (1:4–11)
A. Ezra appalled (9:3)	A. Fasted and prayed (1:4)
B. People gather (9:4)	

The Literary Structure of Ezra 9-10 and Nehemiah 1-3

Ezra 9–10	Neh 1–3
C. Penitential prayer in reported speech (9:5–15)	B. Penitential prayer in reported speech (1:5–11a)
	C. Nehemiah's position (1:11c)
3. Ezra and Shecaniah in reported speech (10:1–5)	4. Nehemiah before the king in reported speech (2:1–8)
A. Crowd gathers before the temple (10:1)	
B. Shecaniah describes the state of the people (10:2)	A. Nehemiah describes the state of Jerusalem (2:1–3)
C. Shecaniah proposes a covenant (10:3–4)	B. Nehemiah requests to rebuild (2:4–5)
D. Ezra rises to initiate the covenant (10:5)	C. Artaxerxes grants the request (2:6–8)
4. Move to the chamber of Jehohanan (10:6–8)	5. Move to the provinces beyond the River (2:9–10)
A. Proclamation to assemble (10:7)	A. Letters sent to officials (2:9)
B. If unheeded, lose possessions and excluded (10:8)	B. Displeased outsiders (2:10)
5. Arrival in Jerusalem within three days (10:9)	6. Arrival and assessment (2:11–16)
	A. Arrival and stay (2:11)
	B. Small group of leaders convened by Nehemiah (2:12)
	C. Nehemiah's survey (2:13–15)
	D. Officials excluded (2:16)
6. Plan of action (10:10–15)	7. Plan of action (2:17–20)
A. Assessment and plan in reported speech (10:10–11)	A. Assessment and plan in reported speech (2:17)
B. Reported response of agreement (10:12)	B. Reported response of agreement (2:18)
C. Request for delay in reported speech (10:13–15)	C. Strife and response in reported speech (2:19–20)
7. Investigating the problem (10:16–17)	
8. List of people resolving the problem (10:18–24)	8. List of people resolving the problem (3:1–32)

Negative Report by Leaders

Nehemiah starts with the prologue "the words of Nehemiah the son of Hacaliah," but the narrative itself begins with the report of the Judeans who returned to Susa (Neh 1:1–3). This report parallels the leaders reporting the state of the people to Ezra in Ezra 9:1–2. Wright and Kratz claim that Ezra 9 draws upon distinctive features of Neh 1:1–11 and so should be read together.[1] Both texts have a group of leaders approaching the prominent character who is narrating in the first-person (Ezra 9:1a; Neh 1:2). Also, they are both presented in a short, recorded speech by the group of leaders (Ezra 9:1b–2; Neh 1:3). Saysell notes that the inclusion of Ammonites in Ezra 9:1 is poignant because Tobiah, one of Nehemiah's adversaries, was labelled an Ammonite in Neh 2:10, 19.[2]

Mourning and Prayer

This section begins with the phrase "when I heard this/these word/s" (Ezra 9:3a; Neh 1:4a). Upon hearing the negative reports, Ezra and Nehemiah both perform mourning actions. Ezra tore his garment and his robe, pulled out his hair, and sat down appalled (Ezra 9:3), and Nehemiah sat down, wept, and mourned (Neh 1:4).[3]

Both passages then contain a recorded prayer.[4] Goswell notes that they both take on the position of Moses in their actions and terminology.[5] Becking observes that Nehemiah addresses his prayer to God, but Ezra only partially addresses God directly. However, this distinction does not

---

1. Wright, "New Model for the Composition of Ezra-Nehemiah," 344; Goswell, *Study Commentary on Ezra-Nehemiah*, 200–201. Wright, *Rebuilding Identity*, 253–55; Wright, "Seeking, Finding and Writing in Ezra–Nehemiah," 287; Kratz, *Composition of the Narrative Books of the Old Testament*, 85–86.

2. Saysell, "According to the Law," 36.

3. A comparison table showing the significant overlap between the two texts is provided in Moffat, *Ezra's Social Drama*, 89. See also Allen and Laniak, *Ezra, Nehemiah, Esther*, 88; Schoville, *Ezra-Nehemiah*, 139; Wright, *Rebuilding Identity*, 253–54; Steinmann, *Ezra and Nehemiah*, 390; Kratz, *Composition of the Narrative Books of the Old Testament*, 84; Plöger, "Reden und Gebete im Deuteronomistischen und Chronistischen Geschichtswerk," 35–49.

4. Wright, "New Model for the Composition of Ezra-Nehemiah," 344; Esler, "Ezra-Nehemiah as a Narrative of (Re-Invented) Israelite Identity," 422.

5. Goswell, *Study Commentary on Ezra-Nehemiah*, 204.

completely separate the two prayers as Becking himself claims, stating that they are both penitential prayers with "a number of elements in common."[6]

Within the prayers, Ezra and Nehemiah include themselves in the sins of the people (Ezra 9:6; Neh 1:6).[7] Jay Hogewood discusses how Ezra's prayer is a confession and functions like the priestly confession. He also notes that the term for confession, התודה, is also found in Neh 1:6.[8] Each prayer also describes how the people have not followed the commandments of God (Ezra 9:10; Neh 1:7) and claims that their current state is a result of their sins. Deuteronomy is in the background of both prayers, almost to the point of direct quotes, according to Baltzer.[9] Mark Boda, though, claims that both these prayers have Deuteronomic language mixed with priestly phrases.[10] One distinction, however, is that Nehemiah's prayer contains a plea for compassion, while Ezra claims God has already been more compassionate than they deserve (Ezra 9:13; Neh 1:11).

Proposal in Reported Speech

After the recorded prayers, Shecaniah speaks to Ezra, and Artaxerxes speaks to Nehemiah. Shecaniah initiates the conversation as does Artaxerxes. However, Artaxerxes only asks questions and grants Nehemiah's requests, while Shecaniah commands Ezra to act (Ezra 10:2–4; Neh 2:2–8). This reverses the expected social roles in both passages. The king would be expected to issue a decree or a command to Nehemiah but instead asks what Nehemiah proposes to do about the problem. Shecaniah, a subordinate to Ezra, would be expected to follow Ezra's lead or ask Ezra what his proposal is for the intermarriage crisis, but instead he commands Ezra to act.

---

6. Becking, *Ezra-Nehemiah*, 172–73.

7. Davies, *Ezra and Nehemiah*, 88.

8. Hogewood, "Speech Act of Confession," 69–82; Myers, *Ezra-Nehemiah*, 78; Clines, *Ezra, Nehemiah, Esther*, 139; Williamson, *Ezra, Nehemiah*, 173.

9. Baltzer, "Moses Servant of God and the Servants," 121; Rudolph, *Esra und Nehemia Samt 3. Esra*, 105; Gabizon, "Development of the Matrilineal Principle in Ezra, Jubilees, and Acts," 149–50; Davies, *Ezra and Nehemiah*, 90.

10. Boda, *Praying the Tradition*, 68–71.

Movement by the Prominent Character

After the recorded speech between the prominent character and the secondary catalyst character, the prominent character moves to a new location in each passage. Ezra moves from the house of God to the chamber of Jehohanan and Nehemiah moves from Susa to the place where governors beyond the River reside (Ezra 10:6; Neh 2:9).

Arrival in Jerusalem: Assessment and Action

The next major movement in each text is the arrival in Jerusalem. In Ezra, the people of Judah and Benjamin arrive within three days (Ezra 10:9). Nehemiah also arrives in Jerusalem and remains for three days (Neh 2:11).

After the arrival in Jerusalem, the two passages present the major narrative movements in different order. Ezra presents a plan of action in recorded speech with a response from the people in recorded speech (vv. 10–15). Then the people investigate the issue (vv. 16–17). However, Nehemiah begins by investigating the issue (Neh 2:12–16) and then proposes a plan of action in recorded speech with a recorded response from the people (vv. 17–18).[11]

Looking more closely at the plan of action in the two passages, Ezra encounters opposition from four named individuals after the recorded speech with the people (Ezra 10:15), and Nehemiah encounters opposition from three named individuals after his recorded speech with the people (Neh 2:19–20). So, even though the major movements of assessment and plan of action are in a different order in the two texts, they are both still present and contain similarities in the details, including a recorded speech by the lead character, a recorded response by the people, opposition by a small number of named individuals, and an investigation of the problem by the prominent character and a small group of people selected by the prominent character (Ezra 10:16; Neh 2:12).

---

11. For a discussion of the use of "we" in the speeches of Ezra and Nehemiah, see Schoville, *Ezra-Nehemiah*, 155. Goswell notes that "I arose" is used to structure the narrative steps here and in Ezra 10. Goswell, *Study Commentary on Ezra-Nehemiah*, 225.

The Literary Structure of Ezra 9-10 and Nehemiah 1-3

List of People Resolving the Problem

The final movement in both texts is the list of people resolving the issue presented at the beginning of the passage. The list in Ezra is the people who put away foreign wives (10:19), which resolves the issue of Israelites marrying foreign women in Ezra 9:1-2. Nehemiah lists the people who built the wall around Jerusalem (3:1-32), which resolves the issue of the wall being broken down and the gates being burned in Neh 1:3. Both passages, then, do not resolve the narrative through the actions of the prominent character but through a list of people who reverse the negative state that was observed at the beginning of the passage.

CONCLUSION

The parallels in the narrative movements of Neh 1-3 and Ezra 9-10 are clear when the literary structure is examined. On the surface, they are thematically distinct—intermarriage and city walls—but the structural similarities bring the passages together. It is significant that there are more points of structural similarity between these two passages than either of them has with passages that contain closer thematic similarity. The return migration in Neh 1-3 is structurally distinct from the other two return passages in Ezra-Nehemiah in the same way that the structure of the foreign wives narrative in Ezra 9-10 is distinct from the other two passages mentioning putting away foreign wives.

The similarity between Ezra 9-10 and Neh 1-3 against other passages that are more thematically related indicates intentional narrative-shaping. One purpose for this structural paralleling could be to draw the books of Ezra and Nehemiah together. The narratives are on either side of the seam between the books, so the overlapping narrative structure could be used to indicate a relationship between the books and events.

While the function of the structural shaping for joining the books of Ezra and Nehemiah could be argued, more important for this study is the theological and thematic purpose. The structural similarity between Ezra 9-10 and Neh 1-3 leads to a renewed examination of the major themes of the two passages. If the narratives have been intentionally shaped to contain similar movements, they may also have been shaped to indicate overlapping themes. The shared theme in the passages will be explored in the next chapter.

Chapter 7

Purifying the Land
Ezra 9–10 and Nehemiah 1–3

IN THIS CHAPTER I will discuss the major theme in Ezra 9–10 and Neh 1–3. Since the prominent character and the primary concern have been identified for each passage in previous chapters, I will focus upon comparing the overlapping theme between two passages. I will show that both passages focus upon building the community and restoring the land through establishing exclusive rights to the land of Judah. Some scholars have noted that Ezra and Nehemiah define "foreigners" differently. Specifically, that Ezra addresses people living in or around Jerusalem and Judah, while Nehemiah identifies them as people from outside the province (e.g., Samaria). This distinction may be valid, but it is not directly relevant for this study. My argument is that the foreigners are excluded from the land regardless of who is defined as "foreign."[1] I will first discuss scholarly literature on the portrayal of land in the two passages. Then I will demonstrate how reading the two narratives together clarifies the concern for removing foreigners from the land, especially in Ezra 9–10 where it is often seen as a secondary theme if it is acknowledged at all.

---

1. For a further discussion of the difference in foreigners, see Becking, *Ezra-Nehemiah*, 170; Vogt, *Studie zur nachexilischen Gemeinde in Esra-Nehemia*, 45; Knoppers, "Nehemiah and Sanballat," 305–31; Williamson, *Ezra, Nehemiah*, 171–72.

Purifying the Land

CURRENT VIEWS OF LAND IN EZRA 9-10 AND NEH 1-3

Interpretations of Ezra 9-10 often consider community identity building[2] or maintaining economic wealth within the Jewish community.[3] Nehemiah 1-3 is often seen as maintaining social boundaries[4] or purifying the entire city of Jerusalem (with parallels to the temple building in Ezra).[5] These thematic elements are valuable in the interpretation of the passages, but I will argue that the theme of dwelling place and land is much more prominent than is normally assumed.

This counters the interpretation of Eskenazi, who claims that Ezra-Nehemiah is a series of three: building the temple, building the community, and building the wall (which essentially sanctifies the city like the temple

---

2. Wright claims that the wall is about Judah's renewed strength and internal unity and also ties this to marriage as disqualification because it breaks the internal unity. Wright, "Writing the Restoration," 27. See also Wright, "New Model for the Composition of Ezra-Nehemiah," 335, where he claims it is about "political disgrace and reproach of the province." See also Bertheau, *Bücher Esra, Nechemia und Ester*; Throntveit, *Ezra-Nehemiah*, 50–51; Clines, *Ezra, Nehemiah, Esther*, 116–17; Myers, *Ezra-Nehemiah*, 77; Rudolph, *Esra und Nehemía Samt 3. Esra*, 89; Williamson, *Ezra, Nehemiah*, 160–61; Ackroyd, *I & II Chronicles, Ezra, Nehemiah*, 261–63; Smith-Christopher, "Mixed Marriage Crisis in Ezra 9–10 and Nehemiah 13," 249; Janzen, "Sacrifice as Cultic Expression of the Law," 196; Redditt, *Ezra-Nehemiah*, 34; Esler, "Ezra-Nehemiah as a Narrative of (Re-Invented) Israelite Identity," 413–26; Moffat, *Ezra's Social Drama*; Goswell, *Study Commentary on Ezra-Nehemiah*, 166; Janzen, "Scholars, Witches, Ideologues, and What the Text Said," 61; Oswald, "Foreign Marriages and Citizenship in Persian Period Judah," 1–17; Johnson, "Ethnicity in Persian Yehud," 177–86; Rothenbusch, "Question of Mixed Marriages between the Poles of Diaspora and Homeland," 65.

3. Van Wyk and Breytenbach claim that separation is about material wealth staying with the returnees who were the elite. Van Wyk and Breytenbach, "Nature of the Conflict in Ezra-Nehemiah," 1260. Tollefson and Williamson discuss political and economic hegemony being challenged in Nehemiah. Tollefson and Williamson, "Nehemiah as Cultural Revitalization," 52; Johnson, *Holy Seed Has Been Defiled*, 87.

4. Grabbe claims that building the walls "seem more to keep outsiders from influencing the Jews than to protect the borders." Grabbe, "Law of Moses in the Ezra Tradition," 110. See also Esler, "Ezra-Nehemiah as a Narrative of (Re-Invented) Israelite Identity," 422; Wright, "New Model for the Composition of Ezra-Nehemiah," 334; Fried, "Who Wrote Ezra-Nehemiah—and Why Did They?," 113–56. A related view is that it was political and created a national identity. See Knauf, "Bethel," 291–349. Another related view is that it was economic. Lipschits, *Fall and Rise of Jerusalem*, 168–73.

5. Janzen, "Sacrifice as Cultic Expression of the Law," 187; Clauss, "Understanding the Mixed Marriages of Ezra-Nehemiah in the Light of Temple-Building and the Book's Concept of Jerusalem," 118–21; Harrington, "Holiness and Purity in Ezra-Nehemiah," 102–03; Goswell, *Study Commentary on Ezra-Nehemiah*, 198.

and the holy people).⁶ It also pushes against the view that Neh 1–3 is specifically about community separation and, at least conceptually and theologically, builds upon the community separation work of Ezra.⁷ Instead, the work of Ezra is removing the foreign influence from the land, and Nehemiah is building a wall to enforce this exclusivist land policy. Before I discuss my view, though, I will explore other interpretations of land in Ezra 9–10 and Neh 1–3.

Ezra 9–10

David Janzen lists three basic explanations for the expulsion of foreign women: first, the community is attempting to prevent apostasy; second, the community is defining its ethnic identity; and third, the community will receive economic or political benefits for removing the foreign wives.⁸ However, only the third option specifically addresses the land issue.

Harold Washington and Eskenazi claim that the community in Ezra 9–10 is concerned about land inheritance, and marrying foreign wives jeopardizes the land inheritance because women could inherit land.⁹ Berquist claims that land inheritance is part of the issue, but it is also wealth in general because marriage within the community centralizes the elite's control over both land and wealth (the elite being priests and leaders).¹⁰ However, wealth and land inheritance would be a more serious problem for

---

6. Eskenazi, *In an Age of Prose*, 40, 77–78; Eskenazi, "Structure of Ezra-Nehemiah and the Integrity of the Book," 652; Campbell, "Structure, Themes, and Theology in Ezra-Nehemiah," 402–5; Clauss, "Understanding the Mixed Marriages of Ezra-Nehemiah in the Light of Temple-Building and the Book's Concept of Jerusalem."

7. Grabbe, "Law of Moses in the Ezra Tradition," 110; Esler, "Ezra-Nehemiah as a Narrative of (Re-Invented) Israelite Identity," 422; Wright, "New Model for the Composition of Ezra-Nehemiah," 334; Fried, "Who Wrote Ezra-Nehemiah—and Why Did They?," 30; Sapolu, "Reconciling Identities," 113–56.

8. Janzen, "Scholars, Witches, Ideologues, and What the Text Said," 49; Janzen, *Witch-Hunts, Purity and Social Boundaries*, 10–19.

9. Washington, "Strange Woman (אשה זרה/נכריה) of Proverbs 1–9 and Post-Exilic Judean Society," 230–35; Eskenazi, "Out from the Shadows," 252–71; Kim, "Foreign Women," 249. Blenkinsopp believes that political and economic interests are present in Neh 6:18–19 and 13:28–29 but is less sure that this is the case in Ezra 9–10. Blenkinsopp, "Social Context of the 'Outsider Woman' in Proverbs 1–9," 472.

10. Berquist, *Judaism in Persia's Shadow*, 118–19. For a similar model, see Smith-Christopher, "Mixed Marriage Crisis in Ezra 9–10 and Nehemiah 13." For a critique of this view, see Southwood, *Ethnicity and the Mixed Marriage Crisis in Ezra 9–10*, 84–88.

Purifying the Land

daughters marrying foreign men because men inherit property, not women. In fact, the exceptions in the Pentateuch for women inheriting property are for daughters, not wives, so the foreign wives would not inherit property because it passes to their children (sons or daughters; cf. Num 27:8–11; Deut 25:5–7).[11]

Dumbrell claims that the end of Ezra is about a reconquest. He states that Ezra 9–10 explains to the golah community that "the sacred character of the promised land now titularly re-occupied Ezra's prayer of Ezra 9:6–15 encapsulates a review of the history of Israel with emphasis upon the loss of the land as a result of former disobedience and the necessity of separation from the Deuteronomic proscribed peoples if the land was to be retained."[12] So, he believes this is reason why the problem in Ezra is not portrayed as inter-Israelite marriage between the returnees and the "peoples of the land" but is directed against Israel's old wilderness and early conquest enemies.

Hoglund claims that intermarriage was an issue for the golah community because it weakened the material wealth of the community.[13] This is similar to the view of Washington, Eskenazi, and Berquist outlined above, with some of the same inheritance issues as noted above, but with a Persian twist. Instead of separation as an ideal solely of the golah community, Hoglund believes this was the Persian policy. The imperial administration desired to keep ethnic distinctions in order to maintain social groups that could be taxed and governed more efficiently.[14] So, this exclusionary act was in the best interest of the golah community and their Persian benefactors. The involvement of the Persian empire in the intermarriage policy of Ezra 9–10 is not stated in the text and so it is outside the scope of this analysis.[15] In addition, the endangerment of their wealth passing into foreign hands is

---

11. For a discussion of other ancient Near Eastern customs for inheritance that show widows were often allowed to live on their deceased husband's property even as the children received the inheritance see Janzen, *Witch-Hunts, Purity and Social Boundaries*, 16; Janzen, "Scholars, Witches, Ideologues, and What the Text Said," 56–58. For additional issues of the viewpoint, see Southwood, *Ethnicity and the Mixed Marriage Crisis in Ezra 9–10*, 78–80.

12. Dumbrell, "Theological Intention of Ezra-Nehemiah," 69.

13. Hoglund, "Achaemenid Context," 67. However, see some significant doubts about how wealthy or elite the golah community was based upon sociological models in Smith-Christopher, "Mixed Marriage Crisis in Ezra 9–10 and Nehemiah 13."

14. Hoglund, "Achaemenid Context," 65–68; Hoglund, *Achaemenid Imperial Administration in Syria-Palestine and the Missions of Ezra and Nehemiah*, 236–40.

15. For a critique of this view, see Southwood, *Ethnicity and the Mixed Marriage Crisis in Ezra 9–10*, 82–83.

a problematic interpretation, as noted above. The focus in the text is foreign women, not foreign men, so they are not addressing the group most likely to benefit from inherited wealth or property ownership.

A final interpretation of land in Ezra 9–10 is based upon the Citizen-Temple Community interpretation by Joel Weinberg.[16] Though Weinberg, and most following his example, analyzes the postexilic period broadly rather than specific passages in Ezra or Nehemiah, this method has been applied to Ezra 9–10. Weinberg focuses upon landholding temples in the Achaemenid period and interprets the postexilic biblical texts as indicating the temple in Jerusalem also held land at the time.[17] This was picked up by Blenkinsopp, who argues that the postexilic texts show the returnees wresting land from the peasantry that had remained in the land and also taking control of the temple, which was "the sociopolitical and religious center of gravity of their existence."[18] So, being excluded from the community for not reporting to the assembly in Ezra 10:8 involves a loss of civic privileges including access to the temple as well as its land, wealth, and political power.[19] This framework is interesting but too broad for a detailed analysis of Ezra 9–10 and Neh 1–3. The political and social developments in Judah and the relationship of the province to the temple or the Persian empire are not presented clearly in the biblical texts. In addition, this theory has come under scrutiny recently, and even Blenkinsopp admits that the biblical texts "are not designed to provide us with the information that we need."[20]

Daniel Smith offers a similar argument to Blenkinsopp, claiming that the golah community found their land occupied by others, and intermarriage was a way to join the aristocracy that had taken over during the exile and retrieve land ownership.[21] Smith's view is less focused upon the temple owning lands and slightly closer to my interpretation of Ezra 9–10 about private land holding in the community, though Smith does not cite the biblical text to support his argument.

16. Weinberg, *Citizen-Temple Community*.
17. Weinberg, *Citizen-Temple Community*, 103.
18. Blenkinsopp, "Temple and Society in Achaemenid Judah," 53.
19. Blenkinsopp, "Temple and Society in Achaemenid Judah," 29; Blidstein, "'Atimia," 357–60.
20. Blenkinsopp, "Temple and Society in Achaemenid Judah," 33; Bedford, "Economic Role of the Jerusalem Temple in Achaemenid Judah," 3–20; Cataldo, "Persian Policy and the Yehud Community during Nehemiah," 240–52.
21. Smith, "Politics of Ezra," 93–96.

Janzen argues against interpreting land ownership as the issue in Ezra 9–10. He claims that divorce without just cause would allow the women to seize control of the property and if the community desired to grow their land holdings, they would have encouraged men to marry foreign women so that they could receive land in the dowries.[22] However, several issues arise in this assertion. First, Janzen assumes the defilement of the foreign wives is not sufficient cause for divorce in the eyes of the Judean community. He derives this from old and neo-Babylonian law codes which primarily list infidelity as a just cause.[23] However, lacking an example of divorce because of inappropriate marital partners (whether ethnic or social standing disparities) does not mean that Babylonian sources did not contain these strictures.

Janzen's argument assumes that scholars have discovered enough law codes to provide a comprehensive list of proper reasons for divorce, which is unlikely even for the reign of one Babylonian king let alone for the entire ancient Near East. The necessity for the list to be comprehensive for the entire ancient Near East is based upon the use of sources that are separated by over a thousand years and over a thousand miles (Old Babylonian documents and Ezra-Nehemiah). Janzen is not using post-exilic Judean documents to examine Ezra-Nehemiah but attempting to make a claim to universal divorce laws in the ancient Near East.

This leads to the second assumption: the post-exilic community followed the same law codes as the Babylonians or viewed "just cause" for divorce the same way. Ideological and religious differences between Judeans and Babylonians are numerous. In addition, some of the laws Janzen is referencing come from the Old Babylonian period. Specifically, he references forfeiture of property in the laws of Eshnunna which was over one thousand years before Ezra-Nehemiah.[24]

In a separate argument, Janzen ties the post-exilic view to the Babylonian laws by way of first century Judaism.[25] Apparently, restrictions on divorce during the time of Jesus reflects the post-exilic community's views. However, Janzen himself notes that the schools of Shammai and Hillel have different lists of appropriate reasons for divorce.[26] So, besides the fact

22. Janzen, *Witch-Hunts, Purity and Social Boundaries*, 17–19.
23. Janzen, *Witch-Hunts, Purity and Social Boundaries*, 17–18.
24. Janzen, *Witch-Hunts, Purity and Social Boundaries*, 17.
25. Janzen, "Meaning of Porneia in Matthew 5.32 and 19.9," 66–80.
26. Janzen, "Meaning of Porneia in Matthew 5.32 and 19.9," 73–74.

that later Judaism does not necessarily reflect the Persian period Judean community, the overlap between Jewish views and Babylonian views are ambiguous at best.

The final point against Janzen's argument ties back to the first. If the defiling element of foreign wives is enough to warrant divorce, then it is likely that the Judean community would avoid inheriting property through these relationships. The exodus and conquest imagery throughout Ezra-Nehemiah would help to solidify this argument. The ancient Israelites were specifically told not to make agreements and trade with the people of the land. They were commanded to drive them off the land. The connections to Deut 7 in Ezra's prayer (Ezra 9:6–15) shows that the people are interpreting their current situation within this framework. So, it is not appropriate to gain property through marriage or any other contract with "foreign" people. The Judean community must remove the foreign influence from the land because they are polluting it. Intermarrying with the foreign women may gain land for the community but it would be polluted land. The only solution was to remove the foreign nations from the land to restore its purity and rightful possession by the Judean community. Janzen also notes this, saying, "God would one day return the people to the land and annul the claims of all others who lived there. . . . What this apparently implied, however, is that no one else should live there and that no one else should become part of the community that did."[27]

Neh 1–3

Though the text of Neh 1–3 is about building a physical wall, most interpreters use a social or holiness interpretation. Eskenazi, and many after, claimed that the wall around Jerusalem expanded the house of God to Jerusalem.[28] The narrative describes "rebuilding of the walls of Jerusalem by the descendants of returnees only, making the city a holy zone/area around the temple, thus protecting it from ritual and ethical contamination."[29] This holiness interpretation has a couple major challenges within the text.

---

27. Janzen, *Witch-Hunts, Purity and Social Boundaries*, 92.

28. Eskenazi, *In an Age of Prose*; Eskenazi, "Imagining the Other in the Construction of Judahite Identity in Ezra-Nehemiah," 235; Goswell, *Study Commentary on Ezra-Nehemiah*, 198. However, see arguments against this interpretation in Kraemer, "On the Relationship of the Books of Ezra and Nehemiah," 75.

29. Redditt, *Ezra-Nehemiah*, 35, 219.

Purifying the Land

First, Neh 1–3 does not reference holiness and impurity as issues directly. Though the city being burned and the people being a reproach might be indications of impurity or defilement, Nehemiah tells the adversaries that they have no portion in Jerusalem, not that they are defiling or polluting the city.[30] The second issue is that Neh 1–3 does not mention the temple at all. Even in the formulations for the house of God, it is called the "house of God which is in Jerusalem," not the house of God which is Jerusalem.[31] So, purifying the city to make it a holy space or equivalent to the temple is not explicit in the text and appears to go against the most straightforward reading in certain places.

A second interpretation, with slightly stronger ties to the land, is social symbolism. The wall has been interpreted as a symbol of God's people being separated from the foreign nations and, more significantly, is "a symbolic conquest of the land with the defeat of Israel's hostile neighbours."[32] This view appears to be more consistent with a clear reading of the text, since Nehemiah encounters, and overcomes, opposition at every stage of the building process (Neh 2:10, 19; 4:1–8).

This social symbolism focuses upon Nehemiah's adversaries and the symbolism of separation but does not adequately address Nehemiah's original intent. The defeat of hostile neighbors is more explicit in Ezra 9 where ancient people groups are cited from Deut 7 (vv.1–2) and intermarriage is equated with prosperity and inheritance (v. 12). The foreign people in Neh 1–3 also appear to live outside of Judah, the land which Nehemiah is claiming, so this would be different from the conquest theme of driving out nations to occupy the land. The main antagonists appear to be near the governors of the province beyond the River (2:10), and specifically Sanballat is in Samaria (4:1–8). These antagonists also have appellations that identify them with other regions near Judah not cities or regions within Judah itself.

If Nehemiah's primary goal was to overcome the Judeans' enemies, it is curious that he only references the city walls in his discussion with

---

30. In fact, the later encounter with removing foreigners from the city (Neh 13:15–22) is about defiling the sabbath. This again shows that Nehemiah is not excluding foreigners from the city or believing that they are inherently polluting or defiling it, as some commentators have claimed. This is unlike Ezra 9–10 where the text clearly claims that the people are being defiled and sinning by their interactions with foreigners (9:2, 11).

31. Kraemer, "On the Relationship of the Books of Ezra and Nehemiah," 75; VanderKam, "Ezra-Nehemiah or Ezra and Nehemiah?," 73.

32. Goswell, *Study Commentary on Ezra-Nehemiah*, 198, 217; Tollefson and Williamson, "Nehemiah as Cultural Revitalization."

Artaxerxes. Nehemiah's response to the adversaries in Neh 2:20 indicates that separation from the foreign people is part of his goal, but he specifically notes that they do not have a portion in Jerusalem. This is not an overarching exclusion from visiting the city (cf. 13:15–22) but a claim to ownership of the city. A symbolic conquering of enemies or symbolic separation from the foreign nations does not address the focus upon the city and land in the text.

EZRA 9–10 AND NEH 1–3: EXCLUSIVE DWELLING IN THE LAND

In this section, I will show the intertwined themes of land and community through each narrative segment of Ezra 9–10 and Neh 1–3. In each section, I will specifically treat how the authors relate the Judean community, exclusivity, and land ownership. My goal is to show that throughout the passages, the exclusionary tactics are broader than the wall around Jerusalem or intermarriage. They are, in fact, claiming ownership of the land of Judah and attempting to restore the land by separate non-community members from it. Reading both passages together clarifies some of the smaller, more ambiguous points but also shows how the two leaders utilize different strategies (wall building and community separation) to obtain a single goal: Judeans dwelling exclusively in the land.

Report of the Leaders

The report of the leaders in Ezra 9:1–2 frequently refers to the foreigners as "peoples of the lands." Luc Dequeker notes this particular term in Ezra-Nehemiah "refers to the non-Jewish population in the area and concerns the problem of segregation."[33] This is only an indirect focus on the land because it is used elsewhere, both singular and plural, as a reference to foreigners, or at least people considered outsiders in the narrative of the text (Ezra 3:3; 4:4; 9:11; 10:2, 11; Neh 9:10, 24, 30; 10:28, 30–31).[34] However,

---

33. Dequeker, "Nehemiah and the Restoration of the Temple after the Exile," 557–58.

34. See discussion of "foreigners" as non-exiled Judeans in Wright, "New Model for the Composition of Ezra-Nehemiah," 343; Leuchter, "Exegesis of Jeremiah in and beyond Ezra 9–10," 62–80; Usue, "Is the Expulsion of Women as Foreigners in Ezra 9–10 Justifiably Covenantal?," 158–69; Becking, *Ezra, Nehemiah, and the Construction of Early Jewish Identity*, 58–73; Moffat, *Ezra's Social Drama*, 77–79; Eskenazi and Judd, "Marriage

Purifying the Land

additional, more direct, indications of the leaders' concern for the land can be added to this indirect reference.

The leaders list nations that Israel was commanded to separate from during the exodus and conquest (Exod 34:11; Deut 7:1; 20:17). Though list of nations in Ezra 9:1 does not follow any of the lists in the Pentateuch passages verbatim, the overlap is significant enough to view these Pentateuch texts as the background even if they are not being quoted exactly.[35] In each of these passages, the list is about the entrance and possession of the land of Israel, specifically driving these groups out of the land.[36] Deuteronomy 7 mentions intermarriage, but that is only part of the separation command (covenants and goodwill towards them are also forbidden [vv. 3–4]).

The reference in Ezra 9:1 also uses broad language of "not separating themselves" (בדל) rather than exclusively marriage terminology.[37] As Ralf Rothenbusch notes, "בדל (Hiphil and Niphal) in this context means the conscious separation from foreign people (Ezra 6:21; Neh 9:2; 10:29; 13:3), which includes the separation or non-separation in mixed marriages (Ezra

to a Stranger in Ezra 9–10"; Japhet, *From the Rivers of Babylon to the Highlands of Judah*, 110–12; Saysell, *"According to the Law,"* 45–49. For the view that it is an internal dispute within the exile community, see van Wyk and Breytenbach, "Nature of the Conflict in Ezra-Nehemiah." Koch claims that the list in Ezra 9:1 shows Ezra was intending to rebuild the nation of Israel. He specifically points out that Samaritans are not included in the list and, he hypothesizes, this was because Ezra saw them as the northern tribes of Israel. Koch, "Ezra and the Origins of Judaism," 193–94.

Against this view, Myers claims that these are people who came into the land and took over after the exile. Myers, *Ezra-Nehemiah*, 77; Würthwein, *"'Amm Haàrez" im Alten Testament*, 51–71.

35. For a table comparing the list of nations in the passages, see Steinmann, *Ezra and Nehemiah*, 326; Dor, "Composition of the Episode of the Foreign Women in Ezra IX–X," 31; Blenkinsopp, "Trito-Isaiah (Isaiah 56–66) and the Gôlāh Group of Ezra, Shecaniah, and Nehemiah (Ezra 7–Nehemiah 13)," 666; Eskenazi, "Imagining the Other in the Construction of Judahite Identity in Ezra-Nehemiah," 245; Larson and Dahlen, *Ezra, Nehemiah, Esther*, 104; Thomas, *Ezra & Nehemiah*, 166; Allen and Laniak, *Ezra, Nehemiah, Esther*, 72; Clines, *Ezra, Nehemiah, Esther*, 119; Goswell, *Study Commentary on Ezra-Nehemiah*, 167–68; Saysell, *"According to the Law,"* 34–41.

36. Moffat, *Ezra's Social Drama*, 74; Van Wijk-Bos, *Ezra, Nehemiah, and Esther*, 40–41; Davies, *Ezra and Nehemiah*, 67.

37. Becking, *Ezra-Nehemiah*, 139; Janzen, "Scholars, Witches, Ideologues, and What the Text Said," 60. For a discussion of separation and the identity and definition of the Jewish people, see Grätz, "Second Temple and the Legal Status of the Torah," 275; Blenkinsopp, *Ezra-Nehemiah*, 195; Janzen, "Sacrifice as Cultic Expression of the Law," 195–96; Harrington, "Holiness and Purity in Ezra-Nehemiah," 112–15. Contra Eskenazi who claims that it does not condemn non-marital relationships. Eskenazi, "Imagining the Other in the Construction of Judahite Identity in Ezra-Nehemiah," 247.

9:1; 10:11)."[38] This term is used in Neh 13:3 to include multiple actions by Nehemiah, including foreign traders on the Sabbath and mixed marriage.[39] It is also used in multiple places in the Old Testament for a mixture of people living close together (Ezek 30:5; Jer 50:37).[40] So, this is not just intermarriage but intermixing with foreign people groups.

Some scholars have questioned why Ezra would use nations that likely did not exist in the post-exilic period and have hypothesized that the author was using traditional enemies to solidify the claim that the group was the true Israel who descended directly from the pre-exilic community of Israel.[41] However, the conceptual reference could also be to the ownership of the land. If the leaders are citing texts about the conquest of the promised land and using ambiguous terminology about "separating themselves from the peoples of the lands," then the exclusiveness of dwelling in the land must be a part of their concern.

Ezra 9:2 then claims that the people took daughters for themselves and their sons but, read with Deut 7, this is not synonymous with "not separating themselves."[42] Instead, this is a further elaboration on one way they have intermingled. The people are to remain separate in general (Deut 7:3; Ezra 9:1) and, even more, they are not to intermarry (Deut 7:4; Ezra 9:2). So, rather than undermining the focus on the land, this confirms that Ezra 9:1-2 is exegeting Deut 7. If the leaders are following Deut 7, then driving out foreign nations and taking possession of the land should also be a part of the theology (7:1). Olyan states, "alleged acts associated with aliens (e.g., 'idolatry', sexual offenses or other 'moral' violations) as practiced by aliens themselves and the Judeans with them threaten the purity of the land and even Israel's continued existence in a text such as Ezra 9:1-2, 10-12, 14."[43]

38. Rothenbusch, "Question of Mixed Marriages between the Poles of Diaspora and Homeland," 70.

39. Rothenbusch, "Question of Mixed Marriages between the Poles of Diaspora and Homeland," 70.

40. Rothenbusch, "Question of Mixed Marriages between the Poles of Diaspora and Homeland," 70. See also Southwood, *Ethnicity and the Mixed Marriage Crisis in Ezra 9-10*, 132-36.

41. Moffat, *Ezra's Social Drama*, 76; Gunneweg, *Esra*, 162.

42. Moffat claims that Ezra is most likely basing this list on Deuteronomy 7. Moffat, *Ezra's Social Drama*, 75. For a discussion of the differences between Ezra and Deuteronomy 7, specifically the fear of apostasy in Deuteronomy but not Ezra, see Conczorowski, "All the Same as Ezra?," 89-108. See also Southwood, *Ethnicity and the Mixed Marriage Crisis in Ezra 9-10*, 75-78.

43. Olyan, "Purity Ideology in Ezra-Nehemiah as a Tool to Reconstitute the

Purifying the Land

The leaders then claim that the "holy seed" has been defiled. N. S. Cezula connects the holy seed with the ideology of an empty land during the exile that the holy people would then inherit when they returned to it. So, the returnees must remain pure to maintain the purity of the land that they are inheriting (reclaiming).[44] This phrase, "holy seed," occurs in one other location, Isa 6:13. The Isaiah passage is about the devastation of the land and the cities (vv. 11–12).[45] Here again, the leaders appear to be focusing upon (re)possession of the land.

The phrase that the leaders use for the defilement of the holy seed is "intermingled with the peoples of the lands," which is another uncommon term for marriage. The word ערב can be interpreted "have fellowship with" or "be mixed up with."[46] Whether fellowship or mingling, the term does not normally refer to marriage. The concept of the "holy seed" need not be only a social or cultic boundary passed down genealogically. This idea of the holy people is present in Deut 7:6 as part of the command to possess the land and remove the other nations. So, if the holy seed is having fellowship with the other nations this does not need to be about building a holy community with ancestral ties but a community called by God to possess the holy land exclusively and drive away the other (unholy?) people groups.

Nehemiah 1:1–3 also focuses upon the land.[47] The leaders describe the state of Jerusalem in more detail than the state of the survivors, and

Community," 4; Usue, "Is the Expulsion of Women as Foreigners in Ezra 9–10 Justifiably Covenantal?," 163; Southwood, *Ethnicity and the Mixed Marriage Crisis in Ezra 9–10*, 210.

44. Cezula, "Concept of 'The Holy Seed' as a Coping Strategy in Ezra-Nehemiah and Its Implications for South Africa," 15–36.

45. Davies, *Ezra and Nehemiah*, 67. E. Allen Jones notes that the "holy seed" constitutes different post-exilic groups in the two texts. This further supports my argument that it is about dwelling in the land rather than genealogy. Jones, "Who Is the Holy Seed?," 515–34. Contra Steinmann, who claims this shows a messianic element in the two passages. Steinmann, *Ezra and Nehemiah*, 320.

46. BDB translates the term in Ezra 9:2 as "have fellowship with." Brown, Driver, and Briggs, "II. עָרַב," 786. HALOT defines the term in Ezra 9:2 as "to be mixed up with." Koehler and Baumgartner, "II ערב," 877. See also Steinmann, *Ezra and Nehemiah*, 323. Davies claims this is related to the mixed multitude in the exodus and the only place where it refers to intermarriage is Ps 106:35, where it references the exodus and people's sin in the land after the conquest. Davies, *Ezra and Nehemiah*, 67.

47. Laird discusses numerous literary parallels between Nehemiah's rebuilding of Jerusalem and the fall of Jericho in the book of Joshua. She claims the theological connection being made by these parallels is holy war. Laird, "Political Strategy in the Narrative of Ezra-Nehemiah," 279–83.

even the term they use for survivors is often connected to possession of the land in Ezra-Nehemiah. As Amzallag notes, פליטה (survivors) is used only once in Nehemiah (1:2) and refers to the people who survived the exile while staying in the land of Judah. Conversely the four occurrences in Ezra (9:8, 13–15) refer to the golah community. However, in both locations, the remnant or survivors are tied to the land: the "tent peg in the holy place" and the rebuilding of the temple and city in Ezra and the burned walls and gates of Jerusalem in Nehemiah.[48] Steinmann claims that this terminology reflects Isaiah's use of the term "remnant" and shows that Nehemiah and Hanani "understood the Judeans to be a fulfillment of Yahweh's prophecies through Isaiah that he would restore a remnant of his people to the land."[49]

Nehemiah asks about the people who escaped and survived the captivity and Jerusalem. When the leaders respond, they mention that the remnant are in great distress and reproach, but their description of Jerusalem is much more detailed. The walls are broken down and the gates are burned. The description of one as broken and the other as burned indicates that the city is a more critical plot point than the people in distress.[50] In addition, this description of the wall and gates being burned is repeat throughout the passage, highlighting the importance of this description (Neh 2:3, 13, 17). So, the leaders use two general terms for the state of the people but specific terms for the state of the city that are then repeated throughout the rest of Neh 1–2.[51]

The initial movements of Ezra 9 and Neh 1 have leaders speaking about issues in the land of Judah to the lead character. The leaders in Ezra 9 use language from the conquest, specifically Deut 7, and language about separation versus fellowship with the peoples of the lands. The leaders in Nehemiah describe the reproach of the remnant and describe the city as burned and broken down, and the latter will become a significant phrase repeated through the passage. These emphases on the land and the Judean

---

48. Amzallag, "Authorship of Ezra and Nehemiah in Light of Differences in Their Ideological Background," 274–75; Moffat, *Ezra's Social Drama*, 96–97.

49. Steinmann, *Ezra and Nehemiah*, 389.

50. The distress of the people and the state of the walls are not entirely separate issues. Frequently, the destruction of the land or the city results in the reproach of the people. So, even in this statement about the state of the remnant, a focus on the land might be present. See Kang, "Positive Role of Shame for Post-Exilic Returnees in Ezra/Nehemiah," 257–59.

51. Wright, *Rebuilding Identity*, 58.

Purifying the Land

people's relationship to it will be reinforced in the prayers of Nehemiah and Ezra.

Prayer

Ezra's prayer claims that sin is the cause of the people's suffering and warns that they are in danger of future destruction if they continue in their sin. The history of destruction culminates in captivity, plunder, and shame (9:7).[52] The grace shown to the people is the "tent peg in his holy place" (9:8). Besides the land imagery of the tent peg being rooted in the holy place, the initial punishment is about being removed from the land.[53] Even if the initial problem presented by the leaders is interpreted as maintaining social boundaries, Ezra's initial recounting of punishment and grace does not appear to be concerned with social boundaries as much as dwelling in the holy land (or being removed from the holy land). Janzen states that the "holy seed" dwells in the "holy place," and so when the foreign women are dwelling in the holy place, they are polluting it.[54] Steinmann claims, "Ezra is clearly stating that God has given his people a firmly established dwelling place: they have been allowed to reinhabit the promised land and live around the rebuilt temple, where God himself will dwell among them in his grace."[55]

McConville believes the "holy place" where the tent peg is placed is Jerusalem, but this does not fit with the imagery of the prayer nor the audience.[56] As Goswell notes, "the phrase 'in his holy place' is balanced by the

---

52. Moffat notes the background of Josh 7 and other Deuteronomic passages used in the prayer. Moffat, *Ezra's Social Drama*, 90–91; Pakkala, "Exile and the Exiles in the Ezra Tradition," 95; Van Grol, "Schuld und Scham," 29–52.

53. For the nomadic practice of staking a land claim, see Fensham, *Books of Ezra and Nehemiah*, 130; Williamson, *Ezra, Nehemiah*, 135; Blenkinsopp, *Ezra-Nehemiah*, 183–84; Musil, *Manners and Customs of the Rwala Bedouins*. In a more metaphorical interpretation, Moffat claims, "All that the community has—its existence as a remnant, its life and presence in Jerusalem and Yehud, its rebuilt temple and its protection—are the result of Yahweh's past mercy." Moffat, "Metaphor at Stake in Ezra 9:8," 298.

54. Janzen, "Scholars, Witches, Ideologues, and What the Text Said," 61.

55. Steinmann, *Ezra and Nehemiah*, 336; Blenkinsopp, *Ezra-Nehemiah*, 183–84; Breneman, *Ezra, Nehemiah, Esther*, 153.

56. McConville, "Ezra-Nehemiah and the Fulfilment of Prophecy," 215; Myers, *Ezra-Nehemiah*, 79. Janzen states that it could refer to both the temple and the city of Jerusalem. Janzen, "Sacrifice as Cultic Expression of the Law," 194. See also Moffat's discussion with the conclusion that the holy place is at least Jerusalem and potentially Judah. Moffat,

expression 'in Judea and Jerusalem.'"⁵⁷ The verse immediately following "the peg in his holy place" refers to a wall around all of Judah, not just the city of Jerusalem (9:9). In addition, the people of Israel are the ones sinning (9:1), not just those in Jerusalem, and the people throughout Judah and Benjamin are gathered in the assembly later in the passage (10:9). Undoubtedly, these people live in other cities, so it is unclear why Ezra would only refer to the people being rooted in Jerusalem alone. The Deuteronomic use of "holy place" could imply Jerusalem as the central authority in the land, but the holy place must be broader than that as well since the concern is clearly for all the people in Judah not just those in Jerusalem.

"Holy place" can signify more than just the temple or Jerusalem, especially in postexilic texts. J. Gamberoni notes that in later biblical texts,

> the term *māqôm* hovers with a certain ambiguity between the Jerusalem temple, Topheth, the city, and the land.... This can hardly be viewed as merely the unintentional result of literary development; rather, later readers, in the shadow of the great catastrophe, expanded to all of Israel the threats which ... had only been directed at the temple.⁵⁸

Therefore, it is more likely that this holy land encompasses the areas that the Judeans are living in (perhaps even the entire promised land given the Deuteronomy quotes in this chapter). So, at a minimum, the holy place should include the cities or towns where the people who gather in chapter ten reside.

The next section of Ezra's prayer claims that God allowed the people to restore the temple and gave them a wall in Judah and Jerusalem.⁵⁹ This last phrase has caused discussion among scholars about whether Ezra 9–10 occurred after Nehemiah's wall-building.⁶⁰ Other scholars have noted that the term for "wall" is not the common one used for Nehemiah's wall, so it

---

Ezra's Social Drama, 98–101.

57. Goswell, *Study Commentary on Ezra-Nehemiah*, 174, 194.

58. Gamberoni, "מָקוֹם (Māqôm)," 542. See also, the use of Jerusalem to represent the people or the state in Tsevat, "יְרוּשָׁלַם (Yerûšālēm/Yerûšālayim)," 349.

59. Goswell claims that both the peg and the wall are metaphors of security that refer to the rebuilt temple. However, he does not clarify how the wall surrounding Judah can indicate the physical temple. Goswell, *Study Commentary on Ezra-Nehemiah*, 174.

60. For the argument that the wall is literal, see Emerton, "Review of Studie zur nachexilischen Gemeinde in Esra-Nehemia," 169–75; Snaith, "Date of Ezra's Arrival in Jerusalem," 58; Fernández, "Esdr. 9,9 y Un Texto de Josefo," 207–8.

Purifying the Land

should be interpreted metaphorically.[61] Some understand this to be a symbolic wall of protection for the community, usually understood as provided by the Persian empire, though occasionally by Yahweh because the term for wall can be a vineyard enclosure leading to the metaphor of Israel as the vine that Yahweh protects.[62]

The use of the term "wall" does not appear to be literal or a reference to Nehemiah's wall. Besides the terminology, גדר instead of the more common חומה, the phrase is "a wall in Judah and Jerusalem." If it was a reference to a physical wall, or specifically Nehemiah's wall, the inclusion of the entire region is hard to understand.[63] On the other hand, if this phrase is about community separation, then the reference to restoring the house of God is also difficult to understand. The description is detailed enough to indicate that raising the house of God and restoring its ruins is a reference to the physical temple, not a metaphorical dwelling. In addition, the book of Ezra places the rebuilding of the temple before Ezra's arrival (6; 8:30–36).[64] A direct reference to the physical city wall does not seem to be the intention, but the description of restoring the ruins of the temple does not appear to be a broad metaphor for community exclusion either.[65]

A more likely interpretation uses both the physical and metaphorical angles and fits with the tent peg of the previous verse. Ezra's statement that God gave them a tent peg in the holy place is a reversal of the captivity and plunder. So, the people are once again rooted in the land of Israel, the holy land. Ezra then describes how, though their stake in the holy place still leaves them in bondage to foreign powers, the foreign kings have given them a place of their own. The Judeans have been able to build a physical temple and have a wall around the province. The wall around Judah and Jerusalem separates the land. The land of Judah, though a province of Persia,

---

61. Becking, *Ezra-Nehemiah*, 149. A metaphorical interpretation of the wall is argued by Williamson, *Ezra, Nehemiah*, 136; Moffat, "Metaphor at Stake in Ezra 9:8," 291; Clines, *Ezra, Nehemiah, Esther*, 124.

62. Yamauchi, "Reverse Order of Ezra/Nehemiah Reconsidered," 11; Brockington, *Ezra, Nehemiah and Esther*, 32; Clines, *Ezra, Nehemiah, Esther*, 124; Myers, *Ezra-Nehemiah*, 75; Steinmann, *Ezra and Nehemiah*, 339.

63. Schoville, *Ezra-Nehemiah*, 123.

64. The exact historical order of events is irrelevant. The point I am making is that the text portrays the temple as being complete before Ezra's arrival, regardless of whether the events happened in this order.

65. Duggan claims that the stake is a reference to the tent peg of the tabernacle and the wall is used for temple precinct partitions but is symbolic of Persian protection for the community. Duggan, "Ezra 9:6–15," 178.

is once again the land of the Judeans with Jerusalem as its capital. They have restored their physical center of worship, the temple, and reclaimed their physical land, Judah and Jerusalem. Even though there is not a literal wall around the province, the idea of a wall around the land indicates that they are once again in possession of the holy land.[66]

The next section of Ezra's prayer returns to the concept of the conquest that was referenced by the leaders at the beginning of Ezra 9.[67] The command that Ezra references is about entering to possess the land and specifically how the peoples of the lands have filled the land with impurity. Christl Maier explains that the impure land contrasts the holy seed so removing the foreign people from the land and settling the holy seed upon it would purify the land.[68] Rothenbusch states, "Since the possession of the country is in danger, the Israelites should not strive for the well-being of these nations. Instead, the Israelites should strive to keep the country for themselves and their offspring."[69] This defilement of the land leads directly into the command not to intermarry with the phrase "and now do not give your daughters" (Ezra 9:12). As Zlotnick-Sivan claims, "Ezra's marital ideology strives, then, to undermine the role of women as potential mediators of peace and prosperity."[70] Eskenazi even argues that the term for uncleanness, נדה, in verse 11 refers to both the women and the land and so ties the two together.[71] Just like Deut 7, Ezra broadens the issue to seeking the peace and prosperity of the people, even though intermarriage is highlighted for special attention. Ezra also claims that the reward for this separation is receiving the land as an inheritance.

The main sections of Ezra's prayer center around land imagery and inheritance. Ezra describes the tent peg that the people have been provided in the land after formerly being removed from it. He then explains how they have been able to restore the ruins of the temple and build a wall around the province of Judah and its capital, Jerusalem.[72] Finally, avoiding marriage,

---

66. Larson and Dahlen, *Ezra, Nehemiah, Esther*, 107.

67. See the list of Pentateuch references in verses 11–12 in Steinmann, *Ezra and Nehemiah*, 340; Schoville, *Ezra-Nehemiah*, 123.

68. Maier, "'Foreign' Women in Ezra-Nehemiah," 87.

69. Rothenbusch, "Question of Mixed Marriages between the Poles of Diaspora and Homeland," 68.

70. Zlotnick-Sivan, "Silent Women of Yehud," 9.

71. Eskenazi, "Imagining the Other in the Construction of Judahite Identity in Ezra-Nehemiah," 250.

72. Van Grol claims these terms come from Isaiah and posits that the prayer might

Purifying the Land

peace, and prosperity with foreigners is rewarded with land inheritance for the Judeans.

Nehemiah 1 contains a prayer recounting the history of Israel's unfaithfulness as well. Nehemiah begins his prayer by claiming that the people have sinned and received the punishment promised by Moses.[73] This punishment is for the people to be scattered among the peoples but, if they return to God, they can be brought back to the promised land (1:8–9).[74]

Interestingly, Nehemiah does not use the term "land" but "the place where I [God] chose my name to dwell" (v. 9).[75] This creates a parallel with Ezra's claim of a tent peg in God's holy place (Ezra 9:8). These are most likely references to the same area: the land of Judah. As Williamson states, "Implicit in the promise is a restoration; a return 'to the place which [God had] chosen as a dwelling place for [his] Name' implies the Divine Presence dwelling with the restored community."[76] So, Nehemiah is not just referring to a return to Jerusalem but the people returning and dwelling in the land in God's presence. Ezra claims the escaped remnant has been given the tent peg, which likely indicates a dwelling place for the people, and Nehemiah claims that God scattered the people and now may bring them back to the dwelling place. As Goswell notes, the language of Neh 1:10 interprets the return from exile as a second exodus.[77] This, then, would exclude the temple as the primary object because the people would not live (or "settle" to use the exodus and conquest phrase) in the temple itself. It also is broader than the city of Jerusalem because "the sons of Israel" (Neh 1:6) did not live

---

also make an allusion to Ezekiel 36:32. Van Grol, "Exegesis of the Exile-Exegesis of Scripture?," 69; Goswell, *Study Commentary on Ezra-Nehemiah*, 172.

73. Donald Polaski notes Deuteronomy chapters 7, 12, and 30 are the background for the language of the prayer. Polaski, "Nehemiah," 41; Van Wijk-Bos, *Ezra, Nehemiah, and Esther*, 51–52; Boice, *Nehemiah*, 19; Clines, *Ezra, Nehemiah, Esther*, 138; Steinmann, *Ezra and Nehemiah*, 393.

74. Kim notes that both prayers reference Deut 7 specifically. Kim, "Historiographic Characteristics of Ezra-Nehemiah," 118–19. Manfred Oeming claims that observing the Torah and gathering the people to Judah are the basis of the prayer and a blueprint to the entire book of Nehemiah. Oeming, "Real History," 140. See also Larson and Dahlen, *Ezra, Nehemiah, Esther*, 134.

75. Burns claims that this phrase is not just a reference to Judah but to Jerusalem specifically. Burns, *Ezra, Nehemiah*, 51; Van Wijk-Bos, *Ezra, Nehemiah, and Esther*, 52; Allen and Laniak, *Ezra, Nehemiah, Esther*, 90; Clines, *Ezra, Nehemiah, Esther*, 139.

76. Williamson, *Ezra, Nehemiah*, 173.

77. Goswell, *Study Commentary on Ezra-Nehemiah*, 207.

Separation of the People, Separation of the Land

only in Jerusalem and, in the parallel passage, Ezra claims they built a wall around the entire province of Judah (Ezra 9:9).

The final piece to understanding the two prayers is their connections to the preceding conversations of the leaders with the prominent characters.[78] Scholars have noted the disconnect between these prayers and the narrative sections that precede them because Ezra only briefly mentions the issue of intermarriage (9:12, 14) and Nehemiah does not explicitly mention the wall or the city of Jerusalem.[79] However, observing the land motif in each prayer can clarify the relationship to the previous conversation with the leaders, especially in Ezra 9.

The leaders in Ezra 9:1-2 claim that the people have mixed with the peoples of the land and, even worse, intermarried with them. This is breaking the command to possess the land, drive out foreigners, and avoid making covenants or seeking their welfare (Deut 7).[80] Ezra responds by referring to the command to possess the land and remove the impurity of the other nations (Ezra 9:11-12). In the same way that the leaders complained of fellowship broadly while highlighting intermarriage, Ezra cites the command not to seek peace or prosperity of the peoples of the lands while also highlighting intermarriage (v. 12). All these activities risk losing the inheritance and good things of the land that God promised and are rooted in the commands given for the conquest and settlement in the Pentateuch.

The lexical connection between Nehemiah's prayer and the leaders' assessment of Judah is weaker than Ezra 9. It is especially challenging because the leaders are describing the current poor state of the people and walls of Jerusalem, but Nehemiah prays that God will gather the people from among the nations.[81] However, the parallel prayer of Ezra with an emphasis on possessing the land and driving out the foreign nations helps to elucidate the connection. Bringing the people to the place where God has chosen to dwell is only partially completed (Neh 1:9). They have arrived in the land but are still a reproach and the city is still in disarray. The phrase

---

78. See the discussion of lexical overlap between the leaders' speech, Ezra's prayer, and Deuteronomy in Duggan, "Ezra 9:6-15," 171-75.

79. Blenkinsopp, "Nehemiah Autobiographical Memoir," 135.

80. Allen and Laniak note that both the leaders' speech and Ezra's prayer rely upon Deuteronomy 7 and 23. Allen and Laniak, *Ezra, Nehemiah, Esther*, 73; Davies, *Ezra and Nehemiah*, 67.

81. For a connection between Nehemiah's prayer and Deuteronomy 7, see Baltzer, "Moses Servant of God and the Servants," 124-25. This is also connected to the leaders' speech in Ezra 9.

"the place where God chooses to make his name dwell" occurs multiple times in Deuteronomy and specifically in connection with the possession of the land.[82] For example, Deut 12 commands that the people observe the statutes of the law when they arrive in the land so that they will possess it forever (v. 1). It then commands them to destroy the cultic areas of the foreign nations who they are driving out of the land and serve God at the place that he will choose to make his name dwell (vv. 2–5). So, the importance of God gathering them to the land is not just a return migration but a full possession of the land like the conquest and part of this possession is the removal of foreign and pagan influences.

Ezra's citation of the Pentateuch clearly connects removing foreign influence with possession and inheritance of the land. Nehemiah's prayer connects these themes but indirectly. The people sinned and were scattered among the nations. Some Judeans are living in the land but have not fully taken possession of it. This is shown by the description of the bad situation of the people and city by the leaders and Nehemiah's subsequent plea for the people to be remembered and God to gather them to his place in language reminiscent of Deuteronomic passages about taking possession of the land and removing foreign nations. Smith details the references to Deuteronomy in the prayers of Ezra and Nehemiah and concludes that they are applying the Deuteronomic theology of hope and possession of the land when following God's covenant but destruction and exile when breaking the covenant.[83]

Proposal Speech

The next section in each text is the proposed solution to the problem (Nehemiah to Artaxerxes and Shecaniah to Ezra). Shecaniah responds to Ezra's prayer stating, "We have been unfaithful to our God and married foreign women from the peoples of the land" (Ezra 10:2). This is normally interpreted as two synonymous phrases where the unfaithfulness to God is identical to, or perhaps through the actions of, marrying foreign wives. However, if this pattern matches Ezra's prayer and the speech of the leaders, it is actually two separate issues. Shecaniah is stating that the people have been unfaithful generally. That is, "the holy seed has intermixed" or they

---

82. For a list of occurrences see Steinmann, *Ezra and Nehemiah*, 385.

83. Smith, "Influence of Deuteronomy on Intercessory Prayers in Ezra and Nehemiah."

have "sought the peace or prosperity" of the peoples of the land (9:2, 12). The people have also been unfaithful specifically in taking foreign wives as the leaders and Ezra have also asserted (9:1, 12). Shecaniah's covenant primarily addresses this second issue by proposing a covenant to put away their foreign wives and children.

Some scholars have noted that in Ezra 10:2–3, the terms for marriage (ישׁב) and sending away (יצא) are not the normal terms for marriage and divorce.[84] They have used this to claim that the people did not actually marry foreign wives (or at least not a legitimate marriage in the eyes of the author of Ezra) or that they did not officially divorce the foreign women but sent them away in some other way.[85] However, as Philip Brown has noted, Neh 13:23 and 27 use the same term for marriage and connect it with Solomon's marriages. He also notes that Ezra uses the more common term in his prayer (Ezra 9:14).[86] Finally, sending the wives away must mean divorce in some way, even though it is not the common term because they are being separated and sent out from the community.[87]

I agree with Brown that the text is clearly indicating marriages to women outside of the golah community, but it also indicates a broader issue of intermixing with the people of the land. As Janzen notes:

> This is why ch. 10 uses *yšb* in the hiphil in order to refer to the breach of this law: Israel has "caused foreign women to dwell" in the place where the people do not belong (10:2, 14, 17, 18). This improper geographic placement of foreigners within Israel is emphasized by the repeated use in ch 10 of terms that refer to the particular exilic descent of Israel. . . . The geographic borders of

---

84. Janzen, "Scholars, Witches, Ideologues, and What the Text Said," 60; Schoville, *Ezra-Nehemiah*, 126; Moffat, *Ezra's Social Drama*, 109–10; Goswell, *Study Commentary on Ezra-Nehemiah*, 180–81. Heth and Wenham, *Jesus and Divorce*, 163; Rawlinson, *Ezra and Nehemiah*, 42; Fensham, *Books of Ezra and Nehemiah*, 135. In addition to the illegality of such marriages and the nonstandard terminology used to describe them, MacLeod argues that "it is hard to understand how the Israelites could make a covenant with God to divorce the pagan women if marriage is a covenant made between a man and a woman in the presence of God." MacLeod, "Problem of Divorce, Part 2," 34–35. Williamson appears to agree with MacLeod but does not come to a definite conclusion. Williamson, *Ezra, Nehemiah*, 150.

85. Thomas suggests that the people might not have been legitimately married. Thomas, *Ezra & Nehemiah*, 184.

86. Brown, "Problem of Mixed Marriages in Ezra 9–10," 456.

87. Brown, "Problem of Mixed Marriages in Ezra 9–10," 457.

Purifying the Land

Israel, in short, have been breached through this illicit act of causing impure foreigners to dwell in the land.[88]

The broader issue of separation, and removal of foreigners, will become clearer in Ezra 10:11.

Artaxerxes questions Nehemiah in recorded speech in this section. The land theme is presented in Nehemiah's speech as he identifies his concern for the city of his fathers' tombs (Neh 2:3, 5).[89] Interestingly, Nehemiah never names Jerusalem but identifies his desire to go to Judah twice (vv. 5, 7).[90] He also uses similar phrasing to describe the burned gates of the city as the leaders' speech (1:3; 2:3).[91]

The important point for this study is Nehemiah's connection to the land. Nehemiah does not claim that he is sad because the people are in great distress and a reproach. He cites the second half of the leaders' speech that the city is desolate and its walls are burned with fire (2:3). Though there is a connection between the state of the city and the state of the people, which will be noted in the next section, Nehemiah does not refer to the people in this conversation. It is even more surprising that Nehemiah is concerned for the state of the land when he does not live in it. If Nehemiah was attempting to make a personal emotional appeal to the king, it would be more logical to claim that his relatives were suffering in the land rather than the walls of the city being in ruins. This is especially true when rebuilding the city walls could be seen as an act of rebellion or military aggression as the adversaries assert multiple times in Ezra-Nehemiah (Ezra 4:11–24; Neh 2:19; 6:6–7).

---

88. Janzen, "Cries of Jerusalem," 128.

89. Some scholars have interpreted this as a Davidic claim, but most reject that assertion or at least admit that the book of Nehemiah does not clearly assert this anywhere. For claims that the passage indicates Davidic lineage, see Kellermann, *Nehemia*, 156–59; Williamson, *Ezra, Nehemiah*, 179. For arguments against the passage indicating Davidic lineage, see Goswell, *Study Commentary on Ezra-Nehemiah*, 213; Becking, *Ezra-Nehemiah*, 181; Williamson, *Ezra, Nehemiah*, 179.

90. Goswell claims Jerusalem was not named because Nehemiah was trying to gain sympathy with the king by couching his request in personal terms. Goswell, *Study Commentary on Ezra-Nehemiah*, 213. Van Wijk-Bos claims a similar view as Goswell but then claims no one was fooled about what city he was referring to, least of all Artaxerxes. Van Wijk-Bos, *Ezra, Nehemiah, and Esther*, 55; Larson and Dahlen, *Ezra, Nehemiah, Esther*, 145. Steinmann claims this is to allow the king to save face when he reverses his previous decision to stop the rebuilding. Steinmann, *Ezra and Nehemiah*, 400.

91. Goswell, *Study Commentary on Ezra-Nehemiah*, 214; Steinmann, *Ezra and Nehemiah*, 400.

Separation of the People, Separation of the Land

So, Nehemiah is clearly concerned about the land to the point that the Judean people are not even mentioned. His definition of it as the place of his fathers' tombs identifies which people have a historic claim to, and interest in, the land. This is his ancestral home, and so he is connecting his genealogy, as a Judean, with the geographic location, Jerusalem and Judah. As will be shown in the next section, rebuilding the city and Judah will remove the reproach of the people, but the focus is upon improving and setting the boundaries for the place where the Judeans dwell.

In this section, both Shecaniah and Nehemiah address problems for the community of Judeans in the land of Judah. Shecaniah discusses intermixing with the people of the land and proposes sending away foreign wives from the dwellings of the Judeans. Nehemiah explains his desire to rebuild the city and province of his ancestors. Both passages are concerned with the connection between the restoration of the community and the restoration of the land.

Movement

The next section in both passages is the movement of the prominent character. Ezra moves to the chamber of Jehohanan and sends out a proclamation to assemble in Jerusalem. The warning of the proclamation is significant because those who fail to assemble will not only lose their membership in the community but also their possessions (Ezra 10:8). Johnson notes that marriage solidified political ties and came with gifts of land and other valuables. So this banishment, and the entire marriage conflict, could be a way for the Judahite elite ("sons of the exile") to maintain control over the property and land that was given to them by the Persian king.[92] Regardless of the motive behind the forfeiture warning, the threat ties the physical aspect of the community with the social aspect. Ezra's threat is not just about the community membership but the homes and possessions of the people. In this way, a person's removal from the community is also a physical separation from their property.[93]

Nehemiah also connects the community to the land when he delivers letters for supplies to build the wall of Jerusalem but encounters resistance

---

92. Johnson, *Holy Seed Has Been Defiled*, 52–54.

93. For a discussion of what political and property ownership changes may have been involved in this banishment, see Blidstein, "'Atimia." For the concept of herem, see Nelson, "Herem and the Deuteronomic Social Conscience," 39–54.

from Sanballat and Tobiah (Neh 2:8–10). The anger of Sanballat and Tobiah is not incited by Nehemiah rebuilding the city of Jerusalem but his seeking the welfare of the people. This again is connecting the community to the land and, in this section, showing that the rebuilding of the city is rebuilding the community. Nehemiah has only addressed the physical issues of the city of Jerusalem in his conversation with Artaxerxes and the letters he delivered for supplies. However, Sanballat and Tobiah are clearly connecting rebuilding the city with the welfare of the community.

The connection between the community and the land is made in the movement section of each passage. The state of the land changes the state of the Judean people in Nehemiah (inciting the anger of Sanballat and Tobiah). The relationship of a person to the community in Ezra changes the relationship of the person to their property (specifically forfeiting their property when they are removed from the community).

Assessment and Action

The two major narrative movements are reversed in this section in Ezra and Nehemiah, but the main theme is found within the plan of action (and conflict) section. Ezra's speech declares to the people, "You have been unfaithful and have married foreign wives . . . separate yourselves from the peoples of the land and from the foreign wives" (Ezra 10:10–11). The first phrase could be equating the unfaithfulness with intermarriage ("you have been unfaithful which is/by marrying foreign wives").[94] However, separate statements for the unfaithfulness and intermarriage happen in both the assessment of the problem and the solution in Ezra's speech. Whereas Shecaniah mentioned unfaithfulness and marrying foreign wives but only proposed separating from foreign wives, Ezra uses the same phrase to describe the situation but proposes solutions to both issues: separating from the peoples of the land and from foreign wives (Ezra 10:2–3, 10–11).[95] This clarifies that unfaithfulness and marrying foreign wives are separate, though overlapping, issues. So, Ezra's concern for intermarriage and mixture with the people aligns with Ezra 9:2 and 12, where both the mixture of Israel with the people of the land and intermarriage are described. As Steinmann

---

94. As argued by Goswell, *Study Commentary on Ezra-Nehemiah*, 186; Moffat, *Ezra's Social Drama*, 121; Batten, *Critical and Exegetical Commentary on the Books of Ezra and Nehemiah*, 344.

95. Schoville, *Ezra-Nehemiah*, 130.

notes, "Ezra first stated 'from the peoples of the land' before 'from your foreign wives.' This order of phrases emphasizes that the primary purpose was to keep Israel separate . . . and this primary concern required the divorce of foreign wives."[96] So, this is a two-part command: separate from the foreign people and from foreign wives.

Besides, being linked with previous passages in Ezra 9 concerned with separation of the land and inheritance (cf. 9:12), the wording in Ezra 10:11 indicates that it is not primarily divorce but removal from the holy land that is in view.[97] Ezra uses the same term as the leaders in Ezra 9:1, בדל "separate." Even more importantly, this word is used in Ezra 10:8 where the person who failed to assemble in Jerusalem would be excluded from the community and forfeit their property. Obviously, the separation of those who failed to assemble in Jerusalem is not "divorce" and so in Ezra 10:11, the term should be interpreted as broader than divorce. The separation from foreign wives is likely divorce or at least removal from the home, but when the phrase includes the separation from "the peoples of the land," it must be removal from the community more broadly.[98]

However, unlike some interpretations, this should not be viewed as strictly social separation. The threat of separation in 10:8 included forfeiture of property. Clines argued it was only movable property but Moffat's argument that חרם usually implies broader, more complete forfeiture or destruction is convincing.[99] As Saysell explains, this is a complete disenfranchisement of the individuals and essentially their "death" in the eyes of the community.[100] When Ezra prayed before the people, he told them the necessity of separation was so that "you may be strong and eat the good things of the land and leave an inheritance to your sons forever" (9:12).

---

96. Steinmann, *Ezra and Nehemiah*, 359.

97. The same call for confession is found in Josh 7:19. Davies, *Ezra and Nehemiah*, 68; Goswell, *Study Commentary on Ezra-Nehemiah*, 188. Compare this Joshua reference with the connections between Josh 6 and Neh 1–3 in Laird, "Political Strategy in the Narrative of Ezra-Nehemiah," 279–83. For more general comparisons to Josh 1–11, see Goswell, *Study Commentary on Ezra-Nehemiah*, 217; Porten, "Restoration of a Holy Nation (445 B.C.E.)," 131. Contra Steinmann who claims that their actions implicitly render praise to God so it should be translated "praise" not "confession." Steinmann, *Ezra and Nehemiah*, 359.

98. See Goswell's discussion of this term as exclusion from the holy community of Israel and consignment to judgment. Goswell, *Study Commentary on Ezra-Nehemiah*, 187–88; Moffat, *Ezra's Social Drama*, 72.

99. Moffat, *Ezra's Social Drama*, 117; Clines, *Ezra, Nehemiah, Esther*, 129.

100. Saysell, "According to the Law," 78–79.

Purifying the Land

Since the other passages on separation focus upon inheritance and possessions in the land, Ezra 10:11 should also be interpreted as more than a social community issue alone.

The response of the people to Ezra's speech also indicates that more is occurring than simply divorcing foreign wives, even though that is a central activity. The counterproposal of the people contains two actions and involves four groups of people. First, the leaders (שׂר) stand for the assembly. Then the people who married foreign wives and the elders and judges of the cities come at the appointed times. The leaders (or princes) are representative of the community, and they are the ones investigating the issue (Ezra 10:16). However, the elders and judges are not said to investigate or represent the assembly at large.[101] Perhaps the elders and judges of the cities represent the commerce or general separation commitment of their respective cities. They are arriving along with the intermarried people, and they are identified by their cities. In this reading, the people who have intermarried arrive before the leaders to resolve the marriage issue, while the elders and judges of the cities come before the leaders to address the more general fellowship with the peoples of the land for their respective cities.

Nehemiah's concern for the separation of the land confirms this reading. Nehemiah's initial proposal to the leaders of the Judeans to rebuild the walls shows his concern for the city of Jerusalem and the people to stop being a reproach (Neh 2:17). However, his concern for removing foreign claims over the city is made clear in the interaction with the adversaries (v. 20). In his initial speech to the Judean leaders, Nehemiah describes the city wall in language reminiscent of the leaders in Neh 1:2 and his dialogue with the king (2:3). In Neh 2:17, however, the burned state of the walls is directly connected to the state of the people as a reproach.[102] The adversaries already appeared to connect the rebuilding of the wall with the prosperity of the Judeans, and perhaps their loss of prosperity, in Neh 2:10. Immediately after Nehemiah's conversation with the Judean leaders, the adversaries

---

101. Dor notes that the activities of the judges and elders in this verse are unclear. Dor, "Composition of the Episode of the Foreign Women in Ezra IX–X," 38. Larson and Dahlen claim that the elders and judges help the commission by testifying about those under investigation. Larson and Dahlen, *Ezra, Nehemiah, Esther*, 119. Allen and Laniak claim that the commission met with local officials who accompanied the accused men. Allen and Laniak, *Ezra, Nehemiah, Esther*, 81; Moffat, *Ezra's Social Drama*, 122; Clines, *Ezra, Nehemiah, Esther*, 130; Williamson, *Ezra, Nehemiah*, 155.

102. Becking, *Ezra-Nehemiah*, 189; Myers, *Ezra-Nehemiah*, 105; Steinmann, *Ezra and Nehemiah*, 410.

question the lawfulness of Nehemiah's actions, but his response indicates deeper implications of their words: they desired to join the rebuilding or at least make a claim of ownership in Jerusalem.

The adversaries mocked and despised the Judeans but then asked what they were doing and if they were rebelling against the king. Nehemiah's response does not address the king nor define what the people were doing. It is likely that the adversaries already knew the rebuilding of the city was sanctioned by the king. Nehemiah had delivered letters for passage and supplies earlier and two of the adversaries heard about it at that time (Neh 2:8-10).[103]

Initially, the displeasure of the adversaries in verse 10 and their mocking and despising in verse 19 would imply that they were attempting to thwart the rebuilding, but Nehemiah's response undermines this simplistic reading. He begins by stating that God will give them success, implying that the adversaries did not believe they would succeed or were attempting to stop them from succeeding (2:20). However, he then claims that the adversaries have no portion, right, or memorial in Jerusalem. Nehemiah is not rebuilding the wall to keep the community in but to maintain the Judeans' ownership (or inheritance). Polaski claims that Nehemiah is showing how he controls memory and power in Jerusalem, likely through written memorials and archives.[104] Likely this exclusion of outside ownership in Jerusalem was already understood by the adversaries when Nehemiah was delivering his letters (2:10). They were displeased because they were being denied their right to the city of Jerusalem, which, in part, also excludes them from the community of Judah.

The terminology that Nehemiah uses for portion and memorial is tied to land appropriation. The land was divided into portions in Josh 18:5 and the reference to the memorial is reminiscent of the stones set up by the community when crossing into the land in Josh 4:7. These concepts are not just community organization and exclusion but physical division of the land.[105]

---

103. Van Wyk and Breytenbach, "Nature of the Conflict in Ezra-Nehemiah," 1260; Burns, *Ezra, Nehemiah*, 56.

104. Polaski, "Nehemiah," 46–47; Larson and Dahlen, *Ezra, Nehemiah, Esther*, 150; Allen and Laniak, *Ezra, Nehemiah, Esther*, 99.

105. See discussion in Becking, *Ezra-Nehemiah*, 191–92; Schoville, *Ezra-Nehemiah*, 156; Goswell, *Study Commentary on Ezra-Nehemiah*, 226. Contra Williamson who thinks these are just metaphorical for community and cult participation. Williamson, *Ezra, Nehemiah*, 192.

Purifying the Land

When the proposals of Ezra and Nehemiah are read together, the importance of the land claim becomes clearer. Ezra argues for separation from the peoples of the land and foreign wives, while Nehemiah tells the foreign leaders that they have no portion, right, or memorial in Jerusalem. Ezra claims that mixing with the foreign people has brought guilt upon them, and Nehemiah tells the Judean leaders that the burned state of Jerusalem has made the Judeans a reproach. Both leaders argue for separating the people and land of the Judeans from foreigners. For each leader, the community is important, and it is shown through their dwelling in the land. The people must dwell in their own space apart from the impurities of the surrounding people.

Resolution to the Problem

The final section of the Ezra and Nehemiah passages sees the people resolving the issue presented at the beginning of each passage. Ezra ends with a list of people putting away foreign wives and children. The focus upon the wives and children for the resolution is likely because this is the most formal, and egregious, contract between the foreign people and the Judeans. Fellowship or mixture with the peoples of the land is a broader category and more general type of engagement, and therefore the solution is less defined. Marriage is a formal contract, so it is easier to identify and dissolve with a formal list of offenders. The vague issue of intermixing would be much more difficult to place into a list. Therefore, this list should not be interpreted as indicating intermarriage was the only form of intermixing, but a list of those who committed the worst and clearest form of fellowship with foreign people.[106]

The connection with the land and the community is clear in the builder list and in the connection of the list with the previous recorded speech by Nehemiah (Neh 2:20). The importance of the wall for the entire Judean community is displayed by the fact that many of the builders are not from Jerusalem itself but other Judean cities (c.f. 3:2, 7, 13–16, 18–19, 22).[107] Combining this with the exclusion of the adversaries by Nehemiah in the previous section, the connection between the land and the community becomes clear. Nehemiah declares that the three adversaries have no portion

---

106. The rest of the passage singles out intermarriage as a particular issue while also acknowledging intermixing broadly. See Ezra 9:1–2, 12; 10:2–3, 11, 14.

107. Thomas, *Ezra & Nehemiah*, 244; Williamson, *Ezra, Nehemiah*, 212.

or memorial in Jerusalem and therefore disallows their involvement in the rebuilding. However, he allows people from other cities in Judah to build the wall even though they do not reside within the city of Jerusalem. Becking notes that this creates a division between people living in the territory of Samaria and the people living in the territory of Yehud.[108] This connection shows how building the walls creates the community and separates the land of the Judeans from foreign people. If the foreign people are excluded from building because they do not have a portion or memorial in the land, then the people who are building the wall have this portion and memorial, even if they do not reside within the city itself.

The list in Ezra 10 and the list in Neh 3 show that they are creating a separate space from the foreign influences. Foreign people dwelling with Judeans are removed in Ezra 10, and the Judeans build the wall to maintain their portion and memorial in the land, to the exclusion of the foreign people in Neh 3.

CONCLUSION

The literary movements of Ezra 9–10 and Neh 1–3 overlap significantly. Within each of these literary movements, the prosperity of the community is connected to their possession of the land. The people of Judah are encouraged to separate from the surrounding people and maintain their claim to the promised land. Each of these passages contain conquest themes that reinforce their exclusionary practices. However, the texts go beyond simply excluding foreigners and tie the community welfare to the land itself. Excluding outsiders, whether in marriage or rebuilding the city wall, is part of the process that results in the community holding the land exclusively. In addition to excluding foreigners, the texts connect the state of the land, unclean (Ezra 9:11) or burned and broken down (Neh 1:3; 2:3, 17), with the state of the community. So, the community is rebuilt by restoring the land of Judah, whether by purifying it or building a wall around Jerusalem. A primary component of these restorative acts is the exclusion of foreign influence. So, one of the primary theological themes that can be seen when the two texts are read together is building the community and restoring the land through the exclusion, and removal, of foreigners.

In conclusion, Ezra 9–10 and Neh 1–3 share the same literary movements in nearly the same order. Neither of these passages share the literary

---

108. Becking, *Ezra-Nehemiah*, 196.

movements of thematically more related passages (foreign wives and return migration passages). This literary shaping at the end of Ezra and the beginning of Nehemiah has implications for the connection between the two books. Whether they were originally a single book or two separate books, this shared connection at the seam between them indicates that they have been shaped to be read together.[109] In addition, reading Ezra 9–10 and Neh 1–3 together can illuminate a shared theological message. When the shared literary movements are read together, their focus upon restoring the community and land through exclusive ownership and removal of foreigners is emphasized.

---

109. Authorship claims have been avoided throughout this study because they are impossible to prove with this literary analysis. The literary shaping of these narratives could be the actions of the original author of a unified Ezra-Nehemiah or a later editor attempting to draw the separate books together. This observation of narrative shaping does not indicate the original form of the texts but only the unity of the books as they currently stand. Whether Ezra and Nehemiah were originally a unified work cannot be determined solely on the mirroring of Ezra 9–10 and Neh 1–3.

Bibliography

Ackroyd, Peter R. *I & II Chronicles, Ezra, Nehemiah*. Torch Bible Commentaries. London: SCM, 1973.

———. *Studies in the Religious Tradition of the Old Testament*. London: SCM, 1987.

Allen, Leslie C. "3344 ידה." In *New International Dictionary of Old Testament Theology & Exegesis*, edited by Willem A. VanGemeren, 2:405–8. Grand Rapids: Zondervan, 1997.

———, and Timothy S. Laniak. *Ezra, Nehemiah, Esther: Based on the New International Version*. New International Biblical Commentary 9. Peabody, MA: Hendrickson, 2003.

Allrik, H. L. "The Lists of Zerubbabel (Nehemiah 7 and Ezra 2) and the Hebrew Numeral Notation." *Bulletin of the American Schools of Oriental Research* 136 (1954) 21–27.

Alter, Robert. *The Art of Biblical Narrative*. Rev. and updated ed. New York: Basic, 2011.

Amzallag, Nissim. "The Authorship of Ezra and Nehemiah in Light of Differences in Their Ideological Background." *Journal of Biblical Literature* 137.2 (2018) 271–97.

Avi-Yonah, Michael. "The Walls of Nehemiah: A Minimalist View." *Israel Exploration Journal* 4.3/4 (1954) 239–48.

Baltzer, Klaus. "Moses Servant of God and the Servants: Text and Tradition in the Prayer of Nehemiah (Neh 1:5–11)." In *The Future of Early Christianity: Essays in Honor of Helmut Koester*, edited by Birger A. Pearson, 121–30. Minneapolis: Fortress, 1991.

Bar-Efrat, Shimeon. *Narrative Art in the Bible*. Journal for the Study of the Old Testament Supplement Series 70. Sheffield: Sheffield Academic, 1997.

Bartlett, John R. "Nehemiah's Wall." *Palestine Exploration Quarterly* 140.2 (2008) 77–78.

Batten, Loring W. *A Critical and Exegetical Commentary on the Books of Ezra and Nehemiah*. The International Critical Commentary on the Holy Scriptures of the Old and New Testaments. New York: Scribner, 1913.

Bautch, Richard J. "An Appraisal of Abraham's Role in Postexilic Covenants." *Catholic Biblical Quarterly* 71.1 (2009) 42–63.

Becker, Joachim. *Esra/Nehemia*. Neue Echter Bibel. Altes Testament 25. Würzburg: Echter Verlag, 1999.

Becking, Bob. "Does Ezra Present the Return from Exile as a Second Exodus?" *Biblische Notizen* 177 (2018) 65–73.

———. *Ezra, Nehemiah, and the Construction of Early Jewish Identity*. Forschungen zum Alten Testament 80. Tübingen: Mohr Siebeck, 2011.

———. *Ezra-Nehemiah*. Historical Commentary on the Old Testament. Leuven: Peeters, 2018.

Bibliography

———. "Silent Witness: The Symbolic Presence of God in the Temple Vessels in Ezra-Nehemiah." In *Divine Presence and Absence in Exilic and Post-Exilic Judaism*, edited by Nathan MacDonald and Izaak J. de Hulster, 267–82. Forschungen zum Alten Testament 61. Tübingen: Mohr Siebeck, 2013.

Bedford, Peter R. "Diaspora: Homeland Relations in Ezra-Nehemiah." *Vetus Testamentum* 52.2 (2002) 147–65.

———. "The Economic Role of the Jerusalem Temple in Achaemenid Judah: Comparative Perspectives." In *Shai Le-Sara Japhet: Studies in the Bible, Its Exegesis and Its Language*, edited by Moshe Bar-Asher et al., 3–20. Jerusalem: Bialik Institute, 2007.

Ben Zvi, Ehud. *Social Memory among the Literati of Yehud*. Beihefte zur Zeitschrift für die alttestamentliche Wissenschaft 509. Boston: De Gruyter, 2019.

Berquist, Jon L. *Judaism in Persia's Shadow: A Social and Historical Approach*. Minneapolis: Fortress, 1995.

Bertheau, Ernst. *Die Bücher Esra, Nechemia und Ester*. Kurzgefasstes exegetisches Handbuch zum Alten Testament 17. Leipzig: S. Hirzel, 1862.

Bertholet, Alfred. *Die Bücher Esra und Nehemia*. Kurzer Hand-Commentar zum Alten Testament 19. Tübingen: J. C. B. Mohr (Paul Siebeck), 1902.

Bickerman, Elias. *From Ezra to the Last of the Maccabees: Foundations of Post-Biblical Judaism*. New York: Schocken, 1962.

Blenkinsopp, Joseph. *Essays on Judaism in the Pre-Hellenistic Period*. Beihefte zur Zeitschrift für die alttestamentliche Wissenschaft 495. Boston: De Gruyter, 2017.

———. *Ezra-Nehemiah: A Commentary*. The Old Testament Library. Philadelphia: Westminster, 1988.

———. "Footnotes to the Rescript of Artaxerxes (Ezra 7:11–26)." In *The Historian and the Bible: Essays in Honour of Lester L. Grabbe*, edited by Philip R. Davies and Diana V. Edelman, 150–58. Library of Hebrew Bible/Old Testament Studies 530. New York: T&T Clark, 2010.

———. *Judaism, the First Phase: The Place of Ezra and Nehemiah in the Origins of Judaism*. Grand Rapids: Eerdmans, 2009.

———. "The Nehemiah Autobiographical Memoir." In *Language, Theology, and the Bible: Essays in Honour of James Barr*, edited by Samuel E. Balentine and John Barton, 199–212. New York: Oxford University Press, 1994.

———. "The Social Context of the 'Outsider Woman' in Proverbs 1–9." *Biblica* 72.4 (1991) 457–73.

———. "Temple and Society in Achaemenid Judah." In *Second Temple Studies*, vol. 1, *The Persian Period*, edited by Philip R. Davies, 22–53. JSOT Supplement Series 117. Sheffield: Sheffield Academic, 1991.

———. "Trito-Isaiah (Isaiah 56–66) and the Gôlāh Group of Ezra, Shecaniah, and Nehemiah (Ezra 7–Nehemiah 13): Is There a Connection?" *Journal for the Study of the Old Testament* 43.4 (2019) 661–77.

———. "Was the Pentateuch the Civic and Religious Constitution of the Jewish Ethnos in the Persian Period?" In *Persia and Torah: The Theory of Imperial Authorization of the Pentateuch*, edited by James W. Watts, 41–62. SBL Symposium Series 17. Atlanta: SBL, 2001.

Blidstein, Gerald J. "ᵓAtimia: A Greek Parallel to Ezra 10:8 and to Post-Biblical Exclusion from the Community." *Vetus Testamentum* 24.3 (1974) 357–60.

Bliese, Loren F. "Chiastic Structures, Peaks and Cohesion in Nehemiah 9.6–37." *The Bible Translator* 39.2 (1988) 208–15.

Bibliography

Boda, Mark J. "Chiasmus in Ubiquity: Symmetrical Mirages in Nehemiah 9." *Journal for the Study of the Old Testament* 71 (1996) 55–70.

———. "Prayer as Rhetoric in the Book of Nehemiah." In *New Perspectives on Ezra-Nehemiah: History and Historiography, Text, Literature, and Interpretation*, edited by Isaac Kalimi, 267–84. Winona Lake, IN: Eisenbrauns, 2012.

———. *Praying the Tradition: The Origin and Use of Tradition in Nehemiah 9*. Beihefte zur Zeitschrift für die alttestamentliche Wissenschaft 277. New York: Walter de Gruyter, 1999.

———. "The Torah and Spirit Traditions of Nehemiah 9 in Their Literary Setting." *Hebrew Bible and Ancient Israel* 4.4 (2015) 476–91.

Boice, James Montgomery. *Nehemiah: An Expositional Commentary*. Boice Commentary Series. Grand Rapids: Baker, 2005.

Botta, Alejandro F. "Nethinim." In *The New Interpreter's Dictionary of the Bible*, 4:260–61. Nashville: Abingdon, 2009.

Breneman, Mervin. *Ezra, Nehemiah, Esther: An Exegetical and Theological Exposition of Holy Scripture*. The New American Commentary 10. Nashville: Broadman & Holman, 1993.

Brockington, L. H. *Ezra, Nehemiah and Esther*. The Century Bible. London: Nelson, 1969.

Brown, Francis, S. R. Driver, and Charles A. Briggs. "II. עָרַב." In *The Brown-Driver-Briggs Hebrew and English Lexicon*, 786. Peabody, MA: Hendrickson, 1997.

Brown, A. Philip, II. "The Problem of Mixed Marriages in Ezra 9–10." *Bibliotheca Sacra* 162.648 (2005) 437–58.

Burns, Rita J. *Ezra, Nehemiah*. Collegeville Bible Commentary 11. Collegeville, MN: Liturgical, 1985.

Byun, Paul. "A Paradoxical Situation and God's Righteousness in Ezra 9:15." *Zeitschrift für die alttestamentliche Wissenschaft* 131.3 (2019) 467–73.

Campbell, George Van Pelt. "Structure, Themes, and Theology in Ezra-Nehemiah." *Bibliotheca Sacra* 174 (2017) 394–411.

Cataldo, Jeremiah. "Persian Policy and the Yehud Community during Nehemiah." *Journal for the Study of the Old Testament* 28.2 (2003) 240–52.

Cezula, N. S. "The Concept of 'The Holy Seed' as a Coping Strategy in Ezra-Nehemiah and Its Implications for South Africa." *Acta Theologica* 38.1 (2018) 15–36.

Chrostowski, Waldemar. "An Examination of Conscience by God's People as Exemplified in Neh 9,6–37." *Biblische Zeitschrift* 34.2 (1990) 253–61.

Clauss, Jan. "Understanding the Mixed Marriages of Ezra-Nehemiah in the Light of Temple-Building and the Book's Concept of Jerusalem." In *Mixed Marriages: Intermarriage and Group Identity in the Second Temple Period*, edited by Christian Frevel, 109–31. The Library of Hebrew Bible/Old Testament Studies 547. New York: Bloomsbury, 2012.

Clines, David J. A. *Ezra, Nehemiah, Esther: Based on the Revised Standard Version*. New Century Bible Commentary. Grand Rapids: Eerdmans, 1984.

———. "Nehemiah 10 as an Example of Early Jewish Biblical Exegesis." *Journal for the Study of the Old Testament* 6.21 (1981) 111–17.

———. "The Force of the Text: A Response to Tamara C. Eskenazi's 'Ezra-Nehemiah: From Text to Actuality.'" In *Signs and Wonders: Biblical Texts in Literary Focus*, edited by J. Cheryl Exum, 199–215. Semeia Studies. Atlanta: Scholars, 1989.

Bibliography

———. "The Nehemiah Memoir: The Perils of Autobiography." In *What Does Eve Do to Help? And Other Readerly Questions to the Old Testament*, 73–109. Journal for the Study of the Old Testament Supplement Series 94. Sheffield: JSOT, 1990.

Cogan, Mordechai. "Raising the Walls of Jerusalem (Nehemiah 3:1–32): The View from Dur-Sharrukin." *Israel Exploration Journal* 56.1 (2006) 84–95.

Conczorowski, Benedikt J. "All the Same as Ezra? Conceptual Differences between the Texts on Intermarriage in Genesis, Deuteronomy 7 and Ezra." In *Mixed Marriages: Intermarriage and Group Identity in the Second Temple Period*, edited by Christian Frevel, 89–108. The Library of Hebrew Bible/Old Testament Studies 547. New York: Bloomsbury, 2012.

Conklin, Blane W. "The Decrees of God and of Kings in the Aramaic Correspondence of Ezra." *Proceedings—Eastern Great Lakes and Midwest Biblical Societies* 21 (2001) 81–89.

Crawford, Sidnie White, and Christopher A. Hoffmann. "A Note on 4Q365, Frg. 23 and Nehemiah 10:33–36." *Revue de Qumran* 23.3 (2008) 429–30.

Daniels, Dwight R. "The Composition of the Ezra-Nehemiah Narrative." In *Ernten, was man sät: Festschrift für Klaus Koch zu seinem 65 Geburtstag*, edited by Klaus Koch et al., 311–28. Neukirchen-Vluyn: Neukirchener Verlag, 1991.

Davies, Gordon F. *Ezra and Nehemiah*. Berit Olam Studies in Hebrew Narrative & Poetry. Collegeville, MN: Liturgical, 1999.

Demsky, Aaron. "'Pelekh' in Nehemiah 3." *Israel Exploration Journal* 33.3–4 (1983) 242–44.

Dequeker, Luc. "Nehemiah and the Restoration of the Temple after the Exile." In *Deuteronomy and Deuteronomic Literature: Festschrift C. H. W. Brekelmans*, edited by Marc Vervenne and James Lust, 547–67. Bibliotheca Ephemeridum Theologicarum Lovaniensium 133. Leuven: Leuven University Press, 1997.

Dor, Yonina. "The Composition of the Episode of the Foreign Women in Ezra IX–X." *Vetus Testamentum* 53.1 (2003) 26–47.

———. "The Rite of Separation of the Foreign Wives in Ezra-Nehemiah." In *Judah and the Judeans in the Achaemenid Period: Negotiating Identity in an International Context*, edited by Oded Lipschits et al., 173–88. Winona Lake, IN: Eisenbrauns, 2011.

Dozeman, Thomas B. "Geography and History in Herodotus and in Ezra-Nehemiah." *Journal of Biblical Literature* 122.3 (2003) 449–66.

Duggan, Michael W. *The Covenant Renewal in Ezra-Nehemiah (Neh 7:72b–10:40): An Exegetical, Literary, and Theological Study*. Dissertation Series / Society of Biblical Literature 164. Atlanta: Society of Biblical Literature, 2001.

———. "Ezra 9:6–15: A Penitential Prayer within Its Literary Setting." In *Seeking the Favor of God*, vol. 1, *The Origins of Penitential Prayer in Second Temple Judaism*, edited by Mark J. Boda et al., 165–80. Early Judaism and Its Literature 21. Boston: Brill, 2006.

Dumbrell, William J. "Malachi and the Ezra-Nehemiah Reforms." *The Reformed Theological Review* 35.2 (1976) 42–52.

———. "The Theological Intention of Ezra-Nehemiah." *The Reformed Theological Review* 35.3 (1986) 65–72.

Dyck, Andrew W. "'My Sad Face': An Interpersonal Metafunction Analysis of the Dialogue between Nehemiah, Son of Hakaliah, and Artaxerxes, King of Persia, in Nehemiah 2,2–8." *Scandinavian Journal of the Old Testament* 34.2 (2020) 161–86.

Bibliography

Dyck, Jonathan E. "Ezra 2 in Ideological Critical Perspective." In *Rethinking Contexts, Rereading Texts: Contributions From the Social Sciences to Biblical Interpretation*, edited by M. Daniel Carroll R., 129–45. Journal for the Study of the Old Testament Supplement Series 299. Sheffield: Sheffield Academic, 2000.

Emerton, J. A. "Review of Studie zur nachexilischen Gemeinde in Esra-Nehemia." *Journal of Theological Studies* 18.1 (1967) 169–75.

Eskenazi, Tamara C. "Imagining the Other in the Construction of Judahite Identity in Ezra-Nehemiah." In *Imagining the Other and Constructing Israelite Identity in the Early Second Temple Period*, edited by Ehud Ben Zvi and Diana V. Edelman, 230–56. T&T Clark Library of Biblical Studies. New York: Bloomsbury T&T Clark, 2014.

———. *In an Age of Prose: A Literary Approach to Ezra-Nehemiah*. The Society of Biblical Literature/Monograph Series 36. Atlanta: Scholars, 1988.

———. "Nehemiah 9–10: Structure and Significance." *Journal of Hebrew Scriptures* 3 (2001) 1–19.

———. "Out from the Shadows: Biblical Women in the Post-Exilic Era." In *A Feminist Companion to Samuel and Kings*, edited by Athalya Brenner, 252–71. The Feminist Companion to the Bible 5. Sheffield: Sheffield Academic, 1994.

———. "The Structure of Ezra-Nehemiah and the Integrity of the Book." *Journal of Biblical Literature* 107.4 (1988) 641–56.

———. "Temple and Society in Achaemenid Judah." In *Second Temple Studies*, vol. 1, *The Persian Period*, edited by Philip R. Davies, 22–53. JSOT Supplement Series 117. Sheffield: Sheffield Academic, 1991.

———, and Eleanore P. Judd. "Marriage to a Stranger in Ezra 9–10." In *Second Temple Studies*, vol. 2, *Temple and Community in the Persian Period*, edited by Tamara C. Eskenazi and Kent H. Richards, 266–85. JSOT Supplement Series 175. Sheffield: JSOT, 1994.

Esler, Philip. "Ezra-Nehemiah as a Narrative of (Re-Invented) Israelite Identity." *Biblical Interpretation* 11.3/4 (2003) 413–26.

Fensham, F. Charles. *The Books of Ezra and Nehemiah*. New International Commentary on the Old Testament. Grand Rapids: Eerdmans, 1982.

Fernández, Andrés. "Esdr. 9,9 y Un Texto de Josefo." *Biblica* 18.2 (1937) 207–8.

Finkelstein, Israel. "Archaeology and the List of Returnees in the Books of Ezra and Nehemiah." *Palestine Exploration Quarterly* 140.1 (2008) 7–16.

———. *Hasmonean Realities behind Ezra, Nehemiah, and Chronicles: Archaeological and Historical Perspectives*. Ancient Israel and Its Literature 34. Atlanta: SBL, 2018.

———. "Jerusalem in the Persian (and Early Hellenistic) Period and the Wall of Nehemiah." *Journal for the Study of the Old Testament* 32.4 (2008) 501–20.

Fleishman, Joseph. "Nehemiah's Request on Behalf of Jerusalem." In *New Perspectives on Ezra-Nehemiah: History and Historiography, Text, Literature, and Interpretation*, edited by Isaac Kalimi, 241–66. Winona Lake, IN: Eisenbrauns, 2012.

Fried, Lisbeth S. "Did Second Temple High Priests Possess the Urim and Thummim?" *Journal of Hebrew Scriptures* 7 (2007) 2–25.

———. "Ezra's Use of Documents in the Context of Hellenistic Rules of Rhetoric." In *New Perspectives on Ezra-Nehemiah: History and Historiography, Text, Literature, and Interpretation*, edited by Isaac Kalimi, 11–26. Winona Lake, IN: Eisenbrauns, 2012.

———. "The Torah of God as God: The Exaltation of the Written Law Code in Ezra-Nehemiah." In *Divine Presence and Absence in Exilic and Post-Exilic Judaism*, edited

Bibliography

by Nathan MacDonald and Izaak J. de Hulster, 283–300. Forschungen zum Alten Testament 61. Tübingen: Mohr Siebeck, 2013.

———. "Who Wrote Ezra-Nehemiah—and Why Did They?" In *Unity and Disunity in Ezra-Nehemiah: Redaction, Rhetoric, and Reader*, edited by Mark J. Boda and Paul L. Redditt, 75–97. Sheffield: Sheffield Phoenix, 2008.

———. "'You Shall Appoint Judges': Ezra's Mission and the Rescript of Artaxerxes." In *Persia and Torah: The Theory of Imperial Authorization of the Pentateuch*, edited by James W. Watts, 63–90. SBL Symposium Series. Atlanta: SBL, 2001.

Fuller, Russell T., and Kyoungwon Choi. *Invitation to Biblical Hebrew Syntax: An Intermediate Grammar*. Invitation to Theological Studies. Grand Rapids: Kregel, 2017.

Gabizon, Michael. "The Development of the Matrilineal Principle in Ezra, Jubilees, and Acts." *Journal for the Study of the Pseudepigrapha* 27.2 (2017) 143–60.

Galling, Kurt. *Die Bücher der Chronik, Esra, Nehemia*. Das Alte Testament Deutsch: Neues Göttinger Biblelwerk 12. Göttingen: Vanderhoeck & Ruprecht, 1954.

———. "The 'Gōla-List' According to Ezra 2 // Nehemiah 7." *Journal of Biblical Literature* 70.2 (1951) 149–58.

Gamberoni, J. "מָקוֹם (Māqôm)." In *Theological Dictionary of the Old Testament*, edited by G. Johannes Botterweck et al., 8:532–44. Grand Rapids: Eerdmans, 1997.

Gitay, Yehoshua. "A Designed Anti-Rhetorical Speech: Ezra and the Question of Mixed Marriage." *Journal of Northwest Semitic Languages* 23.2 (1997) 57–68.

Glatt-Gilad, David A. "Reflections on the Structure and Significance of the 'amānāh (Neh 10,29–40)." *Zeitschrift für die alttestamentliche Wissenschaft* 112.3 (2000) 386–95.

———. "The Voluntary Nature of the Nehemiah Covenant in Rabbinic Literature." *Review of Rabbinic Judaism* 20.1 (2017) 3–20.

Goswell, Greg. *A Study Commentary on Ezra-Nehemiah*. Grand Rapids: EP, 2013.

Grabbe, Lester L. *Ezra-Nehemiah*. Old Testament Readings. London: Routledge, 1998.

———. *Judaism from Cyrus to Hadrian*. Vol. 1. Minneapolis: Fortress, 1992.

———. "The Law of Moses in the Ezra Tradition: More Virtual Than Real?" In *Persia and Torah: The Theory of Imperial Authorization of the Pentateuch*, edited by James W. Watts, 91–114. SBL Symposium Series 17. Atlanta: SBL, 2001.

———. "What Was Ezra's Mission?" In *Second Temple Studies*, vol. 2, *Temple and Community in the Persian Period*, edited by Tamara C. Eskenazi and Kent H. Richards, 286–99. JSOT Supplement Series 175. Sheffield: JSOT, 1994.

Graham, M. Patrick. "A Connection Proposed between II Chr 24,26 and Ezra 9–10." *Zeitschrift für die alttestamentliche Wissenschaft* 97 (1985): 256–58.

Grätz, Sebastian. "The Second Temple and the Legal Status of the Torah: The Hermeneutics of the Torah in the Books of Ruth and Ezra." In *The Pentateuch as Torah: New Models for Understanding Its Promulgation and Acceptance*, edited by Gary N. Knoppers and Bernard M. Levinson, 273–88. Winona Lake, IN: Eisenbrauns, 2007.

Grol, Harm W. M. van. "Exegesis of the Exile-Exegesis of Scripture? Ezra 9:6–9." In *Intertextuality in Ugarit and Israel: Papers Read at the Tenth Joint Meeting of the Society for Old Testament Study and Het Oudtestamentisch Werkgezelschap in Nederland En Belgie Held at Oxford, 1997*, edited by Johannes C. de Moor, 31–61. Boston: Brill, 1998.

———. "'Indeed, Servants We Are': Ezra 9, Nehemiah 9, and 2 Chronicles 12 Compared." In *The Crisis of Israelite Religion: Transformation of Religious Tradition in Exilic*

Bibliography

and Post-Exilic Times, edited by Bob Becking and Marjo C. A. Korpel, 209–27. Oudtestamentische Studiën 42. Boston: Brill, 1999.

———. "Schuld und Scham: Die Verwurzelung von Esra 9,6–7 in der Tradition." *Estudios Bíblicos* 55.1 (1997) 29–52.

Gunn, David M., and Danna Nolan Fewell. *Narrative in the Hebrew Bible*. New York: Oxford University Press, 1993.

Gunneweg, Antonius H. J. *Esra*. Kommentar zum Alten Testament 19. Gütersloh: Gütersloher Verlagshaus Mohn, 1985.

———. *Nehemia*. Kommentar zum Alten Testament 19. Gütersloh: G. Mohn, 1987.

Halpern, Baruch. "A Historiographic Commentary on Ezra 1–6: A Chronological Narrative and Dual Chronology in Israelite Historiography." In *The Hebrew Bible and Its Interpreters*, edited by William Henry Propp et al., 81–142. Biblical and Judaic Studies 1. Winona Lake, IN: Eisenbrauns, 1990.

Hamilton, James M., Jr. *Exalting Jesus in Ezra and Nehemiah*. Christ-Centered Exposition. Nashville: Holman Reference, 2014.

Harkins, Angela Kim. "The Pro-Social Role of Grief in Ezra's Penitential Prayer." *Biblical Interpretation* 24 (2016) 466–91.

Harmelink, Bryan L. "Exploring the Syntactic, Semantic, and Pragmatic Uses of וַיְהִי in Biblical Hebrew." PhD diss., Westminster Theological Seminary, 2004.

Harrington, Hannah K. "Holiness and Purity in Ezra-Nehemiah." In *Unity and Disunity in Ezra-Nehemiah: Redaction, Rhetoric, and Reader*, edited by Mark J. Boda and Paul L. Redditt, 98–116. Hebrew Bible Monographs 17. Sheffield: Sheffield Phoenix, 2008.

Hasler, Laura Carlson. "The Cited Documents of Ezra-Nehemiah: Does Their Authenticity Matter?" *Biblical Interpretation* 27.3 (2019) 372–89.

Häusl, Maria. "Searching for Forces of Group Cohesion in the Books of Nehemiah and Isaiah." In *Ṣedaqa and Torah in Postexilic Discourse*, edited by Susanne Gillmayr-Bucher and Maria Häusl, 55–70. T&T Clark Library of Biblical Studies 640. London: Bloomsbury T&T Clark, 2017.

Hays, Christopher B. "The Silence of the Wives: Bakhtin's Monologism and Ezra 7–10." *Journal for the Study of the Old Testament* 33.1 (2008) 59–80.

Healey, Joseph P. "Nethinim." In *Anchor Bible Dictionary*, 4:1085–86. New York: Doubleday, 1992.

Heltzer, Michael. "The Right of Ezra to Demand Obedience to 'The Laws of the King' from Gentiles of the V Satrapy (Ez 7:25–26)." *Zeitschrift für Altorientalische und Biblische Rechtsgeschichte* 4 (1998) 192–96.

Hensel, Benedikt. "Ethnic Fiction and Identity-Formation: A New Explanation for the Background of the Question of Intermarriage in Ezra-Nehemiah." In *The Bible, Qumran, and the Samaritans*, edited by Magnar Kartveit and Gary N. Knoppers, 133–48. Studia Samaritana 10. Boston: De Gruyter, 2018.

Heth, William A., and Gordon J. Wenham. *Jesus and Divorce: The Problem with the Evangelical Consensus*. Nashville: T. Nelson, 1985.

Hogewood, Jay C. "The Speech Act of Confession: Priestly Performative Utterance in Leviticus 16 and Ezra 9–10." In *Seeking the Favor of God*, vol. 1, *The Origins of Penitential Prayer in Second Temple Judaism*, edited by Mark J. Boda et al., 69–82. Early Judaism and Its Literature 21. Atlanta: Society of Biblical Literature, 2006.

Hoglund, Kenneth. "The Achaemenid Context." In *Second Temple Studies*, vol. 1, *The Persian Period*, edited by Philip R. Davies, 54–72. JSOT Supplement Series 117. Sheffield: Sheffield Academic, 1991.

Bibliography

———. *Achaemenid Imperial Administration in Syria-Palestine and the Missions of Ezra and Nehemiah*. Dissertation Series/Society of Biblical Literature 125. Atlanta: Scholars, 1992.

Hogue, Timothy. "Return from Exile: Diglossia and Literary Code-Switching in Ezra 1–7." *Zeitschrift für die alttestamentliche Wissenschaft* 130.1 (2018) 54–68.

Holmgren, Frederick C. "Faithful Abraham and the 'amānâ Covenant Nehemiah 9,6–10,1." *Zeitschrift für die alttestamentliche Wissenschaft* 104.2 (1992): 249–54.

Horbury, William. "Extirpation and Excommunication." *Vetus Testamentum* 35.1 (1985) 13–38.

In der Smitten, Wilhelm Th. *Esra: Quellen, Überlieferung und Geschichte*. Studia Semitica Neerlandica 15. Assen, Netherlands: Van Gorcum, 1973.

Janzen, David. "The Cries of Jerusalem: Ethnic, Cultic, Legal, and Geographic Boundaries in Ezra-Nehemiah." In *Unity and Disunity in Ezra-Nehemiah: Redaction, Rhetoric, and Reader*, edited by Mark J. Boda and Paul L. Redditt, 117–35. Hebrew Bible Monographs 17. Sheffield: Sheffield Phoenix, 2008.

———. "The Meaning of Porneia in Matthew 5.32 and 19.9: An Approach from the Study of Ancient Near Eastern Culture." *Journal for the Study of the New Testament* 23.80 (2001) 66–80.

———. "The 'Mission' of Ezra and the Persian-Period Temple Community." *Journal of Biblical Literature* 119.4 (2000) 619–43.

———. "Sacrifice as Cultic Expression of the Law: Social and Geographic Separation in Ezra-Nehemiah." In *The Social Meanings of Sacrifice in the Hebrew Bible: A Study of Four Writings*, 185–208. New York: De Gruyter, 2004.

———. "Scholars, Witches, Ideologues, and What the Text Said: Ezra 9–10 and Its Interpretation." In *Approaching Yehud: New Approaches to the Study of the Persian Period*, edited by Jon L. Berquist, 49–70. Semeia Studies 50. Atlanta: Society of Biblical Literature, 2007.

———. *Witch-Hunts, Purity and Social Boundaries: The Expulsion of the Foreign Women in Ezra 9–10*. JSOT Supplement Series 350. New York: Sheffield Academic, 2002.

———. "Yahwistic Appropriation of Achaemenid Ideology and the Function of Nehemiah 9 in Ezra-Nehemiah." *Journal of Biblical Literature* 136.4 (2017) 839–56.

Japhet, Sara. *From the Rivers of Babylon to the Highlands of Judah: Collected Studies on the Restoration Period*. Winona Lake, IN: Eisenbrauns, 2006.

———. "Sheshbazzar and Zerubbabel—Against the Background of the Historical and Religious Tendencies of Ezra-Nehemiah." *Zeitschrift für die alttestamentliche Wissenschaft* 94.1 (1982) 66–98.

———. "Theodicy in Ezra-Nehemiah and Chronicles." In *Theodicy in the World of the Bible*, edited by Antti Laato and Johannes C. de Moor, 429–69. Boston: Brill, 2003.

Jepsen, Alfred. "Nehemia 10." *Zeitschrift für die alttestamentliche Wissenschaft* 66.1 (1954) 87–106.

Jobling, David. *The Sense of Biblical Narrative: Structural Analyses in the Hebrew Bible I*. 2nd ed. Journal for the Study of the Old Testament Supplement Series 7. Sheffield: JSOT, 1986.

———. *The Sense of Biblical Narrative: Structural Analyses in the Hebrew Bible II*. Journal for the Study of the Old Testament Supplement Series 39. Sheffield: JSOT, 1986.

Johnson, Willa Mathis. "Ethnicity in Persian Yehud: Between Anthropological Analysis and Ideological Criticism." *Society of Biblical Literature Seminar Papers* 34 (1995) 177–86.

Bibliography

———. *The Holy Seed Has Been Defiled: The Interethnic Marriage Dilemma in Ezra 9–10*. Hebrew Bible Monographs 33. Sheffield: Sheffield Phoenix, 2011.

Jones, Christopher M. "Embedded Written Documents as Colonial Mimicry in Ezra-Nehemiah." *Biblical Interpretation* 26 (2018) 158–81.

Jones, E. Allen, III. "Who Is the Holy Seed?: Purity and Identity in the Restoration Community." *Journal for the Study of the Old Testament* 45.4 (2021) 515–34.

Joüon, Paul, and T. Muraoka. *A Grammar of Biblical Hebrew: Part Three: Syntax*. 5th ed. Vol. 2. Rome: Editrice Pontificio Istituto Biblico, 2005.

Kang, Bin. "The Positive Role of Shame for Post-Exilic Returnees in Ezra/Nehemiah." *Old Testament Essays* 22.2 (2020) 250–65.

Kellermann, Ulrich. *Nehemia: Quellen, Überlieferung, und Geschichte*. Beihefte zur Zeitschrift für die alttestamentliche Wissenschaft 102. Berlin: Töpelmann, 1967.

Kidner, Derek. *Ezra and Nehemiah: An Introduction and Commentary*. The Tyndale Old Testament Commentaries 12. Downers Grove, IL: InterVarsity, 1979.

Kiel, Yishai. "Reinventing Mosaic Torah in Ezra-Nehemiah in the Light of the Law (Dāta) of Ahura Mazda and Zarathustra." *Journal of Biblical Literature* 136.2 (2017) 323–45.

Kim, Grace Ji-Sun. "Foreign Women: Ezra, Intermarriage and Asian American Women's Identity." *Feminist Theology* 22.3 (2014) 241–52.

Kim, Raeyong. "Historiographic Characteristics of Ezra-Nehemiah." *Korean Journal of Christian Studies* 75 (2011) 105–23.

Klingbeil, Gerald A., and Chantal J. Klingbeil. "'Eyes to Hear': Nehemiah 1,6 from a Pragmatics and Ritual Theory Perspective." *Biblica* 91.1 (2010) 91–102.

Knauf, Ernst Axel. "Bethel: The Israelite Impact on Judean Language and Literature." In *Judah and the Judeans in the Persian Period*, edited by Oded Lipschits and Manfred Oeming, 291–349. Winona Lake, IN: Eisenbrauns, 2006.

Knoppers, Gary N. "Hierodules, Priests, or Janitors? The Levites in Chronicles and the History of the Israelite Priesthood." *Journal of Biblical Literature* 118.1 (1999) 49–72.

———. "Nehemiah and Sanballat: The Enemy Without or Within?" In *Judah and the Judeans in the Fourth Century BCE*, edited by Oded Lipschits et al., 305–31. Winona Lake, IN: Eisenbrauns, 2007.

Knowles, Melody D. "Pilgrimage Imagery in the Returns in Ezra." *Journal of Biblical Literature* 123.1 (2004) 57–74.

Koch, Klaus. "Ezra and the Origins of Judaism." *Journal of Semitic Studies* 19.2 (1974) 173–97.

Koehler, Ludwig, and Walter Baumgartner. "II ערב." In *The Hebrew and Aramaic Lexicon of the Old Testament*, 2:877. New York: Brill, 1995.

Koller, Aaron J. *Esther in Ancient Jewish Thought*. New York: Cambridge University Press, 2014.

Korada, Manoja Kumar. "Seeing Discontinuity in Chronicles-Ezra-Nehemiah through Reforms." *Journal of the Evangelical Theological Society* 61.2 (2018) 287–306.

Kraemer, David Charles. "On the Relationship of the Books of Ezra and Nehemiah." *Journal for the Study of the Old Testament* 18.59 (1993) 73–92.

Kratz, Reinhard Gregor. *The Composition of the Narrative Books of the Old Testament*. Translated by John Bowden. New York: T&T Clark, 2005.

Kugler, Gili. "Present Affliction Affects the Representation of the Past: An Alternative Dating of the Levitical Prayer in Nehemiah 9." *Vetus Testamentum* 63.4 (2013) 605–26.

Bibliography

Laird, Donna J. "Political Strategy in the Narrative of Ezra-Nehemiah." In *The Oxford Handbook of Biblical Narrative*, edited by Danna Nolan Fewell, 276–85. New York: Oxford University Press, 2016.

———. "The Temple Building Account in Ezra 1–6: Refracting the Social World." *Conversations with the Biblical World* 31 (2011) 95–114.

Larson, Knute, and Kathy Dahlen. *Ezra, Nehemiah, Esther*. Holman Old Testament Commentary 9. Nashville: Broadman & Holman, 2005.

Lau, Peter H. W. "Gentile Incorporation into Israel in Ezra-Nehemiah?" *Biblica* 90.3 (2009) 356–73.

Leuchter, Mark. "The Exegesis of Jeremiah in and beyond Ezra 9–10." *Vetus Testamentum* 65 (2015) 62–80.

———. "Inter-Levitical Polemics in the Late 6th Century BCE: The Evidence from Nehemiah 9." *Biblica* 95.2 (2014) 269–79.

———. "The Levites in Exile: A Response to L. S. Tiemeyer." *Vetus Testamentum* 60.4 (2010) 583–90.

Levering, Matthew. *Ezra & Nehemiah*. Brazos Theological Commentary on the Bible. Grand Rapids: Brazos, 2007.

Lipiński, Edward. "נָתַן." In *Theological Dictionary of the Old Testament*, edited by G. Johannes Botterweck, Helmer Ringgren, and Heinz-Josef Fabry, 10:90–107. Grand Rapids: Eerdmans, 1999.

Lipschits, Oded. *The Fall and Rise of Jerusalem: Judah under Babylonian Rule*. Winona Lake, IN: Eisenbrauns, 2005.

———. "Nehemiah 3: Sources, Composition, and Purpose." In *New Perspectives on Ezra-Nehemiah: History and Historiography, Text, Literature, and Interpretation*, edited by Isaac Kalimi, 73–99. Winona Lake, IN: Eisenbrauns, 2012.

Lortie, Christopher R. "These Are the Days of the Prophets: A Literary Analysis of Ezra 1–6." *Tyndale Bulletin* 64.2 (2013) 161–69.

MacLeod, David J. "The Problem of Divorce, Part 2: The Teaching of Scripture—the Old Testament Texts." *Emmaus Journal* 2.1 (1993) 23–44.

Maier, Christl M. "The 'Foreign' Women in Ezra-Nehemiah: Intersectional Perspectives on Ethnicity." In *Feminist Frameworks and the Bible: Power, Ambiguity, and Intersectionality*, edited by L. Juliana Claassens and Carolyn J. Sharp, 79–98. T&T Clark Library of Biblical Studies 630. New York: Bloomsbury T&T Clark, 2017.

Mangan, Céline. *1–2 Chronicles, Ezra, Nehemiah*. Old Testament Message 13. Wilmington, DE: Michael Glazier, 1982.

Margalith, Othniel. "The Political Background of Zerubbabel's Mission and the Samaritan Schism." *Vetus Testamentum* 41.3 (1991) 312–23.

———. "The Political Role of Ezra as Persian Governor." *Zeitschrift für die alttestamentliche Wissenschaft* 98.1 (1986) 110–12.

Mason, Rex. "Some Chronistic Themes in the 'Speeches' in Ezra and Nehemiah." *Expository Times* 101.3 (1989) 72–76.

Mayer, G. "ידה Ydh: III. Usage." In *Theological Dictionary of the Old Testament*, edited by G. Johannes Botterweck et al., 5:431–43. Grand Rapids: Eerdmans, 1986.

McConville, J. G. *Ezra, Nehemiah, and Esther*. Daily Study Bible: Old Testament. Philadelphia: Westminster, 1985.

———. "Ezra-Nehemiah and the Fulfilment of Prophecy." *Vetus Testamentum* 36.2 (1986) 205–24.

Bibliography

Mermelstein, Ari. "When History Repeats Itself: The Theological Significance of the Abrahamic Covenant in Early Jewish Writings." *Journal for the Study of the Pseudepigrapha* 27.2 (2017) 113–42.

Miller, Cynthia L. *The Representation of Speech in Biblical Hebrew Narrative: A Linguistic Analysis*. Harvard Semitic Studies 55. Atlanta: Scholars, 1996.

Min, Kyung-jin. *The Levitical Authorship of Ezra-Nehemiah*. Journal for the Study of the Old Testament Supplement Series 409. New York: T&T Clark, 2004.

Mitchell, Hinckley Gilbert Thomas. "The Wall of Jerusalem According to the Book of Nehemiah." *Journal of Biblical Literature* 22.2 (1903) 85–163.

Moffat, Donald P. *Ezra's Social Drama: Identity Formation, Marriage and Social Conflict in Ezra 9 and 10*. T&T Clark Library of Biblical Studies 579. London: Bloomsbury T&T Clark, 2014.

———. "The Metaphor at Stake in Ezra 9:8." *Vetus Testamentum* 63.2 (2013) 290–98.

Mtshiselwa, V. N. N. "Remembering and Constructing Israelite Identity in Postexilic Yehud: Some Remarks on the Penitential Prayer of Nehemiah 9:6–37." *Verbum et Ecclesia* 37.1 (2016) 1–6.

Musil, Alois. *The Manners and Customs of the Rwala Bedouins*. Oriental Explorations and Studies 6. New York: American Geographical Society, 1928.

Myers, Jacob M. *Ezra-Nehemiah*. The Anchor Bible 14. Garden City, NY: Doubleday, 1965.

Nelson, Richard D. "Herem and the Deuteronomic Social Conscience." In *Deuteronomy and Deuteronomic Literature: Festschrift C. H. W. Brekelmans*, edited by Marc Vervenne and James Lust, 39–54. Bibliotheca Ephemeridum Theologicarum Lovaniensium 133. Leuven: Leuven University Press, 1997.

Newman, Judith H. "Nehemiah 9 and the Scripturalization of Prayer in the Second Temple Period." In *The Function of Scripture in Early Jewish and Christian Tradition*, edited by Craig A. Evans and James A. Sanders, 112–23. JSNT Supplement Series 154. Sheffield: Sheffield Academic, 1998.

Noth, Martin. *Überlieferungsgeschichtliche Studien: Die Sammelnden und Bearbeitenden Geschichtswerke im Alten Testament*. 3rd ed. Tübingen: M. Niemeyer, 1967.

Oeming, Manfred. "The Real History: The Theological Ideas Behind Nehemiah's Wall." In *New Perspectives on Ezra-Nehemiah: History and Historiography, Text, Literature, and Interpretation*, edited by Isaac Kalimi, 131–50. Winona Lake, IN: Eisenbrauns, 2012.

Olyan, Saul M. "Purity Ideology in Ezra-Nehemiah as a Tool to Reconstitute the Community." *Journal for the Study of Judaism in the Persian, Hellenistic, and Roman Period* 35.1 (2004) 1–16.

Oswald, Wolfgang. "Foreign Marriages and Citizenship in Persian Period Judah." *Journal of Hebrew Scriptures* 12 (2012) 1–17.

Pakkala, Juha. "The Disunity of Ezra-Nehemiah." In *Unity and Disunity in Ezra-Nehemiah: Redaction, Rhetoric, and Reader*, edited by Mark J. Boda and Paul L. Redditt, 200–15. Hebrew Bible Monographs 17. Sheffield: Sheffield Phoenix, 2008.

———. "The Exile and the Exiles in the Ezra Tradition." In *The Concept of Exile in Ancient Israel and Its Historical Contexts*, edited by Ehud Ben Zvi and Christoph Levin, 91–101. Beihefte zur Zeitschrift für die alttestamentliche Wissenschaft 404. New York: De Gruyter, 2010.

———. *Ezra the Scribe: The Development of Ezra 7–10 and Nehemiah 8*. Beihefte zur Zeitschrift für die alttestamentliche Wissenschaft 347. New York: W. de Gruyter, 2004.

Bibliography

———. "The Original Independence of the Ezra Story in Ezra 7–10 and Neh 8." *Biblische Notizen* 129 (2006) 17–24.

Plöger, Otto. "Reden und Gebete im Deuteronomistischen und Chronistischen Geschichtswerk." In *Festschrift für Günther Dehn: zum 75. Geburtstag am 18. April 1957 Dargebracht von der Evangelisch-Theologischen Fakultät der Rheinischen Friedrich Wilhelms-Universität zu Bonn*, edited by Wilhelm Schneemelcher, 35–49. Neukirchen Kreis Moers: Verlag der Buchhandlung des Erziehungsvereins, 1957.

Polaski, Donald C. "Nehemiah: Subject of the Empire, Subject of Writing." In *New Perspectives on Ezra-Nehemiah: History and Historiography, Text, Literature, and Interpretation*, edited by Isaac Kalimi, 37–59. Winona Lake, IN: Eisenbrauns, 2012.

Porten, Bezalel. "Restoration of a Holy Nation (445 B.C.E.)." *Dor Le Dor* 7.3 (1979) 127–35.

Puech, Émile. "The Tell El-Fûl Jar Inscription and the Nĕtînîm." *Bulletin of the American Schools of Oriental Research* 261 (1986) 69–72.

Rainey, Brian. "'Their Peace or Prosperity': Biblical Concepts of Hereditary Punishment and the Exclusion of Foreigners in Ezra-Nehemiah." *Journal of Ancient Judaism* 6.2 (2015) 158–81.

Rawlinson, George. *Ezra and Nehemiah: Their Lives and Times*. London: James Nisbet, 1890.

Redditt, Paul L. "The Census List in Ezra 2 and Nehemiah 7: A Suggestion." In *New Perspectives on Ezra-Nehemiah: History and Historiography, Text, Literature, and Interpretation*, edited by Isaac Kalimi, 223–40. Winona Lake, IN: Eisenbrauns, 2012.

———. *Ezra-Nehemiah*. Smyth & Helwys Bible Commentary 9B. Macon, GA: Smyth & Helwys, 2014.

Rendsburg, Gary A. "The Northern Origin of Nehemiah 9." *Biblica* 72.3 (1991) 348–66.

Rendtorff, Rolf. "Nehemiah 9: An Important Witness of Theological Reflection." In *Tehillah Le-Moshe: Biblical and Judaic Studies in Honor of Moshe Greenberg*, edited by Mordechai Cogan et al., 111–17. Winona Lake, IN: Eisenbrauns, 1997.

Rice, John Will. "The Diachronic Composition of the Shema-Reports in Nehemiah 1–6." *Zeitschrift für die alttestamentliche Wissenschaft* 131.1 (2019) 91–104.

Rothenbusch, Ralf. "The Question of Mixed Marriages between the Poles of Diaspora and Homeland: Observations in Ezra-Nehemiah." In *Mixed Marriages: Intermarriage and Group Identity in the Second Temple Period*, edited by Christian Frevel, 60–77. The Library of Hebrew Bible/Old Testament Studies 547. New York: Bloomsbury, 2012.

Rudolph, Wilhelm. *Esra und Nehemia Samt 3. Esra*. Handbuch zum Alten Testament 20. Tübingen: J. C. B. Mohr (Paul Siebeck), 1949.

Sapolu, Pasesa. "Reconciling Identities: Social Identity, Hybridity, and Leadership in the Nehemiah Memoir." PhD diss., Graduate Theological Union, 2020.

Saysell, Csilla. *"According to the Law": Reading Ezra 9–10 as Christian Scripture*. Journal of Theological Interpretation Supplements 4. Winona Lake, IN: Eisenbrauns, 2012.

Schoville, Keith N. *Ezra-Nehemiah*. The College Press NIV Commentary. Joplin, MO: College Press, 2001.

Schultz, Richard. "5987 נָתִין." In *New International Dictionary of Old Testament Theology & Exegesis*, edited by Willem A. VanGemeren, 3:203–4. Grand Rapids: Zondervan, 1997.

Schunck, Klaus-Dietrich. *Nehemia*. Vol. 1. Biblischer Kommentar. Altes Testament 23/2. Neukirchen-Vluyn: Neukirchener Verlag, 1998.

Bibliography

Segal, Michael. "Numerical Discrepancies in the List of Vessels in Ezra I 9–11." *Vetus Testamentum* 52.1 (2002) 122–29.

Shepherd, David, and Christopher J. H. Wright. *Ezra and Nehemiah*. The Two Horizons Old Testament Commentary. Grand Rapids: Eerdmans, 2018.

Sivertsev, Alexei. "Sects and Households: Social Structure of the Proto-Sectarian Movement of Nehemiah 10 and the Dead Sea Sect." *Catholic Biblical Quarterly* 67.1 (2005) 59–78.

Smith, Daniel L. "The Politics of Ezra: Sociological Indicators of Postexilic Judaean Society." In *Second Temple Studies*, vol. 1, *The Persian Period*, edited by Philip R. Davies, 73–97. JSOT Supplement Series 117. Sheffield: Sheffield Academic, 1991.

Smith, Gary V. "The Influence of Deuteronomy on Intercessory Prayers in Ezra and Nehemiah." In *For Our Good Always: Studies on the Message and Influence of Deuteronomy in Honor of Daniel I. Block*, edited by Jason S. DeRouchie et al., 345–65. Critical Studies in the Hebrew Bible 3. Winona Lake, IN: Eisenbrauns, 2013.

Smith-Christopher, Daniel L. "The Mixed Marriage Crisis in Ezra 9–10 and Nehemiah 13: A Study of the Sociology of Post-Exilic Judaean Community." In *Second Temple Studies*, vol. 2, *Temple and Community in the Persian Period*, edited by Tamara C. Eskenazi and Kent H. Richards, 243–65. JSOT Supplement Series 175. Sheffield: JSOT, 1994.

Snaith, Norman Henry. "The Date of Ezra's Arrival in Jerusalem." *Zeitschrift für die alttestamentliche Wissenschaft* 63 (1951) 53–66.

Southwood, Katherine. "An Ethnic Affair? Ezra's Intermarriage Crisis against a Context of 'Self-Ascription' and 'Ascription of Others.'" In *Mixed Marriages: Intermarriage and Group Identity in the Second Temple Period*, edited by Christian Frevel, 46–59. Library of Hebrew Bible/Old Testament Studies 547. New York: T&T Clark, 2011.

———. "'And They Could Not Understand Jewish Speech': Language, Ethnicity, and Nehemiah's Intermarriage Crisis." *Journal of Theological Studies* 62 (2011) 1–19.

———. *Ethnicity and the Mixed Marriage Crisis in Ezra 9–10: An Anthropological Approach*. New York: Oxford University Press, 2012.

Steinmann, Andrew. *Ezra and Nehemiah*. Concordia Commentary. St. Louis: Concordia, 2010.

Talstra, Eep. "The Discourse of Praying: Reading Nehemiah 1." In *Psalms and Prayers: Papers Read at the Joint Meeting of the Society of Old Testament Study and Het Oudtestamentische Werkgezelschap in Nederland En België, Apeldoorn August 2006*, edited by Bob Becking and Eric Peels, 219–36. Old Testament Studies 55. Boston: Brill, 2007.

Thiessen, Matthew. "The Function of a Conjunction: Inclusivist or Exclusivist Strategies in Ezra 6.19–21 and Nehemiah 10.29–30?" *Journal for the Study of the Old Testament* 34.1 (2009) 63–79.

Thomas, Derek. *Ezra & Nehemiah*. Reformed Expository Commentary Series. Phillipsburg, NJ: P&R, 2016.

Thon, Johannes. "Sprache und Identitätskonstruktion: Das Literarische Interesse von Neh 13,23–27 und die Funktion diese Textes im Wissenschaftlichen Diskurs." *Zeitschrift für die alttestamentliche Wissenschaft* 121.4 (2009) 557–76.

Throntveit, Mark A. *Ezra-Nehemiah*. Interpretation: A Bible Commentary for Teaching and Preaching. Louisville: John Knox, 1992.

Tiemeyer, Lena-Sofia. *Ezra-Nehemiah: An Introduction and Study Guide*. T&T Clark Study Guides to the Old Testament. New York: T&T Clark, 2017.

Bibliography

Tollefson, Kenneth D., and H. G. M. Williamson. "Nehemiah as Cultural Revitalization: An Anthropological Perspective." *Journal for the Study of the Old Testament* 17.56 (1992) 41–68.

Tsevat, M. "יְרוּשָׁלַםִ (Yerûšālēm/ Yerûšālayim)." In *Theological Dictionary of the Old Testament*, edited by G. Johannes Botterweck et al., 6:347–55. Grand Rapids: Eerdmans, 1990.

Ussishkin, David. "On Nehemiah's City Wall and the Size of Jerusalem during the Persian Period: An Archaeologist's View." In *New Perspectives on Ezra-Nehemiah: History and Historiography, Text, Literature, and Interpretation*, edited by Isaac Kalimi, 101–30. Winona Lake, IN: Eisenbrauns, 2012.

Usue, Emmanuel. "Is the Expulsion of Women as Foreigners in Ezra 9–10 Justifiably Covenantal?" *Acta Theologica* 32.1 (2012) 158–69.

Van der Merwe, Christo H. J. et al. *A Biblical Hebrew Reference Grammar*. 2nd ed. New York: Bloomsbury T&T Clark, 2017.

Van Wijk-Bos, Johanna W. H. *Ezra, Nehemiah, and Esther*. Westminster Bible Companion. Louisville: Westminster John Knox, 1998.

Van Wyk, Wouter C., and A. P. B. Breytenbach. "The Nature of the Conflict in Ezra-Nehemiah." *HTS Teologiese Studies/Theological Studies* 57.3/4 (2001) 1254–63.

VanderKam, James C. "Ezra-Nehemiah or Ezra and Nehemiah?" In *Priests, Prophets, and Scribes: Essays on the Formation and Heritage of Second Temple Judaism in Honour of Joseph Blenkinsopp*, edited by Eugene Ulrich et al., 55–75. Journal for the Study of the Old Testament Supplement Series 149. Sheffield: JSOT, 1992.

Venema, G. J. *Reading Scripture in the Old Testament: Deuteronomy 9–10, 31, 2 Kings 22–23, Jeremiah 36, Nehemiah 8*. Old Testament Studies 48. New York: Brill, 2004.

Vogt, Hubertus C. M. *Studie zur nachexilischen Gemeinde in Esra-Nehemia*. Werl: Kommissionsverlag Dietrich Coelde, 1966.

Walsh, Jerome T. *Style and Structure in Biblical Hebrew Narrative*. Berit Olam. Collegeville, MN: Liturgical, 2017.

Waltke, Bruce K., and Michael Patrick O'Connor. *An Introduction to Biblical Hebrew Syntax*. Winona Lake, IN: Eisenbrauns, 1990.

Washington, Harold C. "The Strange Woman (אשה זרה/נכריה) of Proverbs 1–9 and Post-Exilic Judean Society." In *Second Temple Studies*, vol. 2, *Temple and Community in the Persian Period*, edited by Tamara C. Eskenazi and Kent H. Richards, 217–42. JSOT Supplement Series 175. Sheffield: JSOT, 1994.

Weinberg, Joel. *The Citizen-Temple Community*. Translated by Daniel L. Smith-Christopher. Journal for the Study of the Old Testament Supplement Series 151. Sheffield: JSOT, 1992.

Welch, Adam C. "The Source of Nehemiah IX." *Zeitschrift für die alttestamentliche Wissenschaft* 47.1 (1929) 130–37.

Werline, Rodney Alan. *Penitential Prayer in Second Temple Judaism: The Development of a Religious Institution*. Early Judaism and Its Literature 13. Atlanta: Scholars, 1998.

Williamson, H. G. M. "The Composition of Ezra i–vi." *Journal of Theological Studies* 34.1 (1983) 1–30.

———. *Ezra, Nehemiah*. Word Biblical Commentary 16. Waco, TX: Word, 1985.

———. "Nehemiah's Walls Revisited." *Palestine Exploration Quarterly* 116 (1984) 81–88.

Wright, Jacob L. "Commensal Politics in Ancient Western Asia: The Background to Nehemiah's Feasting (Part II)." *Zeitschrift für die alttestamentliche Wissenschaft* 122.3 (2010) 333–52.

Bibliography

———. "A New Model for the Composition of Ezra-Nehemiah." In *Judah and the Judeans in the Fourth Century BCE*, edited by Oded Lipschits et al., 333–48. Winona Lake, IN: Eisenbrauns, 2007.

———. *Rebuilding Identity: The Nehemiah-Memoir and Its Earliest Readers*. Beihefte zur Zeitschrift für die alttestamentliche Wissenschaft 348. New York: De Gruyter, 2004.

———. "Seeking, Finding and Writing in Ezra–Nehemiah." In *Unity and Disunity in Ezra-Nehemiah: Redaction, Rhetoric, and Reader*, edited by Mark J. Boda and Paul L. Redditt, 277–304. Hebrew Bible Monographs 17. Sheffield: Sheffield Phoenix, 2008.

———. "Writing the Restoration: Compositional Agenda and the Role of Ezra in Nehemiah 8." *Journal of Hebrew Scriptures* 7 (2007) 19–29.

Würthwein, Ernst. *Der "'Amm Ha'arez" im Alten Testament*. Stuttgart: W. Kohlhammer, 1936.

Yamauchi, Edwin M. "Archaeological Backgrounds of the Exilic and Postexilic Era, Part 4: The Archaeological Background of Nehemiah." *Bibliotheca Sacra* 137.548 (1980) 291–309.

———. "The Reverse Order of Ezra/Nehemiah Reconsidered." *Themelios* 5.3 (1980) 7–13.

———. "Was Nehemiah the Cupbearer a Eunuch?" *Zeitschrift für die alttestamentliche Wissenschaft* 92.1 (1980) 132–42.

Zeelander, Susan. *Closure in Biblical Narrative*. Biblical Interpretation Series 111. Leiden: Brill, 2012.

Zlotnick-Sivan, H. "The Silent Women of Yehud: Notes on Ezra 9–10." *Journal of Jewish Studies* 51.1 (2000) 3–18.

Subject Index

Aaron, 26, 35–36, 41
Achaemenid, 100, 144
Ancestry, 55, 61, 74, 83, 104–5
Aramaic, 66–67, 74
Artaxerxes, 7–9, 16, 29–36, 38–39, 45–48, 51, 53–54, 64–68, 72, 76, 78–79, 82, 86–88, 97, 137, 147–48, 159, 161, 163
Articles, 22–25, 33, 59, 71–72
Author/authorship, 6, 9, 21, 23–24, 30, 34, 37, 40, 52, 59–60, 67, 120, 127, 148, 150, 160, 169

Babylon(ian), 11, 24–25, 29, 60, 64–66, 69, 145–46
Beyond the River, 31–32, 34, 38, 68, 80, 138, 147
Build (building, rebuilding), 3–5, 9–12, 18, 20–25, 29–30, 38–40, 42–51, 53–54, 57, 60, 74, 79, 82, 83, 86, 88, 139–42, 146–49, 151–56, 158, 161–63, 165–66, 168

City, 4, 10, 12–14, 18, 23, 26, 28, 36, 42–45, 47–51, 53, 55, 62–63, 77, 79, 81–84, 86, 95, 98, 139, 141, 146–48, 151–55, 157–59, 161–63, 165–68
Cultic personnel, 14, 16, 23, 25–28, 30, 35–36, 40–41, 50, 54–55, 61, 69–70, 74, 83–84, 87, 128–29
Cyrus, 9, 16, 18–24, 30, 38–39, 51, 53, 57–60, 72, 88

Date formula, 7, 18–19, 29, 37, 40, 45, 52, 65–66, 71, 76, 79, 90, 98, 115–17, 119, 121
Daughter(s), 95, 106, 108, 132, 142–43, 150, 156
Decree, 1–2, 7–9, 13–14, 19–23, 30–36, 38–39, 41, 46, 51–55, 57–59, 66–68, 72, 74, 86–88, 95, 97, 137
Deuteronomic text/language, 6, 8, 78, 105, 112, 137, 143, 149–50, 153–54, 157–59
Divorce, 103–04, 107–08, 145–46, 160, 164
Documents, embedded, 42–43, 67, 98–99, 104–5, 119, 124–25, 131
Documents, transcribed, 16, 19, 30, 38, 51, 57, 66–67, 74, 78, 86–87, 96

Edict, 18, 32, 34, 58, 68, 72
Editor, 5–6, 10, 20, 52, 59, 66–67, 76, 78, 169
Eliashib, 42, 50, 83, 115–16
Exclusion, 3–5, 11–12, 14, 26–27, 47, 53, 55, 61, 74, 81–82, 107, 123, 129, 140, 142–44, 147–51, 155, 157, 164, 166–69
(pre-, post-) Exilic, 4, 11, 22, 24, 26, 29, 32–34, 37–40, 45, 60, 72, 88, 91–92, 94, 100, 112, 116, 119, 122–24, 144–45, 149–52, 154, 157, 159–60, 162
Exodus, 1, 36, 40, 123–24, 146, 149, 151, 157

Subject Index

Feast, 29, 54, 97
Foreign(er), 1, 3–6, 9, 11–13, 25, 33, 88, 95–96, 99–101, 103–4, 106–8, 110–12, 114, 117–18, 120–21, 127, 131–32, 139, 140, 142–51, 153, 155–65, 167–69

Genealogy, 27, 29, 31, 34, 36, 39, 50, 54, 60–62, 64, 69–70, 84, 87, 110, 115, 117, 151, 162
Geshem, 13, 47, 49–50, 55, 82
Governor, 27, 32, 34–35, 38–39, 47–49, 51, 61–62, 72, 80–81, 86, 99, 125, 138, 147

Hebrew, 3, 14–15, 19–20, 38, 74, 123–24, 131
Holy/holiness, 4, 6, 9, 30, 34, 37, 53–55, 100, 118, 125–26, 141–42, 146–47, 151–57, 159–60, 164

Impure, 100, 107, 147, 156, 158, 160–61, 167

Jerusalem, 3–4, 10, 12, 16, 20–24, 29, 31–38, 40, 43–51, 53, 55, 57–58, 60–62, 65–69, 71–72, 74, 77, 79, 81–82, 84, 86–87, 93, 98, 116–17, 138–39, 140–41, 144, 146–48, 151–58, 161–68
Jeshua, 18, 119
Jew(ish), 6, 10, 21, 23, 47, 49, 51, 103, 127–29, 141, 146, 148–49
Joiada, 102–4, 108, 127–29, 131
Judea(n), 4, 11–12, 19, 23–26, 44, 47–49, 54–55, 77, 82–83, 86–88, 95, 103, 106–7, 127, 136, 145–48, 150, 152–57, 159, 162–63, 165–68

King, 7, 9, 14, 16, 18–22, 29–34, 37–41, 45–48, 51–53, 55, 57–59, 64–65, 67–71, 74, 76–80, 82, 86, 95, 124, 127–28, 137, 145, 155, 161–62, 165–66

Laity, 26–27, 35–36, 54, 60, 69, 93
Language, 1, 6, 8, 20, 78, 100, 107, 113, 127, 137, 149, 152, 157, 159, 165

Law, 6, 30–33, 35, 64, 66–68, 78, 87, 94, 97–98, 100, 106, 117–18, 121, 126, 145, 159–60, 165–66
Leader, 1, 3–4, 16, 18, 21–24, 26, 29–32, 35–36, 38–39, 47–51, 54, 58–62, 68–71, 81–82, 86–87, 91–95, 98–99, 104, 110–11, 114–16, 118–19, 122, 125, 136, 142, 148–53, 156, 158–61, 164–65, 167
Levites, 22–23, 25–26, 28, 31–32, 34–38, 40–41, 50, 54–55, 58, 60–61, 66, 70–72, 74, 83–84, 89, 93, 97–102, 104–6, 108, 109, 111–12, 115, 119–20, 122–26, 128, 131
Levitical texts, 23, 54, 122–23
List, inventory, 13, 24–25, 34, 59–62, 74
List, name, 1–3, 7, 11, 13–14, 18, 22, 25–28, 31, 34–39, 41–44, 47–48, 50, 54–55, 59–64, 69–70, 72, 74, 83–84, 86–87, 96, 99, 101, 104–5, 107, 119–20, 122, 125, 131, 139, 149–50, 167–68

Movement, literary, 3–4, 6, 14, 18–19, 29, 44, 58–59, 65–67, 69, 75, 77, 79–81, 85, 88, 105, 111–14, 117, 121, 130, 138–39, 152, 163, 168–69
Movement, spatial/geographical, 13, 44, 53, 59, 65–66, 69–71, 80–81, 116–17, 138, 162–63

Nethinim, 25–26, 28, 35–36, 41, 50, 54, 83–84

Official, 25, 32, 35, 40–41, 47, 49–50, 54, 68, 72, 74, 81, 83, 86, 111–12, 117, 165
Outside(r), 5, 11–14, 44, 46–47, 107, 140–41, 147–48, 160, 166, 168
Ownership, 3–4, 115, 144–45, 148, 150, 162, 165–66, 169

Persia(n), 11, 14, 16–21, 29, 32–33, 36–37, 39–40, 49, 51–53, 55, 57, 64, 67–68, 74, 76, 86, 88, 95, 105–7, 122, 143–46, 155–56, 162

Subject Index

Pilgrimage, 40
Prayer, 3, 6–9, 13–14, 44–45, 48–49, 51–52, 70–71, 77–79, 86, 91–92, 94–95, 97–101, 105–6, 111–14, 116–17, 122–26, 131, 136–37, 143, 146, 152–60, 164
Priest, 22–23, 25–28, 30, 32, 34–37, 38, 40–41, 47, 49–51, 54–55, 58, 60–61, 64, 67, 69, 71–72, 74, 83–84, 93, 98–100, 102–4, 108, 111–12, 115, 119, 125–26, 128–29, 131–32, 137, 142
Priestly text, 6, 23, 54–55, 137
Prince, 90–92, 110–12, 116, 120, 131, 165
Property, 93, 116–17, 142–46, 162–64
Province, 13, 22, 34, 45–46, 48–49, 60, 62, 80, 140–41, 144, 147, 155–58, 162
Purity/purify, 12, 102, 105, 107–8, 140–41, 146–47, 150–51, 156, 168

Remnant, 49, 112–13, 122, 152–53, 157
Reported/recorded speech, 2–3, 9, 13–14, 16, 29–30, 37, 43–48, 51–52, 55, 57, 70–71, 77, 79–83, 86, 91–92, 94, 96, 98, 101–2, 104–5, 110–13, 115, 117–19, 122–125, 127–28, 131, 136–38, 161, 167
Restoration, 13, 40, 44, 77, 100, 105–7, 140, 146, 148, 152, 154–57, 162, 168–69
Returnee, 1–2, 14, 16, 22, 25–27, 29, 31, 35–36, 38–39, 41, 51, 57–62, 69, 71–72, 74, 86–87, 141, 143–44, 146, 151

Sacrifice, 33–34, 38–39, 54, 67, 72, 108, 119–20

Sanballat, 13, 43–44, 47, 49–50, 55, 80–82, 84, 102–3, 108, 128, 147, 162–63
Seam (editorial/literary), 6, 10, 38, 139, 169
Shecaniah, 84, 92–96, 104, 106–7, 113–18, 131, 137, 159–60, 162–63
Sheshbazzar, 1, 7, 16–18, 22, 24, 27, 31, 37–41, 51–55, 56, 59–62, 73–74, 84–88, 108, 130
Social/sociological, 3–5, 11–13, 15, 20, 49–50, 92, 106, 122, 137, 141, 143–47, 151, 153, 162, 164–65
Son (other), 27, 31, 36, 50, 60, 69, 84, 95, 102–4, 106, 108, 110–11, 115–16, 119–20, 127–29, 131–32, 136, 150, 164
Sons of Israel, 18, 35, 49–50, 54–55, 95, 99–100, 112, 119, 121–22, 157–58
Sons of Solomon's servants, 25
Sons of the exile, 119, 162

Tobiah, 13, 43, 47, 49–50, 55, 80–82, 136, 162–63

Unclean, 27, 61, 156, 168

Vessel, 24, 27, 37, 39–40, 53, 58–60

Wall, 4–5, 10–14, 16–17, 42–44, 47–51, 53, 82–84, 87–88, 139, 141–42, 146–48, 152, 154–58, 161–63, 165–68

Yehud, 20, 46, 49, 96, 107, 153, 168

Zerubbabel, 18–19, 60, 84, 87

Scripture Index

EXODUS
34:11	149

NUMBERS
10:13–28	36
27:8–11	143

DEUTERONOMY
4:25–31	44
7	78, 95, 146, 150, 152, 156–58
7:1–2	147
7:3–4	149–50
7:1	149–50
7:6	151
7:12	147
9	6, 78
12	157
12:1	159
12:2–5	159
20:17	149
23	158
25:5–7	143
30	78, 157
30:1–5	8

JOSHUA
1–11	164
4:7	166
6	53, 164
7	94, 153
7:19	94, 164
18:5	166

1 KINGS
8	78
8:33–34	44
8:46–52	44

1 CHRONICLES
13:1	115
24:10	27

2 CHRONICLES
24:26	110

EZRA
3–6	95
3:3	148
4–6	9
4:4	148
4:10–11	67
4:11–24	161
4:13–14	67
4:17	67
4:21	67
5:16–17	67
6	29, 88
6:6	67
6:19–22	29
6:19	29
6:21	149

NEHEMIAH
4	13, 47

Scripture Index

(Nehemiah continued)

4:1	42–43
4:2	43
4:6	42
5	122
6:6–7	161
6:14	128
6:18–19	142
7–8	99
7	9, 21, 60, 62, 87, 98
7:40	84
8–13	9
8	2, 6, 33, 87, 91, 97–98, 121, 126
8:4	118
8:7–8	118
11	98
11:13	84
12:6	84
13:3	149–50
13:14	128
13:15–22	147
13:22	101, 128
13:23–31	106
13:28–31	102

ESTHER

5:3–8	79
7:1–6	79

PSALMS

106:35	151

ISAIAH

6:11–13	151–52
45	19

JEREMIAH

28:1–17	24
29:2	115
50:37	150

EZEKIEL

30:5	150
36	131
36:32	156–57

www.ingramcontent.com/pod-product-compliance
Lightning Source LLC
Chambersburg PA
CBHW072129160426
43197CB00012B/2044